REPORT ON THE HEBRIDES

1. The Rev. Dr. John Walker. (Frontispiece to Sir William Jardine, 'The Naturalists' Library' (1843), vol. 26)

2. Caricature of Dr. John Walker. (From John Kay's 'Original Portraits', vol. II)

The Rev. Dr. John Walker's

REPORT ON THE HEBRIDES

of 1764 and 1771

Edited by

MARGARET M. McKAY

JOHN DONALD PUBLISHERS LTD
EDINBURGH

ISBN 0 85976 043 X

Printed in Great Britain by Bell & Bain Ltd., Glasgow
Phototypesetting by Wright Printers, Dundee

PREFACE

I am very grateful to the British Library for consent to publish the manuscript of Dr. John Walker's 'Report on the Hebrides', King's MS 105, and to the Committee of the Gaelic Society of Inverness for permission to include the sections on Lewis, Harris and Skye which were published in the Transactions of the Society, vols. XXIV (1899-1901) and XXVIII (1912-1914). I am further indebted to the Trustees of the National Library of Scotland for granting permission to reproduce the illustrations of Dr. John Walker, and to K. I. Winch of Cambridge Library for the maps.

My research has been helped greatly by the generous assistance of the staffs of the Scottish Record Office, the National Library of Scotland, Aberdeen University Library, the University Library of Cambridge and the University of Edinburgh Library.

Finally my thanks must go to my husband, W. R. McKay, who compiled the index, and was a constant source of encouragement, and to my daughters, Elspeth and Catriona for their forbearance during the time they lived with Dr. Walker.

Cambridge, 1980

PLATES

1. Rev. Dr. John Walker, from Sir William Jardine's 'The Naturalists' Library'
2. Dr. Walker, from John Kay's 'Original Portraits'

MAPS

		page
1.	The Hebrides in relation to mainland Scotland	34
2.	Lewis, Harris	38
3.	North Uist, Benbecula	62
4.	South Uist, Barra	73
5.	Islay	96
6.	Jura	110
7.	Smaller Islands adjacent to Jura	119
8.	Mull	150
9.	Tiree and Coll	168
10.	Small Isles: Rum, Eigg, Muck, Canna, Sanday	194
11.	Skye	202

CONTENTS

	page
Preface	v
List of Plates and Maps	vi
Introduction	1
'REPORT ON THE HEBRIDES'	31
Author's Address to the Commissioners of Annexed Estates	33
Lewis	37
Harris	51
St. Kilda	57
North Uist	61
Benbecula	67
South Uist	71
Barra	83
Rockall	91
Islay	95
Jura	109
Colonsay	121
Oronsay	127
Gigha	131
Iona	135
Mull	149
Coll	167
Tiree	177
Rum	193
Skye	201
Eigg	221
Canna	227
Notes	230
Index	245

INTRODUCTION

The Author

JOHN WALKER was born in 1731 in Edinburgh, where his father was rector of the Canongate School. He was a gifted child, said to be enjoying Homer in the original and reading James Sutherland's 'Hortus Edinburgensis'[1] at the age of ten. Natural history was to become the driving force of his life and botany especially his dearest pursuit; he was to remark in later life to Lord Kames, when Linnaeus' theory of a connection between man and apes was being considered,

> I have been from my cradle, fond of vegetable life; and though I like my species and the rank I hold in creation, I declare I would sooner claim kindred to an oak or to an apple-tree than to an ape.[2]

Geology was another field of intense interest. At the age of fifteen, he began a collection of minerals and when a student at the University of Edinburgh found inspiration in the teaching of Professor William Cullen, whose chemistry courses he attended and with whom he went on tours to collect fossils and rocks. Cullen's far-reaching range of interests included medicine, botany, chemistry, agriculture and mining, and John Walker received a sound introduction to the work of contemporary scientists and especially to the work of systematisation and classification in botany.

Walker was educated for the ministry of the Church of Scotland. In 1754 he was licensed by the Presbytery of Kirkcudbright and four years later became minister of Glencorse, near Edinburgh. There he met Henry Home, Lord Kames, the renowned agricultural improver, jurist and prominent figure of the Edinburgh enlightenment, who was to become a lifelong friend and correspondent on scientific and agricultural matters. Through Kames, Walker met many of the great savants of the day; he was introduced to Benjamin Franklin, met Rousseau and began a correspondence with Linnaeus. During the years at Glencorse he was able to go on botanical and mineralogical expeditions in the nearby Pentlands, adding to current knowledge of species of plants and rocks. In 1761 he made his first journey in the Highlands and the following year he was in the Hebrides. That year he was translated to the parish of Moffat where he remained minister until 1783 when he moved to Colinton, outside Edinburgh. At both Moffat and Colinton he transformed the manse gardens into botanical wonderlands. Throughout his mature years he carried on a very active correspondence, answering queries from anyone interested in botanical or geological matters until he became blind about 1796. He died in Edinburgh at the beginning of 1804, and was buried in the Canongate churchyard.

Walker's scientific work won him early recognition. In the 1750's he won silver and gold medals from the Edinburgh Society for his collections of marles and other natural manures. Between 1761 and 1764, concentrating on mineralogy and exploring mines in the search for new ores, he made several discoveries, including Strontianite, thirty years before it was formally named. By the end of that period he was well to the fore in the field of classification of both plants and minerals.

In 1764 he received a commission from the Commissioners of Annexed Estates which was to result in the writing of the 'Report on the Hebrides', and at the same time he was asked by the General Assembly of the Church of Scotland and by the Society for the Propagation of Christian Knowledge to report on the state of religion and education in the Highlands and Islands. Walker's reports to the General Assembly and to the S.P.C.K. were completed in 1765 and in the same year he was given an honorary M.D. from the University of Glasgow and the degree of D.D. from the University of Edinburgh. In 1771 he was in the Hebrides again, to complete the surveys of the islands.

In 1775 Dr Ramsay, the first regius professor of Natural History in Edinburgh, died and a rather unpleasant period of acrimonious string pulling ensued. Dr Walker was encouraged by 'various friends . . . who knew his qualifications and were aware that he had been for years preparing himself for teaching natural history'[3] to offer himself as a candidate. He was in fact very eager for the chair and implored Kames to help him. Walker was successful and, though remaining minister of Moffat, became professor of Natural History in 1779. He already had a house in the Canongate and spent increasingly lengthy periods there. From 1781 he gave several series of lectures and thereafter he was at the heart of Edinburgh scientific life. He helped organise the Royal Society of Edinburgh and was appointed one of its first joint secretaries of the physical section in 1783, a post he held until 1796. He was active in the organisation of the Natural History Society of Edinburgh in 1782, was an early contributor to the Highland Society and helped to form the Agricultural Society of Edinburgh in 1792. Dr Walker lectured on agriculture at the university and had hopes of the chair of agriculture when it was founded in 1790 by Sir William Pulteney, but in this he was disappointed. In November 1793 the newly appointed Board of Agriculture asked him to write an account of the state of husbandry in the Western Isles. His work did not form part of the series published by the Board on the agricultural state of the Kingdom but probably became the basis for his 'Economical History of the Hebrides and Highlands', published posthumously in 1808.

Walker could very well be regarded as the epitome of the 'moderate' minister. Not only were his intellectual roots firmly grounded in the Moderate party, but he came to enjoy some success as an ecclesiastical politician and was elected moderator of the General Assembly in 1790. The Moderates were criticised bitterly by their opponents in the Evangelical party as lovers of the high social life, more given to learned disquisitions than God-fearing sermons, happier in the drawing rooms of the upper classes than in their own pulpits, engaging in intellectual exercise for its own sake rather than seeking their own and their parishioners' salvation. At Glencorse the minister was renowned for his bringing in 'weeds' from the hills, and in his second charge he was known popularly as 'the mad minister of Moffat'. In the 1760's and 1770's, when he was collecting his geological and botanical specimens and journeying around the Highlands and Islands, he was away from his parish for months at a time. Clearly, he found his parochial work burdensome and regarded it as depriving him of time which might have been devoted to scientific study. One of his parishioners at Moffat remarked that 'he spent the week hunting butterflies and made the cure of the souls of his parishioners a bye-job on Sunday'.[4]

To some extent the Evangelicals' criticism of Moderate preaching as clear, short and cold was justified in Walker's case. His pulpit manner was evidently marked by stiffness and his sermons were renowned for their dryness.[5] His intellect could not find expression in the 'enthusiasm' of the Evangelicals.

Dr Walker's absenteeism and, after his appointment as professor of Natural History, his pluralism, brought down on his head the wrath of the Presbytery of Lochmaben, but he either ignored the Presbytery's representations to him or treated them with disdain. The Presbytery found his holding the office incompatible with continuing as minister of Moffat, but Walker successfully appealed to the Synod. His presentation to Colinton in 1783 led to another crisis, this time over patronage. It was the first occasion in that parish on which a minister was inducted without reference to the people, and a secession from the parish church was the unhappy result.

There is no doubt that Walker found the company of Kames and his associates congenial and stimulating. He was regularly to be found at their levées and suppers in Edinburgh and at their country mansions. While at Moffat, he found himself in social and intellectual isolation, a circumstance not improved by his remaining unmarried until 1787. He wrote to Lady Kames, in 1776,

> . . . I must confess that all the merit I have in keeping free of the pest (sc. wives) has been against my will . . . I live as all bachelors do, like a wild beast in his den. I pass my hours like an owl in an ivy bush, and very differently from what I have had the happiness to do under your roof, among learned men and elegant women. My next neighbour here is the moon, and a little way off I have the fixed stars. Very peaceable company . . .[6]

In the winter of 1778 he told Lord Kames that he was 'blocked up with snow and not within 18 miles of a person I can converse with'.[7] Life at Moffat was leading him to desperation:

> I am for several reasons sick of this place and anxious to leave it; and was even thinking to give it up if I could have but procured a chaplaincy to go with a regiment to America.[8]

He would surely have been even more out of place in the army than at Moffat. Fortunately, it was not long after this that he was given the chair of Natural History and returned to the cultural life of the capital.

Among the literary preoccupations of many Moderates – including Walker – was the vexed issue of the authenticity of the poems of 'Ossian'. Many of the Evangelical Highland ministers found it difficult to achieve a compromise between the Bible and Gaelic oral literature. They waged a persistent war against 'the vain, hurtful, lying earthly stories' and had an ardent dislike of the Ossianic ballads. The Moderates were free from the necessity of denouncing Ossian: to them the stories were more intriguing than sinful. Walker delighted in identifying places he visited with sites in the stories. He described to Lady Kames 'the spot of Fingal's residence . . . a green promontory skirted with wood' at Selma. In Appin he encountered 'a circle of Druidical stones which alone would almost authenticate his (Ossian's) poems were there nothing else'.[9]

On the other hand Moderates and Evangelicals united in their abhorrence of 'Popery'. Walker never expressed his aversion to Roman Catholicism with the wild extravagance of some of his contemporaries, but it was deep-rooted and reinforced by his discovery that in the Catholic islands and areas of the mainland a marked reverence for traditional ways went hand in hand with a reluctance to adopt the new agricultural techniques. Catholicism was coming between the people and their material salvation, as well as subverting their religious beliefs:

> Even the progress of the arts of industry will be prevented, as Popery prevails. For the Balefull influence of the Popish religion, wherever it is generally professed in the Highlands, is visible, even in the face of the Country. There, not only the morals and manners of the People, but the very Soil, is more rude and uncultivated. The Popish inhabitants . . . become peculiarly averse, to every innovation, that tends to promote industry, or improve the country.[10]

Although he believed that Catholicism went hand in hand with Jacobitism and rebellion, and that under its influence 'the people must be corrupted not only in the Principles of Religion but in those of Government', he did not approve of the penal laws being enforced 'if the hurtful consequences they are meant to obviate can be prevented by other methods; and it seems more worthy of the constitution of this Kingdom, and of the Church of Scotland, to obtain the end proposed . . . by more generous and humane ones, if the means can be obtained'.[11]

In the history of science Walker was overlooked until comparatively recently, but now his work in collection and classification and his influence as a teacher have won him the title of 'father of Scottish Mineralogy'.[12] Walker was the first professor of Natural History who gave lectures, held class meetings, prepared syllabuses for his students and organised work in the laboratory. His pupils included James Hall and Robert Jameson, who following Walker's lead, established Scottish geological studies and in turn taught Charles Darwin, Sir William Jardine and Necker de Saussure. His lectures attracted students from England, Ireland and America; one of them, Samuel Latham Mitchill, became a leading light in American science. For many years Walker worked on the preparation of a 'Flora Scotica' but after the publication of John Lightfoot's work in 1777 laid it aside. After his death, his herbarium was sold but his manuscripts remain as a collection in the Library of the University of Edinburgh. For a time his work in botany remained unnoticed but now a eulogy by a critic of Hooker's work is accepted as being fully justified:

> It is impossible to mention the name of Dr Walker without bewailing the loss which botanical fame has sustained . . . He had explored the vegetable productions of Scotland, not merely with an industrious, but with a philosophical eye, and . . . he was more acquainted with the extent of our Flora than any dead or living botanist . . . such indeed, is the respect which we entertain . . . for the memory of this great but neglected naturalist, that we are persuaded, that had he, in his vigorous days, published a 'Flora Scotica', it would have placed its author among the first botanists of the eighteenth century.[13]

Though he was without personal practical experience in agriculture, it is in that field he has enjoyed the greatest reputation. His ideas were 'mainstream' improvement and almost without doubt came from his association with Lord Kames and other renowned agriculturalists. The improvers were opposed to the runrig method of farming, scourge cropping and inadequate manuring, overstocking and poor ploughing, and they advocated growing root crops in rotation and sowing grass seeds for good grazing and hay. Walker adopted these ideas and also drew on Kames' practical experience and his knowledge of agricultural science. His friend and teacher, professor William Cullen, ran a farm at Ormiston Hill, was an agricultural theorist, and a further source of expertise. Walker also studied in detail the works of Sir Alexander Murray of Stanhope who had attempted improvements in Ardnamurchan and was especially concerned with systems of hill drainage and the use of natural manures.

Lord Kames constantly rebuked Walker for a lack of diligence and assiduity in getting his work ready for publication. Though he contributed a number of papers for learned journals and synopses of geological and botanical studies for his students, the two major works Walker planned, the 'Flora Scotica' and a 'Natural History of the Highlands', were never completed. After his death, his friend, Charles Stewart, the printer, published the two-volume 'Economical History of the Hebrides and Highlands' and 'Essays on Natural History and Rural Economy'. Some of the papers and essays were on learned geological and botanical subjects but others show a continuing interest in the important aspects of the Highlands and Islands and their economy.[14]

There can have been few men so well qualified to undertake a survey of the Hebrides in 1764.

The Commissioners of Annexed Estates and the 'Report on the Hebrides'

Following the 1745 rebellion, the Scottish Court of the Exchequer had been authorised to take charge of the estates which were forfeit to the Crown owing to the owners' attainder for treason. Forty-one estates were taken over. The majority of these were sold to repay debts, but thirteen were annexed to the Crown by act of Parliament in 1752. The rents and profits were to be used 'for the Purposes of civilising the Inhabitants upon the said Estates, and other Parts of the Highlands and Islands of Scotland, and promoting amongst them the Protestant religion, good Government, Industry and Manufactures, and the Principles of Duty and Loyalty to his Majesty, his Heirs and Successors, and to no other use or Purpose whatsoever'. The Commissioners, first appointed in 1755, included some of the foremost men of the day, drawn from Crown officials, judges, noblemen and lairds; one of the most outstanding was Lord Kames. Because of their wide brief, they had to extend their activities far beyond the general administration of the annexed estates. If the revenues were to be spent on 'civilising' the entire Highlands, it was necessary first to ascertain what conditions were like and what resources lay beyond the Highland line. Surveys had to be made.

In March 1764, probably at the instigation of Kames, Walker proposed to the Commissioners that he should 'take a tour thro' the Highlands', and make a 'faithful and distinct report'. The proposal was accepted, expenses of £60 were allowed, and Lord Kames drew up Walker's instructions, 'to examine the natural histories of these countries, their population, and state of their agriculture, manufactures and fisheries'.[15]

Walker's pastoral duties, as he was then minister of Moffat, prevented his simply absenting himself and setting out on his tour. He suggested to the General Assembly that he should take the opportunity given by his commission from the Board of Annexed Estates to report on the religious and educational state of the Highlands for the Church. A few years previously, in 1760, two ministers, Doctors Hyndman and Dick, had journeyed through many of the islands and along the west coast to survey the size of the parishes, the difficulties under which the ministers were working, the size of the population, the numbers of Catholics and the provision of education. The S.P.C.K. had asked for reports on its schools, thus making it a joint commission. Hyndman and Dick had not reached all the southern islands, so Walker suggested he should be given similar commissions by the General Assembly and the S.P.C.K. to complete their work. The General Assembly agreed to the proposal, and pulpit supply was arranged for the duration of the tour. Thus Walker was freed from his parochial responsibilities but faced with the onerous tasks of making reports to each of his three sponsors. Furthermore, Thomas Pennant, the English naturalist, was working on his 'British Zoology', which was to be published in 1766-68, and he seized on his fellow naturalist's tour as an opportunity for further research. He wrote to professor Cullen,

I take the liberty of recommending to Mr Walker a thorough Attention to the Zoology of the western Isles, particularly to such parts as may confirm or confute the Accounts of the old Writers.

To enquire into the Origin of the Report of Sheep being found in some of the islands with blue fleeces - others with teeth of a gold colour - and another kind in the Isle of Hirta with horns as large as those of oxen . . . What is the Lavellan mentioned by Sibbald and the Martrick, another quadruped of the same Author? A bird called the Ailsa Cock in the Isle of Ailsa. And the Birds described by Martin in his Western Isles under local names.

Furthermore he wanted Walker to have the skins of any of them stuffed,

to Observe the species of wild deer . . . to collect the natural history of the seal and to bottle any rare marine substances, insects and small fishes.[16]

Thus burdened, Walker set out, going from Greenock to Campbeltown in the 'custom house wherry' provided for the expedition and then over to Ireland for provisions, where he visited the Giant's Causeway and took 'a fine pillar of it' for the foundation stone of the Edinburgh Museum. From Ireland he went over the short sea crossing to Islay and on the 22nd of June reported his progress to Lord Kames:

I have for several days been employed in scrutinising this Island. And from what has already occurr'd to me, I would fain hope, that my Expectations concerning this Journey, have not been too sanguine, which I was something afraid of. I expect tomorrow to boil water upon the Summit of the Paps of Jura, tho' I am much disswaded from it, as I must march five miles of steep Ascent, to the Haunches in Heather and Mud, and three more upon loose Rocks.[17]

He asked for a further £40 to be sent on to Stornoway to await him.

The next day found him still on Islay, inspecting an S.P.C.K. school at Kilchoman, and it was not until the 27th that the expedition to the Paps took place. It was both more fatiguing and more rewarding than anticipated:

Some Highland gentlemen were so good as to go along to conduct us. And a box with barometrical tubes, a telescope, a large kettle, water, fewel, provisions, and a couple of fowling-pieces, loaded seven or eight servants.

The first part of our progress lay through deep bogs, from which we sometimes found it very difficult to extricate ourselves. We then came to a chain of small but steep hills, where the heather struck us to the breast . . . Here we had before us, a very steep and continued ascent of about one thousand five hundred feet of perpendicular height, and composed entirely of loose rocks and stones. They lay upon the side of the mountain, like a great stream, and upon the least motion, gave way all about us, which made our progress both tedious and dangerous. With great difficulty, we made our way against these hurling ruins of the mountain; and at last, after an ascent of seven hours, with excessive fatigue, we gained the summit.

It was now five o'clock in the afternoon, the day was serene, not a cloud in the firmament, and the atmosphere uncommonly clear; so that the view we now enjoyed, of the earth and seas below, made us forget the toil of our ascent. Every way we turned, we had a prospect of sea and land, as far as the eye could reach . . . In another quarter, we distinctly saw the whole of the Hebrides, and Deucaledonian ocian. Southwards, the vast promontory of Cantire lay under our eye; and beyond it, in one view, all the west of Scotland rising to the great mass of mountains in the head of Clydesdale and Nithsdale: in another view, the spiry summits of Arran, and the whole Irish sea, with its shore, to the Isle of Man. . . . The promontory of the Giants Causeway appeared near and distinct; and beyond it, the high land of Inis-huna, the north extremity of Ireland; beyond this, to the Hebrides, nothing but air and ocean.[18]

Walker was in Colonsay on the 29th of June and then spent nearly the whole of July travelling from Iona, where he camped, collected lichens used for dyeing and toured the Abbey ruins, to Mull, Coll, Tiree, Rum, Eigg and Canna. On the 30th of July he was in Barra and in South Uist on the 31st. It took him a fortnight to see Benbecula, North Uist, Berneray, Vallay, Pabbay, Ensay and Harris, and on the 16th of August he was at Stornoway. Again, a report was sent to Lord Kames:

> I have seen the most fertile lands I ever saw in my life, without cultivation; a people by nature the most acute and sagacious, perfectly idle, the most valuable fisheries, without lines or nets; and in every corner one of the finest harbours that ever nature formed, a beautiful though useless void, as inanimate and unfrequented as those of the 'Terra Australis'.[19]

While in Stornoway, he visited the spinning school set up by the Commission of Annexed Estates and was greatly taken with the Gaelic songs the women sang as they worked, which he told Kames 'gave me more pleasure, if it be safe to own such an unpolite notion, than any concert I was ever at'.[20] After collecting the £40 forwarded by the Commissioners, Walker crossed the Minch, visited Assynt, and then went to Skye. He left the cutter and crossed to Glenelg, saw Kintail, Glenshiel and Lochaber, and then on to Morvern. He went south by Glenspean, Fort Augustus, Badenoch and Taymouth.

On December 9th, the minister of Moffat returned at last to his manse - seven months and two days after setting out. The next day he wrote to Lord Kames, giving him an account of the tour:

> Upon looking into my Journal, I find the Miles I have travelled are as follows
>
> sailed 1,263
> rowed in a boat 280
> rode 1,087
> walked 528[21]
>
> The hardships I met with were greater indeed than I would have chosen, but they were what I expected, and were in most cases, unavoidable. The Entertainment I had from the Business I was engaged in, and the surveying a sort of new World, made me even bear them with Pleasure, and I expect still more in reflecting upon them.[22]

He had augmented his collection of plants and had as many as had been recorded in England, even though he had seen only a fifth of Scotland; on Skye he had found a new species in a class of plants Linnaeus had asked him to work on. He had been 'encouraged to collect extensively all the singular minerals I met with, and in large masses, as their conveyance home by cutter was so easy'.[23]

Later he told his fellow naturalist, Lord Bute,

> You may be certain, that not withstanding the Attention I payed on this journey to (the economic, religious and educational state of the Islands) of which indeed they most justly command, I did not neglect the Natural History of the Country which you know was one principal motive for my undertaking it.
>
> I had many a toilsome Day rendered very agreeable, by a Harvest of Plants I had never before seen, many of which have not as yet been viewed by Botanick Eyes . . .
>
> Of fossils, I collected everything the Country affords which I put up at different places in Parcels of Boxes. They are daily coming home and I think the very carriage of them shall take half a year's stipend . . .

> In the animal Kingdom I met likewise with a great deal of Entertainment. I preserved a great number of Birds and Fishes, two chests of which, I lately got home, which I know not what to do with as they require so much Room and so much attention to preserve them properly . . .
>
> The Islands do not abound in Insects, yet I got a few that were very uncommon, and a great Variety of Sea Insects, Corallines and other Zeophyla, which I have preserved in Spirits for further inspections.[24]

Walker's impression of the situation of the people he encountered during the journey was a good deal more charitable than the contemporary Lowland view, summed up by a correspondent of the Duke of Newcastle who found that the Highlanders 'not being brought up to mechanical trades or other occupations loiter away their time in dancing, attending on their chiefs and chieftains, and in stealing from other people in order to support their idleness'.[25] Walker believed that the islanders were 'an acute and sensible people, extremely desirous of instruction, and capable of great attainments, both in Knowledge and Industry'.[26] He had become 'more and more convinced, that the mind of man is to be observed more and more perfect as one moves northwards, and that a penetrating air seems to produce penetrating souls and that wind and weather, the keener they are appear to give the sharper edge to the human understanding'.[27] Where there was a lack of education and religious guidance, however, he believed there was a certain irregularity in morals and lack of civilised manners and way of life.

Walker's attitude to the Gaelic language seems also to have been unusually sympathetic for a Lowland minister in the middle of the eighteenth century. He did not believe, it is true, that children could be taught to read in Gaelic and considered that knowledge of English acquired in school was the key which would open the doors of civilisation to the islanders. On the other hand he objected to the General Assembly's order that part of every sermon should be in English, and there is evidence from his manuscripts that he himself acquired later in life some knowledge of Gaelic orthography, which he obviously lacked when he wrote this Report.

Walker was anxious immediately on his return to complete the report for the Commissioners of Annexed Estates. To Lord Kames he wrote,

> I am now going to sit down, and prepare for the view of the Board, what I have written upon my Expedition, which is a great Quantity, but in great Dissorder . . .
>
> I will immediately enter upon it, with all Diligence and Despatch of which I am capable. Let me do my best, I am certain it will require a great deal of Time. The Account of the Islands which will itself make a large volume, I propose to have finished against March or April . . . which with my whole year's work on a very large parish and other necessary Avocations will cost me excessive labour.[28]

By January 1765, Walker was hoping to have the report finished by June. At the same time he had to complete the report on the religious and educational state of the Hebrides for the General Assembly in May 1765[29] and finish his report to the S.P.C.K.[30] As a result, the vastly more detailed 'Report on the Hebrides' was not ready for the Commissioners of Annexed Estates until

March, 1771. Then, the report was received very favourably and there were suggestions that it should be published, but these Walker resisted, maintaining that it 'was intended for their private Use, and not at all for Publication at least in its present form'.[31] Walker was intending to use the material in the report for a 'Natural History of the Hebrides'. During the tour of 1764, he had not managed to reach Scarba, Seil, Luing, Lismore and several other islands, as it had been too dangerous for the boat he was travelling in to reach them, and soon after the presentation of the report he asked to be allowed a second commission to complete his work by visiting these islands. The Commissioners granted him a further 100 guineas and once more the General Assembly allowed him leave of absence in return for another report. The expedition of 1771 produced the second report for the Church[32] but nothing for the Commissioners. They had promised him a further payment when he completed the proposed 'Natural History of the Hebrides', but it was never finished. The original 'Report on the Hebrides' of 1771 was sent to the king and was seen no more until it was discovered at the end of the nineteenth century in the King's Library, by then part of the British Museum Library. The folio MS volume stands next to the anonymous report, 'The Highlands in 1750', which was edited by Andrew Lang in 1898. It is possible that Lang found the MS 'Report on the Hebrides' and told others of its existence. It came to the notice of Sir Kenneth Mackenzie of Gairloch, who had the sections on Lewis and Harris copied, and these were published by the Gaelic Society of Inverness. The section on Skye was printed in a later volume. Apart from this, the 'Report on the Hebrides' has remained unnoticed in the British Library, although it seems possible that there are manuscript copies of individual sections extant in private collections. The report is an invaluable account of the Hebrides as they were immediately before 'improvement' became widespread.

The report is based on the mass of material Walker brought back from his tour. Unfortunately neither this nor the journal he kept appears to have survived and it is not known who gave him the very detailed figures of exports, prices, wages and population totals. His most likely contacts were of course the ministers, and Walker acknowledged their assistance to Lord Bute:

> Though the Commission I had from the General Assembly cost me a great deal of Time and Travel, yet it was very usefull to me upon many accounts, especially in procuring me the Assistance and Information of the Clergy, in everything I wanted.[33]

Walker was sent data after his return which appear in the text of the report. His correspondence with Macnicol, minister of Lismore, too late to be of use in 1771, perhaps gives an indication of what demands he made on his fellow ministers; he asked for information on fish, their Gaelic and English names, snakes, deer bones, seals, tides, numbers of people over eighty, what 'Selma' meant and any other Ossianic names Macnicol could suggest, the rents of farms and the kind of flax sown.[34]

The S.P.C.K. report of 1765 shows that during the tour of 1764 Walker had been in contact with the parish elders, some of whom were proprietors or their heirs, and would have information he needed; among others he met Macneill, younger of Colonsay, Young Clanranald, Young Boisdale, and Gillanders, Mackenzie of Seaforth's tyrannical factor on Lewis.

Walker also did a considerable amount of background research. His manuscript papers in the library of the University of Edinburgh show detailed work on the Sibbald manuscripts in the Advocates' Library (he owned a 1742 catalogue of the Library), including notes on the animal and bird life of the Hebrides, natural products and numbers of fighting men. He transcribed information on natural manures and minerals from Sir Alexander Murray's 'True Interest of Britain and Ireland' and a chronology from Boece, giving forty kings of Scotland with notes on each. Besides his large collection of botanical and geological treatises, Walker's own library contained works of Sibbald, Pennant's 'British Zoology', Martin Martin's 'Voyage to St Kilda', a 'Confession of Faith' in Irish, Sacheverell's 'Account of the Isle of Man', and a 1675 edition of Ptolemy's 'Geography'.[35] Walker also drew on Martin Martin's 'Description of the Western Isles' and George Buchanan's 'History of Scotland' which used Dean Monro's description of the Hebrides. His 'Economical History of the Hebrides and Highlands' shows he was acquainted with Webster's account of the population of Scotland and the General Assembly's 1750 report[36] which contained estimates of population.

After Walker's death, his library, containing some six hundred titles, was sold. The sale catalogue, which survives,[37] shows how broad his scientific reading was of the authors mentioned in the report. Apart from Linnaeus, who figures very prominently, the library contained, for example, Wallerius' 'Mineralogie' (1753), 'Chemica Physica' (1760), 'Systema Mineralogica' (1768) and 'Elementa Mineralogica' (1768). There were also volumes of Bauhin's 'Historia Plantarum' (1650-51) and 'Pinax and Prodromus' (1671), and John Ray's 'Historia Plantarum' (1686), 'Observations' (1673), 'Catalogus Plantarum Angliae' (1677) and 'Synopsis' (1724). It seems Walker read French (probably only reluctantly), but not German. He was of course fluent in Latin.

Aspects of the Islands c. 1764

It is not the intention of this introduction to attempt to survey the history of the islands in the mid-eighteenth century. This was not John Walker's aim and the necessary local detailed studies have not yet been made in any number. It seems more worthwhile to expand on some of the topics which particularly interested Walker.

The Land

Walker's estimates of the extent of the islands are far from accurate, and vary wildly from over- to under-estimates: Rum with nearly 30,000 acres is credited with only 15,360; Tiree which contains just under 19,000 acres is said to be nearer 31,000; Islay, at 150,000 is given as 211,200. Only Colonsay and Barra of the larger islands are near their true extent. Very few estates in the Highland area had been surveyed by 1764 and the figures seem to be based on hearsay or guesswork. When Macleod of Macleod put Harris up for sale in 1771 the extent of the island was not known and Walker's report was used as the basis for the description of the estate. It was criticised even then for its inaccuracy. Unfortunately, the lack of accuracy must cast doubt on Walker's breakdown of the totals into land that had been tilled, what was considered reclaimable and what even he thought was beyond all hope of cultivation. But if his figures are anywhere near accurate or if their ratios are true, they are startling and confirm that cultivation must have extended to ground that today would not be considered inbye at all, leave alone be used for tillage. James Macdonald's report on the Hebrides to the Board of Agriculture in 1811 gives adequate evidence that this was indeed the case, and it is confirmed by traces of tillage still to be seen in the most unlikely places; but Walker's figures put the extent of tillage higher even than Macdonald's and would repay detailed investigation as an invaluable source for estimates of the amount of land lost to grazing between 1765 and the first decade of the nineteenth century.

His first category of land includes the infield and all the outfield. Not all this category would be in cultivation at once, the outfield being worked in patches for a number of years; hence Walker's care to define it as land worked by plough or spade at one time or another. The ratios of land used for cultivation to the total available appear in Table 1. Also in that table for comparison are Sir Frank Fraser Darling's ratios for inbye land, not tilled land, to total acreage. They show how narrow the ratios were according to Walker. Fraser Darling considered Tiree's ratio of inbye to total acreage of 1: 3.5 as extraordinarily narrow but in 1764, if Walker is to be believed, it was far narrower still.[38]

Table 1
*Walker - Ratios of tilled land to total acreage;
†Fraser Darling - Ratios of inbye land to totals.

Island	Walker*	Fraser Darling†
Lewis	1: 11.23	1: 21 (Lewis and Harris)
Harris	1: 12.57	
N. Uist	1: 8.11	1: 6 (N. Uist to Barra)
Benbecula	1: 2.4	
S. Uist	1: 5.5	
Barra	1: 2.56	
Islay	1: 4.22	1: 7.5
Jura	1: 7.67	1: 135
Colonsay	nearly all arable	1: 12
Mull	1: 4.61	1: 36
Coll	1: 2	1: 12
Tiree	1: 1.54	1: 3.5

Walker's second category of land included all that he regarded as reclaimable: 'extensive tracts of moorish soil, covered with heather or grasses of the coarsest nature . . . all the tracts where the soil is good, but so encumbered with fixed stones as to be unserveable for cultivation . . . fields of blowing sand . . . which by skill and industry may be so fixed, as to be rendered not only harmless but useful'.[39] The only land he considered totally irreclaimable was 'the mountainous tracts, which from their great height or rocky and precipitous situation can only serve for the pasture of sheep or of small black cattle in the summer season'.[40]

Thousands of acres of arable land had been lost beneath blowing sand and Walker is witness to further inundations. The islands with large tracts of machair land, the Harris islands, North and South Uist, Benbecula, Barra, Coll and Tiree were vulnerable to sand from the dunes that fringed the western shores separating the true machair from the beach becoming unstable and being blown over the cultivated machair lying behind them. The blow destroyed not only arable land but entire 'villages' or townships. In 1697 great damage had been done in the south of Pabbay, Harris and the farm of Middleton disappeared from the rent rolls; on Berneray, Sheapie was overblown to a depth of several feet, again in 1697; on Coll a teind decreet of 1726 mentions two farms having to be removed a mile owing to inundation. In this report Walker records the houses in the Baleshare township on North Uist being blown up to the roofs; on Barra good land had been covered following a great storm in 1749, and entire villages had to be removed in several parts of the island. The initial cause of the dunes appears to be tidal and climatic but their repeated blowing depends on how well plants can form a stabilising cover to resist the wind. In 1695 an Act had been passed forbidding pulling up bent, juniper and broom bushes by the roots because 'many land, meadows and pasturages lying on the sea coasts have been ruined and overspread in many places . . . by sand driven over from adjacent sandhills.' This was directed at the blowing sands of Culbin but the problem was much more widespread. Bent had many uses for the people of the Hebrides (*vide* the Coll section of this report), and at least one of the stabilising plants, the Lady's bedstraw, was used for dyeing; one pound of the roots of this small plant were needed to dye just a single pound of wool. It came to be an offence on many estates to pull bent or to collect the roots of the bedstraw. The lack of provision of winter fodder for the cattle led to their being driven to eat the bent shoots, thus preventing it from establishing itself on the dunes. Overstocking must have played a major part in maintaining the blow and reducing the arable acres. The significance of the effect of the blowing sand on the ability of a population to live on an island is pointed out by Walker in describing how Barra, once exporting significant amounts of grain, was no longer able to provide enough for its own food, and the people were provided for only by the introduction of potatoes. Thus the all-important relationship between population and resources was being disturbed. Furthermore, the population was far from stable, and increasing numbers had to be fed from a declining acreage. There is no evidence in Walker, however, that the sandblow was the result of the increase in population.

Grain Production

The report demonstrates how important it is to regard each island as a separate economic unit. There is a considerable difference, for example, in the islands' ability to grow sufficient grain to feed their populations and, for that matter, in their dependence on grain for food. In Jura the people were living mainly on milk, butter, cheese, mutton, fish and venison; on Rum for the whole summer they lived on animal food and an old man was said to have lived for fifty years without tasting bread, dependence on which he regarded as a sign of decadence; in North Uist the labourers had lived on fowl, fish and milk with very little bread until the manufacturing of kelp began and they needed more sustenance and presumably could afford it. Some of the islands were able to export grain: Tiree annually exported about 400 bolls of bear and meal; Barra 'commonly' exported a little bear. Others had grain to spare in good years: Islay sold a considerable quantity in some years and usually had enough whatever the season; Coll exported a considerable quantity in good years despite using a good deal for distilling. South Uist exported after a good harvest but had to import after a dry summer. Harris and Lewis usually managed to provide enough. Benbecula managed in a good season but had to import a good deal if the summer was dry. Mull always imported, not so much from a lack of arable land, but because too much was turned over to pasture. North Uist had not enough arable to support its population and imported. Jura suffered great scarcity and Rum produced enough grain to feed its population for only a few months of the year.

The grey oat (*avena strigosa*) was grown everywhere and yielded an average of 3:1, although in potentially fertile Tiree it returned only an abysmal 2½:1. The use of the caschrom could produce 5:1 in some areas. At the present time 10:1 is expected from grains in good conditions for growth. A Scots acre sown with a boll of grey oats was producing a return of seed and between half a boll and one and a half bolls of meal. Bear (the four-rowed barley, *hordeum vulgare*) was grown in all the islands, although comparatively little was sown in Skye. In most of the islands it produced a return of about 5:1, varying from about 3:1 to 8:1, but in the Outer Hebrides and especially Lewis, South Uist and the Harris islands, the returns could reach as much as 30:1, with an average of nearer 15:1, when the ground was prepared with the caschrom (which dug deeply and turned the sod right over) and was covered with seaweed. The best returns came from ground left uncultivated for some time. In the very best conditions, when the season was favourable and produced enough rain during the growing period and the seed was sown very thinly, bear on Pabbay, Harris produced 17, 12 or 10 ears of barley for one grain sown. A good head of bear contains fifty grains. High yields such as these had been produced at least since the seventeenth century and probably much longer. In the report, Walker urges that in some islands the two-rowed barley should be introduced, but by the time he wrote the text of the 'Economical History of the Hebrides and Highlands', probably at the end of the 1790's, he had become persuaded that there was nothing to be gained by its introduction to the islands, as it required earlier sowing and a longer growing period than bear. For oats, he urged the introduction of the white oat (which had a higher yield than the grey and could be successful if planted early) and of the most suitable variety which could withstand wind well and grow in exposed situations.

Walker set out in 1764 to observe the state of agriculture in the Hebrides so that the principles of improved farming could be applied to them most advantageously. Therefore he noted the yields of crops, compared the advantages of cultivation with caschrom and plough, recorded dates of sowing and reaping and where natural manures such as seaware, sea-sleech, shell and stone marles, coral, limestone and shell sand could be obtained. After the report was written, he turned his mind to constructing an agricultural system that could be applied to the islands. His ideas were published posthumously in his 'Economical History of the Hebrides and Highlands' (1808). Although Walker accepted that the land in the Hebrides was more fit for pasture than crops, he did not believe that it was therefore better for the people to rear cattle or sheep and to import grain. He realised that a pastoral system would lead to depopulation, which he wanted to avoid, and instead he proposed an intensive system of crop raising which would provide sufficient grain and potatoes for the people to live on and at the same time rear more and better quality cattle or sheep if conditions suited them better. He was governed by social rather than economic criteria and advocated agricultural techniques to achieve his aims.

The system of agriculture he proposed was based on drainage, enclosure and a rotation of crops including green crops, turnips, beans and potatoes. The infield would continue under cultivation but with a rotation that would not scourge it; the whole of the outfield, formerly used in small patches, was to be brought into cultivation, and potatoes were to be used to extend the arable acreages. Food crops could be produced in far greater quantity because of the increased acreage under cultivation; the use of natural manures would increase yields; and winter feed would be produced for the stock; there would be little encroachment on the summer pastures.

Walker wanted true 'improvement', not what went under that name and led to the impoverishment of the land, a failure to use its potential and depopulation throughout many of the islands.

Weights and Measures

Walker's statements on weights and measures are very precise and reveal a considerable degree of discrepancy among the islands. They reflect the state of unutterable confusion which existed in 1764 in Scotland. Amsterdam, Scottish Troye and Scottish Trone weights were all in use and of different values. The old Scottish Trone weights had been abolished in 1617 when Scottish Troye had been made standard, but they continued to be used. Trade and the union with England brought into use the Amsterdam and English weights. The Act of Union had enacted that the same weights and measures were to be used throughout the United Kingdom, but English and Scottish weights were both retained. In 1765 two bills had been presented to the Commons to establish 'uniform and certain standards of weights and measures throughout the Kingdom of Great Britain', but they were not passed.

In 1779 John, Lord Swinton published a pamphlet entitled 'A proposal for Uniformity of Weights and Measures in Scotland', which set out tables of equivalent values for all the systems in use. Using English Troy grains as the base:

English Avoirdupois —	437.6 grains = 1 oz; 16 oz = 1 lb; 14 lbs = 1 stone. *i.e. 1 stone = 98,022 grains*
Scottish Trone —	476 grains = 1 oz; 20 ozs = 1 lb; 16 lbs = 1 stone. *i.e. 1 stone = 152,320 grains*
Scottish Troye —	476 grains = 1 oz; 16 ozs = 1 lb; 16 lbs = 1 stone. *i.e. 1 stone = 121,856 grains*

Amsterdam weight was theoretically the same as Scottish Troye, but the weights used were often heavier.

In practice, Lord Swinton found a degree of variation greater still and he had to set out tables of equivalents for all the counties of Scotland and in many cases for different centres within the counties. Walker mentions that on the islands the standard weights and measures of Scotland were 'altogether unknown'. He found that 'the inhabitants deal with one another according to certain local weights and measures of their own, which are unpractised and even unknown in their immediate neighbourhood. Nay, in many places, as in the Isle of Mull, they have none that are in general use, and the People buy and sell almost quite by guess.' He gives details of weights for butter and cheese: in Lewis the stone was 23 English pounds; in North Uist it was 16 lbs Trone weight or 22 lbs English; in South Uist, 21 lbs; in Mull, 22 lbs at 16 oz to the pound for butter and 24 lbs at 16 oz to the pound for cheese; on Tiree and Coll, 22 lbs at 22 oz to the pound and on Islay butter and cheese were sold at 22 oz to the pound.

Measurement of grains and meal was just as complicated. In 1618 the Linlithgow boll had been established as the unit for dry measure. It contained 16 pecks of 4 firlots and each firlot was a declared number of pints. Before this there had been differences in measuring wheat, rye and meal on the one hand

and barley and oats on the other: the former were streaked, that is, the measure was levelled off, but the latter were heaped above the level of the measure. To maintain the difference, two bolls were established containing firlots based on pints of differing capacity. In 1696 the Linlithgow boll was abolished and grain was to be sold by weight at eight stone Troye weight to the Linlithgow boll. In practice it continued to be used, and in 1765 the boll was still the general measure all over Scotland and, far from being uniformly the equivalent of eight stones, in many instances it was not equal even to the former Linlithgow standard and could be measured in pounds or pints or a combination of both. Lord Swinton found that, in 1779, 'there are hardly two counties in Scotland where the boll-measure is exactly the same, and there are some counties, where the boll contains more than double what it does in others'. Walker found considerable variation: on Lewis the boll of grain was said to contain 16 pecks, each peck of 8 pints, that is, a quarter more than the Linlithgow peck which contained 6 pints; on Jura a boll of fern ashes contained 16 pecks, with each peck 10 lbs, making a boll of 160 lbs compared to the eight stones or 112 lbs of the standard boll; on Tiree and Coll the boll was 'near double that of Lithgow'; on Mull the boll of oatmeal was five stones to the boll and eight cogs to the stone and the boll of bear was larger than the meal boll; on Skye the boll of oatmeal weighed 'rather more than ten stone whereas that of Lithgow weighs only eight'. It is a hazardous undertaking to attempt a statistical analysis based on the boll or grain prices in eighteenth-century Scotland.

Church and Education

At the re-establishment of Presbytery after the Revolution, the Church of Scotland's influence in the Hebrides had appeared somewhat tenuous and threatened by both Episcopalians and Catholics, and without the manpower or the organisation to combat them. By 1764, time and the Episcopalians' support of the Jacobite cause had resulted in ministers in every parish and a majority of the heritors firmly presbyterian in belief and practice. It was not so easy to triumph over 'popery', and there were fears expressed by Walker and his fellow ministers that it was still on the increase.

Catholicism had become established in some of the islands during the seventeenth century when missionaries, mainly Franciscans and Lazarists, had come among a people who for the most part had been neglected from the time of the Reformation - as indeed the Presbyterians admitted. The Franciscans who came from Ireland in the 1620's and 1630's found the population clinging to a memory of Catholic beliefs and some undoubtedly pagan practices. A few areas appear to have been more definitely Catholic. The missionaries found great encouragement and success and sent back to the Committee of Propaganda in Rome news of great numbers of converts coming from a wide area, including Islay, Colonsay, Jura, Skye, Barra, South and North Uist, Benbecula, Rum, Eigg, Canna and Mull. They were, however, given very little support from Rome in either money or men, and political events led the chiefs, on whose welcome success depended, to become less hospitable. By the 1690's Catholicism was centred on the islands where Catholic chiefs could protect the priests - South Uist, Benbecula, Barra and all the Small Isles; the southern islands and Skye, except for brief periods of intermittent missionary endeavour, had been recovered for Protestantism, although Martin Martin's description of beliefs and practices casts some doubts on what that Protestantism really meant.

The situation was a considerable source of concern and even humiliation to the Church of Scotland. At the turn of the century there were more priests than ministers within the area of the Presbytery of Skye and it was reported to the General Assembly that

> The number of these trafiquing Priests and Jesuits increase in their number and labours day by day . . . They throng upon Ardinmurchan, Morvern, Tiri, Coll and North Uist and other islands who own the reformed Protestant religion where they have perverted some already and many are endangered.[41]

In 1694, for the first time since the Reformation, a Catholic bishop was appointed and later began visitations to the Highlands and Islands. In 1714 it was reported that there were six priests and a friar in the islands, a priest in South Uist was saying mass publicly, and on Rum, Eigg and Canna the people 'keep their priest and pay him their tithes'.[42] In 1720 it was said that the minister of South Uist had lived forty years on the island but had never had above eighteen hearers at once.[43] Barra had had a Catholic school for many decades, but Protestant fears were aroused by the establishment of a seminary at Scalan, Glenlivet in 1717. In 1721 the Pope ratified the division of Scotland into two Vicariates, and in 1731 a bishop, a son of Macdonald of Morar, was appointed to the Highlands. Except for Rum and Muck, where the lairds of Coll and Muck were attempting to establish Protestantism, the Catholic islands remained beyond the reach of the Church of Scotland and the penal laws were unenforced. At the end of the 1730's a report was prepared for the General Assembly drawing attention to the fact that

> Diverse Acts of Parliament have been made in Scotland against (Popery), but not put into execution, and almost in everything, these laws have been trampled upon by Papists and (it appears) that diverse of them continue to succeed to lands, or do elude the law by deeds of Trust, and their children are brought up and educate in the errors of the Church of Rome and some have been sent abroad for that end, papists have had and continue to have their Masses, and places of meeting of their Idolatrous Worship publicly, and keep schools.[44]

Catholicism was increasing, 'where the heritors are Popish, and Priests and Emissaries of Rome are resett and encouraged, and where there are none in Authority to support and protect, such as incline to favour the Protestant Ministers and other Missionaries, but the people left to the Arbitrary Will of Papists, Particularly in Bara, South Uist, Egg, Muck and Cana, Knowdart, Morshire etc. . . . When Papists send their children to the (S.P.C.K.) schools, the Priests do threaten the parents with Excommunication, and they are laid under the displeasure of their Popish Landlords; yea popish Schools and

Seminaries are kept in places yet, and popish Bishops have their meetings with their clergy, and send Youth abroad to Popish Colleges, and many of them when returned, are put in orders, and sent to their respective pretended functions, and marry and Baptise Papists and Protestants, and Intrude themselves on Sick Persons, whereby some few have been brought over to Popery.'[45]

By 1760, despite Walker's fears, the position from the Church of Scotland's point of view had improved greatly. The Catholic hierarchy and priests were deeply implicated in the Jacobite rebellions and the '45 is said to have held back the Catholic Scottish Mission for more than a quarter of a century.[46] Orders were given to demolish 'papist chapels' and arrest the priests. There had been three priests on Barra and South Uist for many years. In 1746, one was arrested on Barra and did not return; Alexander Forrester, priest on Uist, left the island until 1748 and then had to work in hiding and from time to time go to the mainland. He was not permanently settled again until about 1763 when he was old and weakened by prison and exile.[47] The priests were brought up to numerical strength again and Bishop John Macdonald for a time was stationed in the islands, but Catholicism never regained its outgoing dynamism and vigour. Soon after Walker's visit there was no prominent Catholic proprietor in the Hebrides. Despite fears to the contrary, Catholicism in the islands had been contained. This had been achieved partly by Catholic involvement in rebellion and partly by the efforts of the Church of Scotland to put its house in order.

The causes of the Church's difficulty in meeting the Catholic challenge in the islands are not far to seek. Before the Reformation there had been nearly fifty parishes in the islands, but the end of the sixteenth and the beginning of the seventeenth centuries saw a series of unions that produced the monolithic united parish of Stornoway, Gress, Eye, Lochs and Uig on Lewis; the united parish of Portree, Raasay, Snizort and Uig on Skye and the united parish of Sleat, Strath and the Small Isles, so vast they were impossible to serve adequately. Even where parishes remained separate, a serious shortage of manpower meant they were in practice united. When Bishop Knox reported on his diocese in 1626, there were only two ministers and a reader serving the whole of Skye, one 'verie auld man' responsible for North and South Uist and Benbecula, two ministers in Islay, two in Lewis, three in Mull, and Barra was looked after by the minister of Harris. The first attempts to reform the parish structures were made after the Synod of Argyll had been set up by the General Assembly in 1638, but the 1661 Act Rescissory at the Restoration annulled them. Nothing more was done, even after Presbytery was restored, until the threat of 'Popery' forced the church into action. In 1724 the Synod of Argyll's area, which had stretched from the Butt of Lewis to Islay and took in a large section of the mainland, was divided in two. The new Synod of Glenelg was made responsible for the northern half including Skye, the Small Isles and the Long Island, and the Synod of Argyll kept the southern, including Islay, Jura, Colonsay, Mull, Coll and Tiree. The Presbyteries were divided into workable units that could hope to provide supervision and support for the ministers in the difficult areas; the Presbytery of Skye, which had included all the Long Island as well as Skye and the Small Isles, was divided into the two Presbyteries of Skye and the Long Island in 1724; the Presbytery of Mull was separated from that of Lorne in 1726, and in 1742 the Long Island was further divided into the Presbyteries of Lewis and Uist. Disjunctions of the parishes were authorised by the Commission of Teinds: in 1722 Lochs and Uig in Lewis were separated from Stornoway, Gress and Eye; in 1726 the Skye parishes of Snizort, Uig, Portree, Sleat and Strath together with the Small Isles were all made separate parishes; in 1733 Barra was severed from South Uist.

Nevertheless, the neglect of a century and a half could not be overcome immediately and its signs were still all too apparent when the Assembly sent Doctors Hyndman and Dick in 1760 and Walker in 1764. By then the parishes numbered twenty-four but in these, although the heritors should have built a church and manse and provided a glebe, one church was being built, two were ruinous, and six parishes had none at all; only two of the ministers had both manse and glebe but most of them held farms from the proprietors. The parishes were still so vast that there were fifty-three 'other places of worship' provided, an indication of how many parishes were really needed. The parish of Jura still included Colonsay, Oronsay, Jura, Scarba and several other small but inhabited islands and for years had suffered gross neglect because its ageing minister could not cope with its excessive demands. In many parishes it was not until towards the end of the century that churches and manses were built, and it was not until well into the nineteenth century that they were made into workable units by the provision of chapels and Parliamentary churches. During this time, the sad state of the parish system was relieved only by the quality of a majority of its ministers - several of whom were renowned classical and Gaelic scholars - and by assistance from the S.P.C.K. and the Royal Bounty Committee of the General Assembly.

The Scottish Society for the Propagation of Christian Knowledge had been granted a royal charter in 1709, and from 1710 it erected schools and supplied teachers to the Highlands and Islands. Under its charter the Society was to 'eradicate error and to sow truth, to teach true religion and loyalty and to strengthen the British Empire by the addition of useful subjects and firm Protestants'. To carry out its work the Society was given financial support from the General Assembly, and in return the teachers worked as catechists for a specific number of days a week, until 1758 when the contract between the two bodies ended.

In 1723 a grant of £1,000 was made by the king to the General Assembly to help in the fight against Catholicism. From 1725 it became an annual grant, administered by an Assembly committee known as the Committee of the Royal Bounty. Part of the grant was used to provide missionary ministers to assist in the parishes who were usually itinerants, wandering from township to township, preaching and reading the scriptures. In 1764 there were ten of them, said to be well qualified and able. The Bounty was also used to support catechists, in addition to the S.P.C.K. teachers, who were to teach the people the catechism and Lord's Prayer in preparation for the minister's annual catechising and, in districts far from a church, 'to meet with them every Sabbath, to read the Scriptures, and to join with them in psalms and prayers'.[48] Between 1725 and 1728, seventy were appointed. Walker met eighteen of them in the islands on his tour and was horrified to discover that a few of them were virtually illiterate. The holders of the Committee's bursaries for Gaelic-speaking students in Divinity were expected to act as catechists during their vacations.

Adequate provision for education was a key factor in the Government's and Church's attempts to 'civilise' the Highlands and Islands. Some schools had been provided in the seventeenth century: the Synod of Argyll by 1700 had Grammar schools in Skye and Islay and eleven schools teaching English in other islands; there was a famous school at Orbost in Skye, and a Grammar School founded by a Macdonald of Sleat at Duntuilm; in Stornoway the Earl of Seaforth started a school in 1680 which at the end of the century was teaching Latin and English. The 1696 Act under which heritors had to build a school in each parish was largely disregarded and the only source of education in many parishes was the charity or S.P.C.K. school or those supported by a grant from the Royal Bounty Committee which assisted four 'Principal' or 'Grammar' schools, some of them the descendants of seventeenth-century foundations and some new, in Lewis, North Uist, Skye and Mull. It was hoped that they would provide Gaelic-speaking students for the ministry.

In 1760, Doctors Hyndman and Dick found only three parochial or 'legal' schools in all the islands they visited, one in North Uist and two in Skye, serving four parishes.[49] By 1764 the position had improved under pressure from the S.P.C.K. There were then only a few islands without a school at all, but still the goal of providing an educational system that could have any effect on the main body was far from realisation.[50]

Population

It is beyond the scope of this introduction to attempt an appraisal of the highly complex demographic history of the islands in the eighteenth century.[51] Nevertheless, Walker's work in demography was considerable and deserves evaluation, especially as it throws further light on the statistical basis of the demographic study of the period.

The mid-eighteenth century brought a surge of interest in the movement of population and its structure. Walker was caught up in this movement and concerned himself with the 'outlines of Life and Death' in which he felt 'many considerable blanks still remain'.[52] As with all demographers of the time, he was working without a basis of reliable statistics. Before the first official census of 1801 and compulsory registration of vital statistics from 1855, there was no reliable quantitative basis for the demographer's work and he had to rely on the Church of Scotland's ministers who held annual visitations of their parishes and either kept lists of those they catechised or had a good idea of their number.

Before 1750 the only indication of the population of the islands had come from presbytery and synod reports to the General Assembly mainly concerning the threat of popery,[53] and a report made to the General Assembly by a deputation sent to the isles in the 1730's.[54] In 1750 the General Assembly was concerned with the ministers' stipends and asked for details of the population of each parish. Some parishes did not produce the figures and most of the others must be regarded as estimates.[55] In 1760 Doctors Hyndman and Dick produced a list of the island parishes, giving the numbers of Catholics and Protestants and in some instances the total number of souls or catechisable inhabitants.[56] On a different scale altogether was Dr Alexander Webster's account of the population of Scotland.[57] In 1755 he collected returns from the ministers, giving in some cases total population figures and in others the numbers of examinable persons. These formed the basis of his 'census' compiled shortly after 1755, which gave not only totals for the parishes but also a breakdown of the population into ages. As the numbers of examinable persons did not include children up to an age varying from six to ten, or the elderly, Webster calculated the totals, using a formula based on Halley's life tables.

Walker wanted to find the total population of Scotland but he wanted it more accurately based than Webster's. Ideally he wanted all the inhabitants numbered and their ages specified - a much closer approximation to a true census than Webster's had been. He was, of course, aware that this was impossible:

> There are few who have the proper opportunity and still fewer, who to obtain a single fact of this nature, would submit to the drudgery of such an operation.[58]

He accepted his limitations and concentrated on getting the data he wanted from one Hebridean parish - the Small Isles. To obtain the statistics he asked the catechist, 'a sensible and careful man', to note the numbers of individuals, their ages, the numbers of the sexes, families, marriages and children, as he went on his annual visitation. Walker believed from his own observation that the statistics would be fairly representative of all the Hebridean parishes. The table and other data thus produced were recorded in this 'Report on the Hebrides'.

Walker arranged his material in a professional way, beginning with children under one and entering totals for the parish as a whole and for the individual islands. Unfortunately in the table there is no division of the sexes. Although the accuracy of any eighteenth-century list of ages must be suspect to some extent, there seems no reason to doubt the children's ages here. There is distinct 'bunching' in the higher age-groups, suggesting some of the informants were not altogether accurate, and it is perhaps wise to use the totals for decades as the basis for analysis. Walker thus provides a rare opportunity to look at the population structure of a parish in the mid-eighteenth century.

One of the most significant observations to be made from the table is that Webster's formula which he used to convert numbers of examinable persons into totals would not have produced Walker's observed figures if it had been applied to the Small Isles returns. The actual total was 1,159; using Webster's figures and taking the age at which catechising began as 7, he would have calculated the total as 1,138, an underestimate of 1.8%; if the age of nine is taken, the total calculated would have been 1,105, an underestimate of 4.7%. It suggests that Webster's figures hide a considerable degree of regional variation or that the Breslau breakdown of population cannot be applicable to the Hebrides in the mid-eighteenth century.

A breakdown of the population of the Small Isles into decades (Table 2) can be used to calculate the percentage of the people in the various age-groups (Table 3). This can then be compared with Webster's data for the whole of Scotland in 1755. The differences in some instances are in demographic terms quite considerable (Table 4).

Table ×
Population of the Small Isles

	EIGG	RUM	MUCK	CANNA	PARISH
0- 9	122	95	41	65	323
10-19	65	54	28	60	207
20-29	90	48	15	41	194
30-39	64	38	25	26	153
40-49	34	20	19	22	95
50-59	39	21	6	25	91
60-69	28	19	6	12	65
70-79	14	4	2	1	21
80-89	3	3	1	1	8
90-99	0	2	0	0	2
	459	304	143	253	1159

Table 3
Percentage of Population in various age-groups

	Webster's Scotland	Small Isles	RUM	EIGG	MUCK	CANNA
0- 9	25.48	28.10	31.25	26.80	28.67	25.69
10-19	18.64	18.80	17.76	14.16	19.58	23.71
20-29	16.65	15.52	15.79	19.61	10.49	16.21
30-39	13.87	14.28	12.50	13.94	17.48	10.28
40-49	10.65	8.99	6.58	7.40	13.29	8.70
50-59	7.50	7.30	6.91	8.20	4.20	9.88
60 and over	7.23	8.20	9.22	9.8	6.30	5.32

Table 4
Differences in the percentage age-groups of the population, Walker (Small Isles, 1764) – Webster (Scotland, 1755)

	Small Isles:	Rum	Eigg	Muck	Canna
0- 9	+2.62	+5.77	+1.32	+3.19	+ .21
10-19	+ .16	− .88	−4.48	+ .94	+5.07
20-29	−1.13	− .86	+2.96	−6.16	− .44
30-39	+ .41	−1.37	+ .07	+3.61	−3.59
40-49	−1.66	−4.07	−3.25	+2.64	−1.95
50-59	− .20	− .59	+ .70	−3.30	+2.38
60 and over	+ .97	+1.99	+2.57	− .93	−1.91

The parish and all the individual islands have a higher percentage in the 0-9 age-group, Rum showing a highly significant discrepancy of 5.77, indicating a higher birth-rate and/or a greater survival rate. After 10, the islands become widely idiosyncratic, except in the 40-49 age-group in which all the islands except Muck are lower than Webster's national figure. Rum and Eigg show remarkably high figures for the over 60's. The table certainly suggests that in 1764 the composition of at least one parish in the islands was far from the national pattern as suggested by Webster in 1755. How far this is true of the other island parishes is open to conjecture.

Although he did not divide the population of the Small Isles by sex in the tables of age-groups, Walker was very aware of the importance of the balance of the sexes in population study. He gives two breakdowns of the sex distribution of the parish; in the 'Economical History of the Hebrides and Highlands' he gives statistics which give ratios of males per 100 females as 108.2 for the under 7's; 117.6 for the 7 to 16-year-olds; 77.6 for the 16 to 60's and 88.5 for those above 60; this gives an overall ratio of 97.97. In this report, sex totals are given for the individual islands, giving ratios: Rum, 93.6; Eigg, 66.3; Muck, 101.4 and Canna, 96.1. The overall ratio is 89.35. This discrepancy must cast doubt on the accuracy of all the figures, and deductions based on them would be suspect. This is a great loss, since some of Walker's figures are potentially very informative. This is especially true of the great imbalance of the sexes on Eigg and of the imbalance of the vital 16-60 age-group. The number of marriages in the households suggests that the ratio of the report may be nearly accurate: Rum, Muck and Canna, with more nearly balanced ratios, had a marriage in each household, but Eigg had no marriage in 10 households, which is over 10% of its total of households. Pennant maintained that in Canna marriage was held in such esteem that an old maid or bachelor was scarcely known.

The average size of the households is high and probably reflects a high birth-rate. Furthermore, Walker specifically states that many of the children had left the islands and were not in his lists. Rum has 5.33 in each household; Eigg, 5.22; Canna, 5.75 and Muck, 5.11.

Age at marriage is not given by Walker, who simply comments that it is early. Pennant, however, states that on Canna the youths married at twenty and the girls at seventeen. The high birth-rate, large size of household and numbers of children all point to a high degree of fertility, and commentators on the islands in the seventeenth and eighteenth centuries bear this out.

The other parish population figures given by Walker in the report are not based on the same kind of enumeration as that made of the Small Isles, but for the most part come from information from the parish ministers. These figures appear initially to have great potential value in assessing the rise of population in the islands between Webster's 'census' of 1755 and the 'Old Statistical Account' or the 1801 census. Indeed, in his 'Economical History', Walker attempts a comparison of this kind, using the General Assembly's account of 1750, Webster's figures, a list of his own dated 1771 and the Old Statistical

Account of the 1790's.[59] Nevertheless, his conclusions, and his assumption that the lists of 1750, 1755, 1771 and 1790 represent the total population of the parishes at these dates and so can be compared, are highly suspect. Although he wanted to be able to produce a statement of population for a specific year, his sources of information limited him to a collection of data covering a wide period. The accuracy of the parish totals given to him in 1764 was totally dependent on the parish ministers, who might base it on a recent list or, by default of information, on a list taken a decade or even more before. The last time any attempt had been made to count the population of Colonsay and Oronsay and probably Jura had been in 1724. For a considerable time before his death in 1757, the minister had been sick, and before that he had found the vast parish so difficult that Colonsay was very rarely visited. The same figure was given to Walker as went to the Presbytery in 1724, although a new minister found in 1766 that the population had increased by more than two thirds.

Walker wanted to compile the most accurate list he could and therefore he was constantly amending the figures he was given. As a result, the lists he presented at various dates do not tally. Altogether he produced three lists of the island population: in the 'Economical History' there is a list of the islands and their population totals, dated 1764; in the same volume there is a list of island parishes, dated 1771; and there is a further manuscript list in the Scottish Record Office, dated 1778.[60] Besides these, there are the totals given in this report and those in his reports to the General Assembly and the S.P.C.K. in 1765. These are set out in Table 5, in the order in which they appear to have been compiled.

None of the figures must be taken as representing the population of any island at the date given without a very careful examination of its sources. In some cases this is impossible, as the source remains unknown. Much research remains to be done.

Table 5

	A. 1765 S.P.C.K. and General Assembly	B. 1771 'Report on the Hebrides'		C. 1764 Island List, 'Economical History'		D. 1771 Parishes	E. 1778 MS.
LEWIS		Stornoway	2286	Lewis	7281		
		Lochs	1187	Rona	9		
		Uig	1687	Shiant	22		
		Barvas	1777				
		Total	**6937**	**Total**	**7312**	**7281**	**7312**
HARRIS		Harris	1363	Harris	1672		
		Islands	630	Islands	616		
				St Kilda	90		
				Flannan Isles	14		
		Total	**1993**	**Total**	**2392**	**2085**	**2486**

Table 5 (continued)

	A. 1765 S.P.C.K. and General Assembly	B. 1771 'Report on the Hebrides'		C. 1764 Island List, 'Economical History'		D. 1771 Parishes	E. 1778 MS.
NORTH UIST			2110	Mainland	2215		
			100	'Heray'	100		
			40	Vallay	40		
			60	Boreray	72		
			70	Heisker	70		
			85	Grimsay	34		
				Rona	7		
				Oronsay	18		
				Kirkibost	28		
		Total	**2465**	**Total**	**2584**	**2565**	**2584**
BENBECULA and SOUTH UIST			600	Benbecula	600		
			1580	South Uist	1580		
				Eriskay	8		
	2200	**Total**	**2180**	**Total**	**2188**	**2180**	**2188**
BARRA				Mainland	1097		
				Islands	298		
	1350		**1285**	**Total**	**1395**	**1395**	**1404**
ISLAY	Kilchoman 4000	Kilchoman	4000	Islay	7000	4300	Kilchoman
				Texa	8		
	Kildalton 3000	Kildalton	3000			3200	Kilchoman
	Total 7000	**Total**	**7000**	**Total**	**7008**	**7500**	**7008**
JURA	Jura 466		466	Jura	630		750
	Scarba 60		12	Lunga	40		
	Others 60		60	Scarba	60		
			1 family	Belnahua	95		
			1 family	Garbh Eileach	11		
			1 family	Eileach an Naoimh	8		
			6	Fladda	14		
	Colonsay, Oronsay 440		760	Colonsay	760		790
			30	Oronsay	30		
	Total 1026	**Total**	**c.1350**	**Total**	**1648**	**1456**	**1540**
GIGHA and CARA				Gigha	452		
				Cara	9		
			463	**Total**	**461**	**550**	**461**
MULL		Torosay	1200	Mull	5316		
	Iona 200	Kilninian	2449	Iona	200		
		Kilvickeon	1676	Ulva	266		
				Gometra	50		
				Inchkenneth	20		
				Calve	6		
		Total	**5325**	**Total**	**5858**	**5481**	**5481**

Table 5 (continued)

	A. 1765 S.P.C.K. and General Assembly		B. 1771 'Report on the Hebrides'		C. 1764 Island List, 'Economical History'	D. 1771 Parishes		E. 1778 MS.
COLL	1200		1200		1200	1200		1206
TIREE	1880		1681		1681	1681		1681
SMALL ISLES			459	Eigg	451			
			304	Rum	304			
			143	Muck	143			
			253	Canna	253			
		Total	**1159**	**Total**	**1151**	**1157**		**1157**
SKYE		Sleat	1868	Skye	14724	1868	Sleat	
		Strath	1200	Raasay	400	1200	Strath	
		Bracadale	3333	Rona	36	2000	Bracadale	
		Snizort	1700	Scalpay	84	1700	Snizort	
		Kilmuir	1900	Oronsay	7	1900	Kilmuir	
		Duirinish	3600	Soay	14	3600	Duirinish	
		Portree	1466	Ascrib	6	1466	Portree	
				Isay	9			
				Trodday	5			
				Flodigarry	114			
		Total	**15067**	**Total**	**15399**	**13734**		**15346**

Lewis - Walker states in the report that this figure (B) is based on information from 1766. In the 'Economical History', on the other hand, he states that the total given there (C and D) comes from a count in 1761.

Harris - The figure in the report (B) is the same as appears in the 1750 General Assembly record and presumably comes from at least as early as that. The source for C, D and E is not known.

North Uist - The report figure (B) is said by Walker to have been taken from a recent 'accurate account' made by the minister.

Benbecula and South Uist - The source for this total is not known. It is very close to Hyndman's and Webster's and is probably too low for 1764, as 'a careful count' taken for Bishop Hugh Macdonald's 'Report on the Highland Vicariate' in 1764 put the population at 2,503, and in addition there were the families of the landowner and some of the gentry who were not Catholic.[61]

Barra - The figure given in the report (B) is the same as in the General Assembly's 1750 record. The source for Walker's revised figure of 1,395 is not known. The earlier total is given some credence by Bishop Macdonald's report which records 1,200 Catholics and, in addition, some Protestant gentry.

Islay - The source is not known for this total (B). Webster did not have information for one of the Islay parishes, nor did the 1750 General Assembly record.

Jura - B includes Colonsay and Oronsay. The entire parish appears to have been reviewed in 1766, and a new count made.

Gigha and Cara - The total of 463 comes from at least as early as the 1750 General Assembly record. The source for the revised figure in D is not as yet known.

Mull - Nothing is known of the sources of these figures.

Coll - Boswell records in his 'Tour of the Hebrides'[62] that Hector Maclean, the minister, had made a list of his parishioners, on the order of the General Assembly, some years before. The minister had found 900 examinable persons over seven. Allowing for 200 under seven and 50 above seventy, the total of about 1,200 had been reached. The list was made probably at least as early as 1760, as Hyndman gives 900 catechisable persons for Coll, and possibly before 1755.

Tiree - In the 1765 reports to the Assembly and S.P.C.K., the total of 1,800 is given which tallies with the 1,793 given in the MS "Dr Walker's 'Observations on Tirey' c1765" in the Inveraray Castle papers.[63] It was changed to 1,681 probably after James Turnbull's farm-by-farm enumeration of the island in 1769 which gives a total of 1,676. At all events, this later figure of Walker's appears the more accurate.

Small Isles - This is based on the enumeration made by the catechist, although there is no explanation why the total has been reduced by two. In the text of the report Walker gives slightly different totals for two of the islands.

Skye - The source for these figures is unknown.

The 1764 list in the 'Economical History' (C) contains most of the updated figures. The 1778 MS list (E) is based on the 1764 (C) list, the individual islands being added together in nearly every instance to give the totals. The 1771 parish list (D) from the 'Economical History' for the most part repeats the 1764 Island list except that the islands have been totalled into parishes. There are, however, a number of anomalies.

Given Walker's difficulties in obtaining population figures for a specific year for the island parishes, the sources used by Webster should be looked at with care. It is doubtful whether the figures he gives derive in every case from 1755. Indeed, several of the island figures are the same as those in the General Assembly's 1750 report and others are very near. It is known that the South Uist figure was based on a list of Protestants made in 1752 and one of Catholics made in 1754.

One of the major factors in Webster's interest in population stemmed from his involvement in the Church's scheme to provide for ministers' widows and children. Walker was likewise concerned with longevity. One of his objectives in 'numbering the population' was to find the extent to which the reputation of the Hebrideans for longevity was borne out, and to produce reliable data on a subject dominated by speculation and rather dubious deduction:

> We know not yet the precise quantity of longevity in any European nation. From the data afforded by bills of mortality, calculations have been formed of the chances of life, and the comparative degrees of health in different towns and countries. But the fixed quantity of longevity, in any given number of inhabitants, has never been attempted by actual experiment. To determine this properly, it would be necessary to have the inhabitants numbered to a man, and the age of every individual specified.[64]

The elderly in the Small Isles were enumerated and he carefully collected verifiable accounts of people over 80 on the other islands. He found altogether three over 100, five over 90 and 17 over 80. Walker summarised his findings:

> Every 12th person was found to be 60 years of age, or upwards; which appears indeed to be a very great proportion. Among each 100 inhabitants there was one person of 80 or upwards, but only one person of 90 years old, above it, among 500 people.

Walker quite rightly commented that his figures by themselves were not very revealing:

> These facts ascertain only the absolute quantity of longevity. For, without a comparison with other places, we cannot say with certainty, even from these facts, whether the Hebrideans are remarkable for being long-lived or otherwise. Their comparative longevity, therefore, cannot be determined; but it will appear, when the same observations come to be made in other countries.[65]

Webster provides the statistics to compare Walker's figures for the Small Isles in 1764 to Scotland in 1755. According to Walker, .86% of the population were over 80 and .17% over ninety; according to Webster's figures, 2.59% of the total population were over 80, including 0.56% over 90. If Walker's and Webster's figures are truly representative, the widespread belief in the longevity of the Hebrideans was far from being reflected in reality.

In this report, Walker supports the popular belief that the Hebrideans were a healthier people than the population in general. Furthermore, he maintains that the health of the islanders had improved greatly 'within thirty years past'. He ascribed the improvement to 'an increase in the quantity of grain, the introduction of garden stuffs, and especially of potatoes'.[66] He found rheumatism, scurvy and jaundice the most prevalent 'chronical disorders' but that they were less serious than the 'acute diseases' - a continued fever, pleurisies, diarrhoea, spotted fever and the 'scarletina of Cullen' which was very contagious and mortal. Smallpox, whooping cough and measles accounted for nearly as many deaths as all other diseases put together. Large numbers of the population of the islands could be swept away in a series of epidemics. Walker records that Barra, with a population of 1285, lost 80 in 1758 from smallpox and 70 in 1762 from an 'epidemical fever'. Tiree apparently lost 105 children from smallpox in 1756 and 40 from whooping cough in two or three months of the winter of 1763. Rum was said to have been nearly depopulated by smallpox in previous outbreaks, as was St Kilda.

Certainly smallpox appears the most devastating scourge to hit the island population at the beginning and the middle of the century. Martin Martin recorded that smallpox came to Bute every sixth or seventh year, and every seventeenth year to North Uist. Walker found it came to Islay every year but still killed more proportionately than it did on the mainland. The more remote islands, as was to be expected, were afflicted less often but with greater severity. Walker believed that if inoculation became a widespread practice, the islands would be filled with more inhabitants than they could support.

In 1764 inoculation had been introduced into the islands only very recently. Since its first introduction into Scotland in 1726, it had not made much headway with the mainland population, some of whom regarded it as tempting God's providence. Their children were affected by an annual visitation which did not result in the devastation that occurred on the islands. Inoculation was introduced into the Orkneys in 1758 and its success was reported widely. Walker records the first inoculations by surgeons in the Hebrides - Clanranald's children in 1763 and 324 children in Skye between November 1763 and September 1764. Some of the people did not wait for assistance from a surgeon; it was reported by Alexander Monro, professor of Anatomy in Edinburgh in a pamphlet of June 1764, that he had 'received from a good friend the history of a person in the Isle of North Uist, entirely ignorant of medicine, who being informed of the success of inoculation in Skye, and seeing the smallpox generally very favourable, put threads thro' some variolous pustules and applied them to the arms of two of his own children, who having mild distinct smallpox, he made use of the matter from them in the same manner, to the children of several of his neighbours; who all recovered from the smallpox without any bad symptom'.[67]

It is difficult to get any indication of the numbers of deaths from smallpox in the islands. Writers tend to be vague, referring to smallpox sweeping away very many young people or occasioning 'great mortality'. The Tiree epidemic that killed so many children was regarded by Walker as a 'devastation of peculiar Malignity'. Perhaps the 1758 'Scots Magazine' record of an outbreak in Kirkwall, which killed 'no less' than 70 out of the 273 people affected, is nearer the norm.

Certainly in the years immediately preceding Walker's visit to the islands, the Seven Years' War appears to have accounted for a far greater loss of population than the 'mortal' diseases. Many were killed and even more appear not to have returned home. Harris had sent 118 men to America, of whom only 14 had returned by 1764; North Uist sent 60 and South Uist 72; Benbecula had provided 28; of the 31 who went from Barra, all had died except for the six who had returned by 1764; Islay had sent 500 and Skye another 500; Tiree had seen only 12 return out of 57, and only 50 had returned to Mull out of 350.

Walker also thought that the southern islands of Mull, Iona and Islay had already lost significant numbers through emigration to Ireland and to the mainland by 1764. Indeed, he believed Islay's losses from this cause were greater than her losses from all diseases put together and that land on Mull had gone out of cultivation at least partly owing to depopulation. This is a remarkably early date for so pronounced an emigration, and it is unfortunate that few indications of the numbers involved can be given.

The 'Report on the Hebrides' is a folio MS volume of 264 pages, in the binding of the King's Library. In editing the MS the original spelling has been retained except for a few minor scribal errors which have been corrected, and the punctuation has been modernised to a certain degree. Place names have been given in the notes and on the accompanying maps according to Ordnance Survey practice. Patronymics used as surnames have been given in lower case type throughout.

REPORT ON THE HEBRIDES

TO
HIS MAJESTIES COMMISSIONERS
AT THE BOARD
OF
ANNEXED ESTATES

My Lords and Gentlemen

The following History of the western Islands, undertaken at your Desire and executed under your patronage, I have endeavoured as much as possible to render subservient to your excellent and Patriotic Designs, for the Improvement of these wild and remote Parts of the Kingdom.

It consists for the most part of a Narration of Facts designed to serve as so many Data, from which, every intelligent Person, though he has never seen these Countries, may form a proper Idea of their Oeconomy and Improvement. And, in this View, it is hoped, they may be of Use to those who have the Police of these distant parts of Scotland, under their immediate Inspection.

They were collected with the utmost Care, during the Course of above Seven Months, in a Journey by Land and Water of upwards of 3,000 Miles, through the Islands North of Cantire and the adjacent parts of the Highlands. Being conscious of no Intention to Mislead, I persuade myself no Person will here be missinformed through Design though I cannot be equally certain, that amidst such a Multiplicity of Facts, I have been no where Missled. What I saw I can affirm; but many things related, must rest on the authority of others; though no Informations were admitted, whose Evidence was not in a high Degree unexceptionable.

Many curious Discoveries in natural History ocurred in the Course of this Journey. But here I judged it more proper to confine myself to a general Description of the Countries; of their Soil and Climate, and of the Customs and Manners of the People. To mark everywhere the Prices of Labour and of Commodities: the Nature and Extent of the Exports and Imports: and the Causes of Population and Depopulation. To describe the present State of Agriculture; Manufacture and Fishery, and to point out the most obvious Methods for the Advancement of these Usefull Arts. Natural History however could not be wholly omitted as it affords such frequent and favourable Opportunities, of turning the Truths of Science to the Purposes of Life.

There is no Corner of Europe, so little known even to the Inhabitants of Britain, as the Islands which are here described. We have long had more Information concerning the Islands of Asia; and it is likely will soon be better

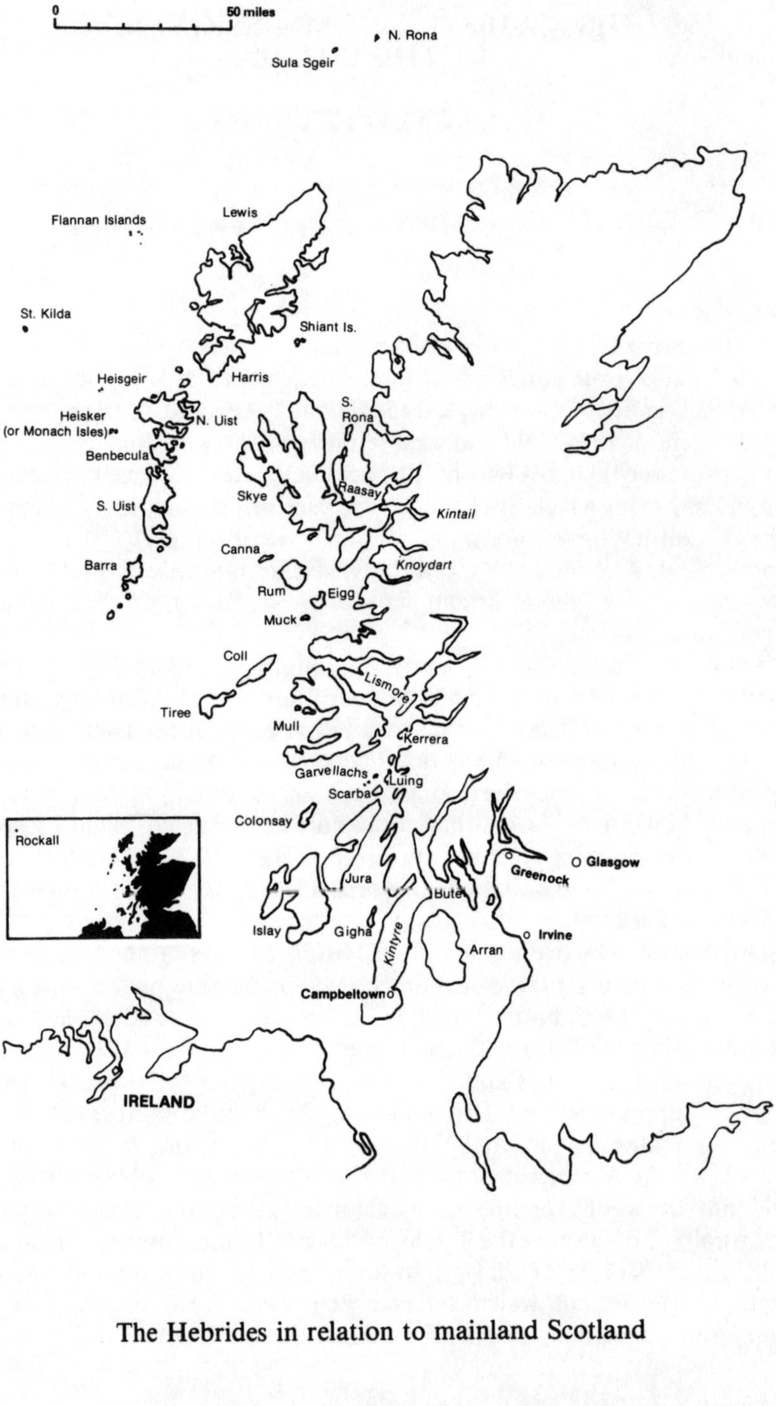

The Hebrides in relation to mainland Scotland

acquainted with those in the far distant parts of the Southern Hemisphere; than we are with the Islands adjacent to our own Coasts, and which make part of the Kingdom.

This is the more to be regretted as the Improvement of the Hebrides is undoubtedly a great national Object. Their Extent is important: upwards of two Millions of Acres. Their Inhabitants numerous: being above Seventy thousand Persons, yet the number is small compared to the Territory they inhabit. Thirty Acres for each Individual, is a Proportion hardly known in any other European Country: and shews; how little these Islands have hitherto felt of the Beneficial Influence of Arts and Industry.

Their Soil remains, as it was left at the Creation: The Inhabitants, when compared to their Fellow Subjects, with Respect to Arts; are in almost the same Situation as in the Days of Oscian, yet they are Countries capable of being greatly advanced by Agriculture; capable of many of the most important Species of Manufacture: possessed of the most valuable Fisheries in Europe: and inhabited by a sensible, hardy, and laborious Race of People.

I call them laborious, contrary indeed to a received Opinion. But it is only from a superficial View, that they are represented as inconquerably averse to Industry and every kind of Innovation. The Culture of their Fields, carried on by the Spade, with the Strength of their Arms, instead of that of Cattle, and many other Operations, in their rude System of Husbandry, exhibits powerfull though indeed ill directed Efforts of Industry. Their extensive Cultivation of Potatoes, by Hand Labour: their Hardships and Assiduity in the Manufacture of Kelp: the Success of the Linen Manufacture, wherever it has been introduced and the amazing Progress of Inoculation; show, that the Highlanders are as capable to judge of, are as ready to embrace and can as vigorously pursue any Innovation that is advantageous or Salutary as any other People whatever.

Unassisted Exertions of Industry are not to be expected from a People still in the Pastoral Stage of Society; nor from unenlightened Minds are we any where to expect the sudden Discontinuance of Bad Customs. But, wherever the Highlanders are defective in industry, it will be found; upon fair Enquiry; to be rather their Misfortune than their Fault: and owing to their want of Knowledge, rather than to any want of the Spirit of Labour. Their Disposition to Industry, is greater than is usually imagined, and if judiciously directed is capable to rise to the greatest Heights.

I have the Honour to be with the greatest Respect

My Lords and Gentlemen

Your most obedient and most humble servant

LEWIS

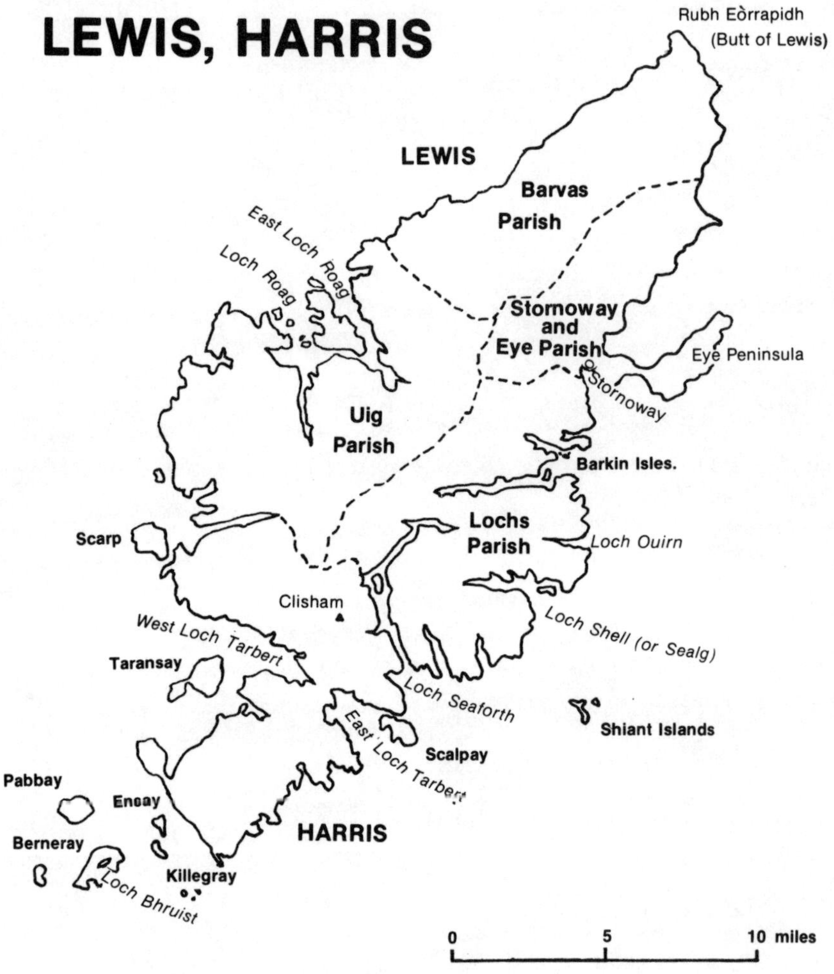
LEWIS, HARRIS
Rubh Eòrrapidh
(Butt of Lewis)
LEWIS
Barvas
Parish
East Loch Roag
Loch Roag
Stornoway
and
Eye Parish
Eye Peninsula
Stornoway
Uig
Parish
Barkin Isles.
Lochs
Parish
Loch Ouirn
Scarp
Clisham
West Loch Tarbert
Loch Shell (or Sealg)
Taransay
Loch Seaforth
Shiant Islands
East Loch Tarbert
Scalpay
Pabbay
Ensay
HARRIS
Berneray
Killegray
Loch Bhruist
0
5
10 miles

LEWES

Situation and Extent

The Country of Lewes is connected to that of Harris, by a Narrow Isthmus, from which it extends Northwards about 54 Miles in Length to Europapoint;[1] which lies nearly under the same Parallel with Cape Wrath, the most remote Place on the Northwest of the main Land of Scotland, and is distant from it about 30 Leagues. The Extent of the Lewes from east to west is various, being deeply cut by several extensive Arms of the Sea, but at a medium its Breadth is nearly 18 Miles.

This vast Country which must contain about 449,120 Acres is let by Mr Mackenzie of Seaforth[2] who is Sole Proprietor for 1,200£ with the adjacent Islands included so that it is rented at present for about one Half penny p. acre.

Numbers of People

The Lewes contains 4 Parishes, which are peopled entirely with Protestants. The Parish of Stornoway, which consists of the united Parishes of Stornoway and Ey,[3] and lies along the east Coast is 22 Miles long, and 10 Miles broad, but the Inhabited part of it scarcely extends anywhere above 3 miles from the Sea. The number of People in it amounts to 2,286.

The Parish of Lochs which comprehends all the South east part of the Island is about 24 Miles long, and 8 Miles broad; it contains the Islands of Schant, and has 1,187 Inhabitants.

The parish of Wig[4] which lies on the Southwest side of the Country is 27 Miles long and 11 broad, the number of People in this Parish is 1,687.

The Parish of Barras,[5] consisting of the united Parishes of Barras and Ness, is the most northerly one in the Lewes. It is 24 miles long but of very different Breadth in different places and contains 1,777 People.

The total number of People in this Island or Peninsula of Lewes amounts to 6,938 and by comparing this Number, with the Number of Acres which the Country contains, it appears, that there are 64 Acres to each Person, a most amazing Proportion! Such as there is certainly, no Instance of in any other Country in Europe.

Of all the People in the 4 Parishes in the Lewes, there are scarce any who understand English, except a few in the Town of Stornoway and its neighbourhood. These amount not to above 200 and here the Minister preaches an English Sermon once a fortnight, but at the other two places of Worship in his Parish, and in the other three parishes in the Island the Ministers preach allways in Galic having no Hearers at these places, who can understand them in English.

The small Progress which the English Language has made in this Country, is chiefly owing to the Want of Schools, for the Inhabitants having little Intercourse with any People who speak English they can have no other way to obtain it, but by being taught to read and speak the Language, when they were young. The Committee for managing the royal Bounty have established a School for English, Latin, Writing and Arithmetic at Stornoway, and the Society for Propogating Christian Knowledge supports two Charity Schools in this Parish. These Schools are full, and well taught, and are at present of great use in Spreading the English Language in that part of the Country, but till last Year when Mr Mackenzie the Proprietor erected a Legal parochial School in the Parish of Lochs, there was no other in all the Lewes. There is still no School of any kind in the Parishes of Wig and Barras, and in the whole Country there are at least 6,000 Persons, who can neither speak English, nor read the scriptures in any Language. The Lewes sent to the Army during the last War 170 Men: of these 34 have returned Home since the Peace, 18 of whom have Chelsea Pensions. The Rest were mostly slain in action in America.

An exact account having been taken of the People in the Lewes in the year 1763 an abstract of it shall be here subjoined according to their different Ages and Sexes.

MALES		**FEMALES**	
Men above 60 years of Age	241	Women above 60	348
Men from 16 to 60	1331	Women from 16 to 60	1265
Boys from 7 to 16	1069	Girls from 9 to 16	1207
Boys under 7	714	Girls under 9	763
Total of Males	3355	Total of Females	3583

Total of Inhabitants 6,938

Of this Number, there are 9 Men above 80 and 12 Women. None of the former are 100, but two of the latter are above it, one being 102 and the other 105.

Soil

By the nearest Computation there may be about 40,000 Acres of Land in the Lewes, which have at some period or other been turned by the Plough or Spade, which consist, for the most part, of a thin hazely Soil, of a reddish

Loam, or of a Soil composed mostly of Sand. It contains about 200,000 Acres, which though never hitherto touched by the Labour either of Men or Cattle, are capable of being reclaimed and consist chiefly of wide extended Heaths or Sandy Downs. The remaining part of the Island, which amounts to no less than 209,120 Acres appears totally irreclaimable, and is composed of Steep Mountains, large tracts of Rocks, fresh Water Lakes, deep Mosses and Blowing Sand.

The number of Tenants in the Island is about 668, and their whole Rent paid to the Proprietor amounts only to 1,200£. Their Possessions at an average are under 40 sh. per Annum. There is one Farm in the Island whose Rent is 50£ but the greatest number run from 10 to 20 sh.

Price of Labour

They know little or nothing of Day Labourers in any of the Islands. When People have occasion for more Labour, than that of their own Servants, they borrow their neighbours, so that they have scarce any Price upon a Mans Labour by the Day.

Here the whole Wages of a Man Servant during the year, come only to 28 sh. and those of a Woman Servant to 8 sh. and the Mans Sustenance in a Family, amounts only to 2£ and the Womans to 1£ 5 sh. There is certainly no European Country, at present, that equals this Cheapness of Labour.

At Stornoway, 12 and 14 Heer Yarn is spun at 10d per Spyndle. Yarn of 18 Heer is spun at 1sh. per Spyndle.

Of the 18 Heer Yarn a Woman spins one Hank a Day, or one fourth of a Spyndle which amounts to 3d.

Price of Commodities

	£	s	d
The best driving Cows, at a Medium, each	1	6	0
The Lewes Stone of Butter, 23 lb. English p Stone		7	0
The Stone of Cheese		2	6
The Stone of washed Wool		9	0
Grass of a Cow for the whole Summer		1	8
Kelp p. Tun	3	5	0
Aqua Vitae p. Anchor, containing 20 Scots Pints	1	5	0
Dog Fish Oil p. Barrel	2	5	0
Herrings p. Barrel	1	2	0
Salmon p. Barrel	1	16	0
Dried Ling p. Hundred	3	15	0

Quality and Price of Grain

The Lewes Boll of Bear, which sells usually at 16 sh. heaped Measure, affords a Boll of Meal streaked Measure.

The Lewes Boll of Grey Oats, which is ¼ more than the Lithgow Boll, sells usually at 8 sh.

The Lewes Boll of Grain is 16 Pecks, the Peck consisting of 8 Pints liquid Measure, whereas the Lithgow Peck contains only 6.

This Boll of Grey Oats affords commonly but 9 Pecks of Meal. When distilled it yields 10 Pints of Aqua Vitae and this again twice Rectified, is reduced to 4 Pints of the strong ardent Spirit called Trestarig.[6]

In general, they find that the yeild of Spirits from Oats is exactly in Proportion to the Quantity of Meal which the Oats would afford. Whatever Quantity of Oats affords 3 Firlots of Meal, Lewes Measure, will make 2 Scots Gallons of Aqua Vitae, so that it is the farenaceous part of the Grain alone that yeilds Spirits.

Exports

	£	s	d
The Lewes exports annually to the Main Land of Scotland 700 Black Cattle; about 100 are sold to the Shipping that put in at Stornoway, and 300 are sent salted to the Ports upon Clyde.[7] The value of the whole is about	1430	0	0
Last Year 50 ton of Kelp was made and exported	162	5	0
There are 12 Stills in Lewes, and from these, there was last year exported —			
200 Anchors of Aqua Vitae	250	0	0
Dog Fish Oil, 140 Barrels	315	0	0
Dried Ling 17,000	637	10	0
Herrings 750 Barrels	1575	0	0
Salmon 48 Barrels	80	8	0
The Spinning School at Stornoway from October, 1763 to December 1764 produced 2,288 Spyndles of Linen Yarn, from 8 to 18 Heer in the lb. of Flax which at 2 sh. per Spyndle at an average, amounts to	228	16	0
Dried Cod 50 Barrels			
Mud Cod 117 Barrels			
Above 2,000 sheep skins with the Wool upon them			
About 38 Stone of Feathers are also exported which are the Product of Suilskeray[8] and the Rona and Flannan Isles			
The Lewes neither imports nor Exports Grain.			

State of Agriculture

Agriculture is not perhaps conducted in any part of the World, in a more rude and artless manner than in this Country. They know of no grain, besides Bear and grey Oats, no Manure but Sea Wrack, and scarce any Instrument of

Agriculture, but the Carschrome, which is a crooked Spade, and a little Harrow with wooden Teeth which is drawn by a Man. The Plough is a thing but lately known to the Inhabitants of the Lewes, and they are still but few of them in the Country. There is not one in all the Parish of Wig, the Land in that part of the Island being still cultivate entirely with the Spade. It is but 9 years since Potatoes were first planted in the Lewes, and the making of Hay is still a more late Improvement and as yet practised but in a few places. They do not shear their Sheep, but pull the Wool off their backs. Neither do they reap their Bear as in other places, but pull it up by the Roots. After it is in the Barn, they cut off the Roots, with a part of the Stem. This Stubble they strow irregularly upon their House Tops, and tie it down with Ropes of Heath, without Turf below it, the Scarcity of Wood oblidging them to have the Timber of their Roofs so slight, that it will bear no greater Burden. They then cut the Heads off it, and these they burn, having no other way of drying their Grain, and at length the middle part of the Straw goes to the Cattle.[9]

State of the Fisheries

Though the Fisheries have never been so much prosecute in the Lewes, as they deserve, yet the People pursue them to a greater Extent, than any others of the Islanders. The Town of Stornoway has 30 Fishing Boats; there are about 20 more upon the adjacent Coasts in that Parish, and besides these, there are about 50 in the other parts of the Island. In Each of these Boats there are 5 Hands at a medium; so that the whole for several Months of the Year, employ 500 Men, but the Fisheries on the Coasts of this Extensive Island are capable to furnish Employment for ten times the Number.

Ling

All along the East Coast of the Island, and in most places within two Miles of the Shore, there runs an extensive Bank which abounds in Ling, but there are scarce any Fishers upon it, except for a few Miles in the Parish of Stornoway, where the People are more industrious in Fishery than in the other parts of the Island, by having better opportunity of being furnished with Salt. Here they generally make and export annually about 13,000 Ling, which at 23 Fish to the hundred, the usual Number, amounts to 30 Ton, but last year they caught and exported 17,000.

Cod

The above Bank running along the east Coast of the Lewes, from which the Ling are taken likewise abounds in Cod, which is a singular Case, as these two kinds of Fish are seldom found in Considerable Quantities, upon the same Bank. Here about 50 Barrels of dried Cod and 117 Barrel of Mud Cod, were caught last Season and exported from Stornoway to Liverpool. Here is also plenty of Cod off Loch Roag, upon the West side of the Country.

Herring

The Situation of the Lewes is extremely favourable for the Herring Fishery, especially in the beginning of the Season. The great Shoal which enters the Minch, that is, the Sea between the Long Island and mainland, always doubles the Butt of the Lewes in its way from the North West sometime in the Month of July, and generally enters some of the extensive Lochs on the East Coast of the Lewes. At this first Appearance of the Herrings, they are in their greatest Perfection and of the greatest Value for the European Market, but as they are not then so stationary, they require to be fished with greater adress and Dispatch than in the Winter Season. By this usual Progress of the Herring, the Lewes is more conveniently situate for the early Fishery than any other of the Islands, and besides this, its Lochs are very frequently their Residence during the Spawning Season. A Few Years ago, Loch Roag upon the West Coast of the Island was the Chief Seat of the Winter Fishery, and every Year they are to be found during that Season, in greater or less Quantities, in the Lochs of Stornoway, Birken Isles,[10] Hornon,[11] Shell, or Seaforth on the East Coast. In some, or in all of these Lochs, they are generally to be found in large Shoals during the Spawning time and continue till about 1st of February; nay they have even been caught in great Quantities at Stornoway, between the 8th and 15th of that Month, but about this time, or soon after, they pretty regularly remove from the Coasts of the Lewes. During the whole fishing Season, the Inhabitants of this Island generally cure and export about 750 Barrels of Herrings. Sometimes they are confined to 500 and sometimes they have compleated 1,000; but this various success arises from the precarious way in which they are furnished with Salt, not from the uncertainty of the Shoals, which are very steady in their Appearance upon the Coasts. And was there easy access to Salt and Cask, it is not improbable that 10,000 Barrels might be annually exported by the Industery of its own Inhabitants.

The People of Stornoway made Trial last Year of the Buss Fishing with one Vessel.[12] She sailed from Stornoway for the Rendevouze at Campbelton about the middle of August, and at Loch Tarbert in the Isle of Harris, very near compleated a Cargo of Herrings, which She carried to Campbelton, and sailed from thence upon the Bounty in the middle of September. This one Experiment points out Stornoway as the Place most advantageously situate of any in Scotland for carrying on the Buss Fishing, while the present Bounty Law continues in Force, and indeed without any Experiment, it is abundantly evident.

By that Law, the Herring Busses are oblidged to rendevouze at Campbelton on or before the 15th of September, when they proceed to the Winter Fishery. In the Voyage to this Rendevouze, a Vessel from Stornoway may be pretty certain of making a compleat Cargo of Herrings, provided She is ready to leave that Port at the Proper time, that is, upon the first Information of their Appearance in the Minch, which is always about the middle of July. While she follows them in their Progress Southwards, she is continuing her Voyage, and has a fair chance of arriving at Campbelton fully loaded, where she can dispose of her Cargo to advantage, and be furnished with fresh Supply of Salt and Casks. She may by this means, have the opportunity of making two Cargoes, during one Fishing, while the Busses from the South can only have the opportunity of obtaining one, and the only Inconvenience or additional Expence she need incur for this great advantage, is that of leaving the Port of Stornoway, a Month or six Weeks sooner than she would otherwise do.

To every other method of prosecuting the Summer Fishery in the Western Islands, there is this Discouragement that by Law there is a Debenture only for a Bushel of Salt for each Barrel of Herrings that are cured and Exported. A Bushel is indeed sufficient to cure a Barrel during the Winter Fishery but in the Summer Season, from the first Appearance of the Shoals in the middle of July, to the middle of September, each Barrel requires two Bushels of Salt to cure it well, so that the Fishers Premium, by the Debenture, amounts only to the Duty upon the one half of his Salt. This must effectually Discourage the People of the Islands from pursuing the Summer Fishery, who have no other Premium than the Debenture upon Salt, but to a Buss upon the Bounty sailing from the Lewes to her Rendevouze, it needs be no Impediment to her making a Cargo in Summer, as her Voyage becomes thereby highly Profitable, notwithstanding this Disadvantage. It may be observed likewise in favour of this method of following the Summer Fishery that it may be practised by all Vessels who sail to the Campbelton Rendevouze, from any place between the Lewes and the Isle of Mull, and further, that as the one half of all the Salt in this way pays the full Duty, should this Method of Fishing be enlarged the Revenue must be proportionably increased.

Mackrel

The Mackrel do not reach the Coast of the Lewes, till the first of August, and might then be had oftimes in large Quantities, but the Inhabitants are at no pains in Catching them, except when they cast up in their Herring Nets, and then they have Salted them to very good Advantage. The Fishers on the west of the Island cure a great deal of Mackrel, which are barreled and sent to the west Indies where they keep equally well with Herring, and it were certainly worthwhile to make Trial of the same kind of Trade in the Lewes, and in others of the western Islands, where this Fish is found in great Plenty.

Salmon

Though there are several Rivers in the Lewes that abound in Salmon, it is but of late, that they were ever turned to any account. Last Year they were fished with some Care, and afforded 48 Barrel for Exportation, and this Quantity will probably increase, as the People become more expert in catching and Curing Salmon which is a Business they have been but lately made aquainted with.

Dog Fish

Many of the People on the west Coast of the Lewes are very industriously and profitably employed during some part of Summer and Harvest, in catching the Dog Fish, from which they extract a Fish Oil of an excellent Quality. Though it is only the Liver that affords the Oil, yet the Fish abounds on that Coast, to such a Degree, that 140 Barrels of the Oil were last Year made and exported from the Lewes, at 2£ 5sh. per Barrel which amounts to 315£. Upon the Coasts of many others of the Islands, the Dog Fish is equally numerous, but is no where fished, to manufacture Oil for Exportation, but at this Place.

State of Manufacture

From the above Account it appears, that the different kinds of Fishery give a good deal of Employment to many of the Inhabitants of the Lewes, yet notwithstanding this and the usual Labour of their Husbandry, the greater part of the Men are either not half occupied throughout the year, or unprofitably employed. Yet here, as in almost all the other parts of the Highlands, there is still a greater Superfluity of Idleness among the Women, occasioned by the Want of the Woolen and Linen Manufacture.

Wool

The only article of Woolen Manufacture that the People of the Lewes pursue, is some coarse Blanketing which they send to Clyde, but their negligence even in the article, appears from their sending annually above 2,000 of Wool [*sic*] out of the Country unmanufactured.

Linen

Though they have been in the practice of sowing Lint for above 60 years, yet for want of being properly supplied with foreign Flax seed, their Lint is degenerate to such a Degree, that it is not worth Cultivation, and its Produce serves only to afford to a few of the Inhabitants a little Linen Cloth of the coarsest Quality. They are entire Strangers to all the Proper Methods of executing the Linen Manufacture, and are even ignorant of the whole Progress of Watering Flax. In place of which, they dry their Lint before the Fire, as it is taken off the Ground, and then beat it upon a stone.

In an Island, where there are about 3,000 Women in a great measure idle, who might be all profitably employed in the Linen Manufacture, such a Situation is really deplorable. The Commissioners therefore upon the annexed Estates erected a Spining School at Stornoway in October 1763, which has already been attended with excellent Effects. There was at first indeed great

Opposition made to it by the People, but this was soon overcome, by the Care and Vigilance of the Gentleman who has the management of Mr MacKenzie's Business in that country, and of Mr MacPherson who is the Undertaker for the Factory.

The Women at first were averse to come to the School, from groundless Reports of a Design to send them to the Plantations, but these Fears being dispelled, the School was immediately filled. They find their Labour both easy and profitable, and pursue it with a great Degree of Spirit and Chearfullness.

The Spining Mistress was brought from Fife, and her Husband is the Heckler. Though she has no Galic, she says the Girls in two or three Days, understand everything she means with regard to their Work, that they are extremely quick and docile, and is certain, that such Girls in the low Country could not make equal Proficiency under a Person who was ignorant of their Language. In August last there were 51 Girls in the School from 9 to 25 Years of Age, who in about 3 Months had learnt to spin Linen Yarn from 8 to 18 Heer out of the Pound of Lint, with sufficient Dexterity. When the School was erected, it was proposed, that 150 Women should be taught to Spin in the Course of 3 Years, but by the Diligence of Mr MacPherson the Undertaker, that number was sufficiently instructed in the Business last October, that is in the Course of one Year after the School was opened. If he is sufficiently supported there is no Doubt of his rendring the Manufacture of Linen Yarn universal throughout the Lewes in three or four Years.

The advantage of this Spinning Station, though still in its Infancy have [*sic*] been very considerable. Above 2,288 Spyndles of Linen Yarn have been sent in the Course of 14 Months, from a Country, which never exported a Thread before. The Inhabitants have already imbibed a Strong Inclination for pursuing the Manufacture, so that besides the Yarn which the Spining School has produced, the People of the Country have purchased from the Undertaker, about 1,500 Pound of Tow, from one penny to 5 Pence per Pound, and a considerable Quantity of dressed Lint at 10 Pence which they have Manufactured upon their own Account.

All this however has been produced from Riga Flax, and in order to perfect the Manufacture in the Lewes, the first and most necessary thing wanted, is a Skillfull Flax Raiser to initiate the People in the Cultivation and Dressing of Lint. The Soil and Climate are favourable enough, for the Production of such Lint as is most proper for them to Manufacture. For though any Lint Crops they at present have, are very contemptible, yet this is owing to the Degenracy of the Lintseed, not to any Fault in the Soil. In the Year 1756 some Foreign Lintseed was brought into Lewes, and it produced as good Crops as in most other places.

An Expert Weaver settled at Stornoway, would also be of great Benefit. There is no Weaver at present in the Lewes, capable of working Linen at above 1 sh. per Yard. From the Foreign Flax brought lately into the Country there has been a great deal of Yarn Spun to a pretty fine Grist, but the Proprietors were oblidged to send it to Ireland in order to be weaved.

Hemp

They sow a good deal of Hemp in the Lewes, and though their manner of cultivating and dressing the Plant is very defective and erroneous, yet all their Nets which are used in the Fishery, are made of it. Last Season, the Vessel which sailed to the Fishery upon the Bounty, from Stornoway, had 670 Nets on Board, from 10 to 52 Fathoms long, and from 3 to 5 Fathoms deep of an exceeding good Quality, and all made in the Lewes, from the Hemp of the Country. Though their Hemp is greatly degenerate, as they never get any foreign Hempseed, but a few Pounds now and [then] from Ireland, yet on the 16th of August last, the Male Plants just come to the Flower, measured 4 Feet 3 Inches in Length. This shews, that the Soil and Climate, are extremely favourable for the Production of this valuable Plant, and were the Inhabitants properly supplied with foreign Hempseed, and instructed in its Cultivation it would establish a very usefull Branch, both for Agriculture and Manufacture, as there can be none more proper in a Country, where Fishery is to be considered as the chief Employment of the People.

NATURAL PRODUCTIONS

Eider Down

The Anas Mollissima of Linnaeus, or Eider Duck abounds in the Rona and Flannan Isles, and the uninhabited Island of Soulisker.[13] This Bird is of a Size, between that of a Duck and a Goose, and affords the Eider Down, which is so much Esteemed, and so high priced being the highest and most elastick that is known. Of this fine Down, the Bird divests itself, for building its Nest, which is very large, and almost wholly composed of it, and from the Nests only, it is collected. The Eggs are as large as those of a Goose, and of a green Colour, which it hatches in the End of June, the proper Time for gathering the Downs.

The Danes furnish the rest of Europe, at present, with this costly Plumage from Iceland and the Coasts of Norway. The Bird abounds in several of the western Islands, and the great Value of its Feathers, was known even in Buchanan's Time, who particularly describes it by the name of Colca, in the Description of Scotland, prefixed to his History. Their Value, however, is altogether unknown to the Inhabitants of the Lewes. For though there is a large Quantity of Eider Down brought annually from Rona, Flannan and Soulisker, it turns to no Account, as it is mixed by the Simple Inhabitants of those remote Islands, with the Feathers of their other Sea Birds.

Martrick[14]

The Martrick which is the Mustela martes of Linnaeus, Inhabits many of the wild rocky places of the Lewes. It is a carnivorous Quadruped, larger than a Cat, of a blackish brown Colour, and affords an exceeding good Fur. They are taken by the Inhabitants in Gins, set for the Purpose, and their Skins usually sell at Five Shillings a Piece.

Sperma Ceti

The Whale which affords the Sperma Ceti or the Physeter macrocephalus of Linnaeus is frequently put ashore upon the Lewes, but the People are entirely ignorant of the Value of that Commodity and the manner of preserving it. In August last, a Fish of that kind, 50 feet long was cast in near Stornoway, which was immediately cut up and divided into Shares by the People who found it. A White Substance they observed in the Head, which they took to be the Brains, and being more than ordinary fat and mellow, they unluckily mixed and boiled it up with the Blubber. The Consequence was, that both Oil and Sperma Ceti were in a great measure lost. The Oil Merchant at Stornoway, would not buy it, being half frozen up with a Substance he knew nothing about, and even at Liverpool, either through Ignorance or unfair Dealing, it was dissadvantageously Sold and turned out to no Account.

Seath Fish[15]

The Seath Fish abounds throughout all the Western Islands, and is a principal part of the Support of the Islanders during all the Summer Season, who then take it in great Numbers with Fishing Rods and Hand Lines.

The Poor people observe, that when they live upon any other Fish, without Bread, which is often the Case, they are never sufficiently nourished, but a Weakness of their whole Body ensues, but when they feed upon Seath, whither with Bread or not, it proves equally healthfull and nourishing. As the Preservation of a Fish of such an excellent Quality deserved a Trial, the People of Stornoway, in August last, were persuaded to make the Experiment. They then began to Fish them with Nets, which had not formerly been done, and were very Successfull, a single Net at one Haul, bringing in from one to 300 of them, which at an Average were 18 Inches long. While the Weather answered which was but for a little Time, they splitted, salted and dried them, and these turned out to very good Account. But when the weather failed for this purpose, they were oblidged to preserve them in the way of Mud Fish which did not answer, either from the peculiar Nature of the Fish from their not being in Season, or from Inexperience in the proper manner of curing them. One beneficial Article of Knowledge, however, results from this Experiment, that the Fish is capable of being preserved to Advantage dry. And as it is to be had in great plenty, during all the Spring and Summer Months, the People of the Islands should be encouraged to make a Trial of it at the Market along with their Cod and Ling.

HARRIS

HARRIS

Situation

The Country of Harris is divided from that of Lewes, by a narrow Tarbert or Isthmus, about half a mile over. It composes one extensive Parish, which comprehends seven lesser adjacent Islands, which are inhabited: Pabbay, Ensay, Killigray and Bernera, which ly to the South, in the dangerous Channel between Harris and North Uist. Taransay and Scarp, which ly upon the west Coast; and Scalpa, which is situate upon the East.

Extent and Rental

The main Land of Harris is 36 miles long and in different places from 8 to 18 miles broad, but its mean Breadth will be about 12 miles.[1] According to these Dimensions, it contains 276,480 Acres, and the Seven lesser Islands contain 24,960, in all 301,440 Acres which are rented at 600£, that is, at less than one half penny per Acre.

The Small Islands contain a much larger Proportion of Arable and fertile Ground, than the main Land of Harris. Their Rent amounts to 257£ so that they are set at between Twopence half penny and three Pence p. Acre: but the main Land being let at present for about 343£ it is rented at less than one third of a penny p. Acre. Mcleod[2] is the sole Proprietor of these Islands, which are all inhabited by the People of his Family and Clan.

Number of people

Upon the main Land of Harris, there are 1,363 Inhabitants, and 630 upon the Seven adjacent Islands belonging to it; the Number of People in the whole Parish being 1,993, which makes 151 Acres to each Person. In the Seven lesser Islands there are indeed but 39 Acres for every Inhabitant but upon the main Island of Harris, this Proportion amounts to a prodigious Number, 202.

There are no Papists in Harris, but of all its Inhabitants, there are not above 100 that understand English. There is a legal and a Charity School in the Parish, but the Bulk of the Inhabitants, receive but little Benefit from them, by their dispersed Situation through so wide a Country, and so many Islands divided from each other, by very dangerous Seas. These Schools have hitherto been kept at two particular Places, but they would be rendred much more usefull if they were removed to different parts of the Parish, every three or four years.[3]

From this Parish, there went to the Army during the late War 118 Men who were all sent to America. Only 14 of these have as yet returned, 8 of whom are Chelsea Pensioners.

Soil

All the East Coast of the main Land of Harris, and all its interior parts, are rocky and mountainous. Here the Mountain of Clisham is situate, which is the highest in all the long Island, and appears to be about 2,000 Feet high. There is an extensive Forest here, formerly much better replenished with Deer than at present, the Eagles being so numerous that very few of the Fawns escape. It still contains however, 700 Head, which brouze upon the Mountains in Summer, and upon the Shores in Winter, where they feed much upon the Sea Weeds. The West side of the Island, near the Sea is mostly arable; the Soil is all sandy but fertile, producing very rich Grass and good Crops of Grain.

In this Island it is judged there will be about 22,000 Acres that have been turned by the Spade or Plough, 60,000 that may be brought into Culture, consisting chiefly of dry Land upon the skirts of the Mountains, Heaths, Sandy Downs, and Bogs that might be profitably drained. The remaining 194,480 Acres seem totally irreclaimable and comprehend all the High Lands upon the Mountains, Steep Declivities, great Tracts of Rocks, Deep Mosses and blowing Sand. The Proportion of wild Land is much less in the Seven adjacent Islands, for of the 24,960 Acres which they contain 15,000 have at least been cultivate.

In several parts of the Harris, the Sand Drift from the Sea Shore, has made great Encroachments upon the Land. There are about 300 Acres of what was formerly the best Arable and pasture Land in the Island of Pabbay, that are at present overwhelmed with Sand. As the Sand blows from the Shore, the Sea advances, and accordingly upon the South West side of this Island, the Sea flows for a great Space, where many People still alive have reaped Crops of Grain. There are about 300 Acres of the best Land in the Island of Bernera, entirely blown up with Sand in the same manner, and the Drift has encroached so much upon Loch Bruist, a fresh Water Lake in the Island, that it is now firm Ground, where there was formerly a great Depth of Water interspersed with Islands. The Sand Drift is continuing to make great Devastation in the same way, along all the west Coast of the main Land of Harris, and in all the other lesser Islands which are adjacent.

Exports

	£	s	d
The Harris affords 100 Ton of Kelp[4] which at 3£ 5sh. p. Ton amounts to	325	0	0
About 250 black Cattle are exported alive and 100 salted which at 1£ 6sh. each amounts to	455	0	0

The Harris seldom exports or imports any Grain; but exports a little Butter and Cheese som Wool, and the Skins of Sheep, Otters and Seals.

State of Agriculture

There is no kind of Grain sown in Harris but Bear or Grey Oats. They used to sow a great deal of Rye, but have given it up of late years, as they found it prejudicial to their Soil, which in general is very light and Sandy, but affords exceedingly good Crops of Bear, when manured with Sea Weeds, and Cultivate with the Spade. An Increase of twenty fold is frequent in that Grain, but they sow it extremely thin.

The Plough which is used here, and in most places of the Long Island, is of a very particular Construction. Its whole Length is but 4 Feet 7 Inches and is drawn by 4 Horses abreast. It has but one Handle by which it is directed, the Mold Board is fastened with two Leather Thongs and the Soke and Coulter are bound together at the Point by a Ring of Iron.[5]

There is another Instrument also used in the Harris and the other parts of the Long Island, in the Cultivation of their arable Land, called a Ristle. It is of the Shape of a Plough, but is only two feet and an half long and drawn by one Horse. It has no Soke, but has a sharp crooked Coulter, which is drawn through the Soil, near 10 Inches deep. The use of it, is to be drawn before the Plough, in order to cut the strong twisted Roots, of a number of repent Plants, with which the Sandy Soil in the long Island is particularly infested; and which are powerfull enough to obstruct the Progress of so weak a Plough as that which is commonly used.

Manufacture

Besides Kelp, there is nothing of Manufacture kind, that the Inhabitants of Harris are employed in, except a little coarse Woolen Yarn and some Blanketing, which they send yearly to Glasgow. They raise a little Flax of which they make some coarse Linen for their own use, but import all the fine Linen which they consume. In the year 1756, an American Vessel in Distress, was obliged to put out three Hogheads of Lint seed in Harris, which was sown; and afforded Crops of Lint which were above double the Value of the usual Crops, yet since that Time no foreign Lintseed has ever been brought into the Country, and there had been none before in the Memory of any Person alive. The second Crop of this American Lintseed sown in the Harris, was greatly inferior to the first; the third continued to be worse, yet was still better, than any Crop from the Lintseed of the Country; but all the Succeeding Crops have been neither better nor Worse than those raised from the Lintseed that has been sown immemorially in the Harris.

Fishery

There is Plenty of Cod upon the Coasts of the Harris, and especially upon the west side of the Island, in the great Loch or Arm of the Sea between Harris and the Lewes, but the Inhabitants have never availed themselves of this advantage any further than by taking a few with Hand Lines for their own Consump. There are but two long Lines in all the Harris, the one belonging to Mr Mcleod of Pabbay,[6] and the other to Mr Campbell of Scalpa,[7] but they have never used them except for taking Ground Fish as the Cod do not resort near either of these Islands.

The East and West Lochs of Tarbert in the Harris are every Year visited by the Herring Shoals, in their Passage towards the South, or upon their Return. During five years from the year 1743 to the year 1747 the west Loch was the principal Seat of the Herring Fishery. About 30 Vessels from 18 to 40 Ton, belonging to Campbelton, Greenock and Irvine, were compleatly loaded, each of these years, at this place. They lay in Docks in the east Loch and their Boats were hauled over the Isthmus to the west Loch, where the Fishery was carried on.

The Herrings generally enter the East Loch of Tarbert in the End of July. This Loch is a circular Bason of about 4 Miles Diameter perfectly land locked, by the Island of Scalpa, surrounded with lofty Mountains and interspersed with fine green Islands. To the beginning of August last, it was so full of Herrings, that a Fleet might have been loaded in a few Days; by the Moon Light, the water was seen heaving with the Fish, and the very Air was strongly impregnate with the Smell. Yet they came and returned unmolested, except by one Vessel from Stornoway, and a few highland Yauls, who caught them in great Quantities, though with very little Art, for the Consumpt of the Country, and who were anxious to sell them at the Rate of 120 for 4 pence having no Salt to preserve them.

Notwithstanding this advantageous Situation, the Country of Harris does not export one Barrel of Herrings. It could at present furnish above 50 Boats, manned with about 300 men, for carrying on the Herring Fishery if they were but provided, with Salt and Cask at a reasonable Price.

ST. KILDA

E

ST. KILDA[1]

This remote and romantick Island lies out in the Atlantick, to the westward of all the Hebrides, and is about 20 Leagues distant from the nearest parts of the long Island. It is about 3 miles long and 2 broad, and must therefore contain about 3,840 Acres. The Rent paid to Mcleod who is the Proprietor, is but about 200 Merks, so that it is let at less than one Penny sterling p. Acre.

St. Kilda was visited by the small Pox for the first time thirty eight years ago, when it was very near stript of all its Inhabitants by that Desease.[2] It reduced them to 5 Families containing only 18 Persons, but since that time they have increased to 92, which is their present Number. During this Period there has not one Person left the Island, and of its present Inhabitants, there are only 10 Persons who are not Natives;[3] so that exclusive of all Intrants and Emigrants, the People of St. Kilda are 4 times more numerous than they were 38 years ago, and was it not for a particular and very mortal Desease, with which the Children are seized 6 or 7 Days after their Birth, they would increase in a much larger Proportion.[4] It is but of late years that the People of St. Kilda were furnished with Salt: before that Period, they were grievously afflicted with the Leprosy,[5] which has disappeared, since they had Access to the Use of Salt; but it would require more particular Information, to be certain that the Extirpation of the Desease was entirely owing to this Cause.

This small and remote Island can never promise to be of any Importance to the Publick except in the way of Fishery; but it has been judged that in this way, it might be a place of considerable moment.

From the Accounts given by Sir William Monson in his Naval Tracts,[6] it has been supposed that there are Cod Banks of great Extent, lying to the westward of the long Island, from the Extremity of the Lewes, to Tilly Head in Ireland, which is a Distance of above 100 Leagues, and especially about St. Kilda and the little solitary Island called Rocca, which lies about 50 Leagues to the westward of Barra.

To make Trial of these Banks two Wherries fitted out for the Cod Fishery sailed from Greenock in April last upon a Bounty granted by the Trustees for Fisheries and Manufactures,[7] and a Brig also sailed from Campbelton, upon the same Design, without any Bounty. These Vessels sailed round the Butt of the Lewes in May, and reached St. Kilda after a very bad tedious Passage, in which, one of the Wherries had a Suit of new Sails torn to pieces. They continued at St. Kilda till they had made Trial of the Fishing about that Island, but meeting with little Success, they returned home in the Month of June.

The Master of the Brig which sailed from Campbelton reported that for 15 Leagues Westward, northward, and eastward from St. Kilda, the water is from

35 to 80 Fathom deep, bottomed with Stones and Gravel, but that upon this Station he caught only 3 dozen of Cod, which were indeed the largest and finest he had ever seen.

The Truth of what Sir William Monson relates concerning the great plenty of Cod found in these Seas in his Time which is above 150 years ago is not at all invalidate by this Account: the Depth of Water about St. Kilda is very proper for Cod, the few that are still to be caught about the Island, shew, that it is a Station well calculated for that Fish, and it is well known, that the Cod is a Fish which frequently shifts its Quarters, that it frequently retreats from the Banks where it has once abounded, and after a Period of Years, does sometimes return.

NORTH UIST

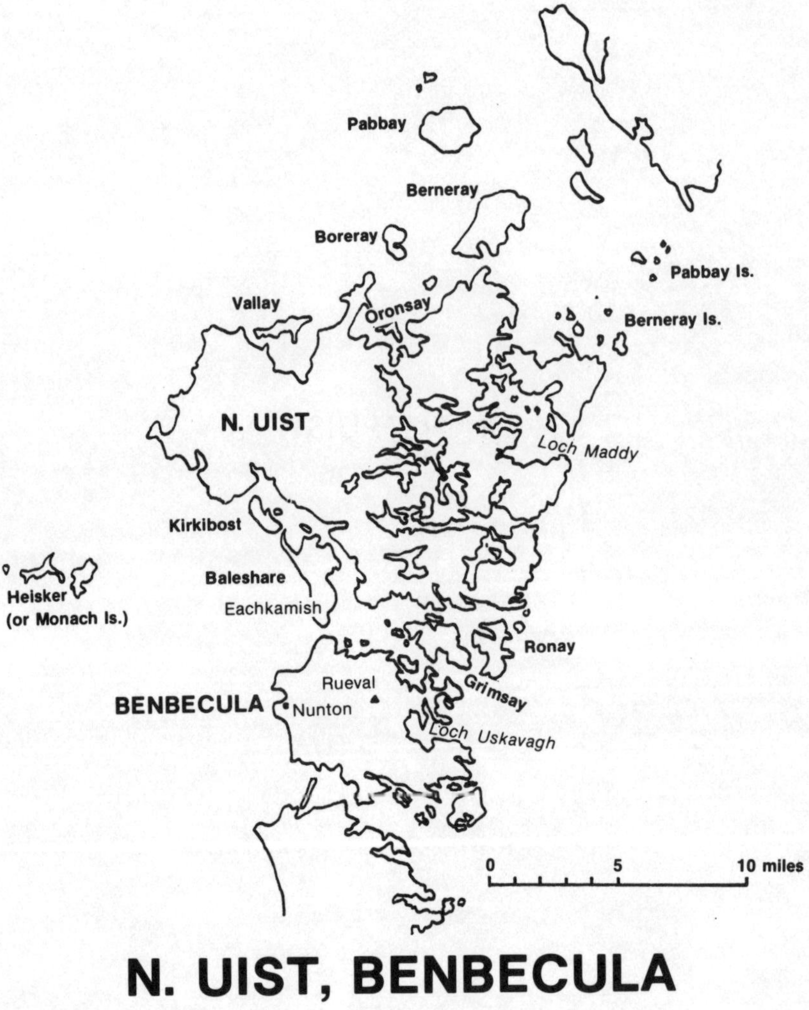

N. UIST, BENBECULA

N WIST

Situation and Extent

The Island of North Wist is seperated from that of Harris by a Channel 4 Leagues in Breadth. It is about 15 Miles long and 12 broad and contains nearly 57,000 Acres. There are several other lesser Islands adjacent to it, which are usually considered as making part of the same Country.[1]

Heray lies upon the South Coast of North Wist, and is separated from it by a Channel of the Sea, which is fordable at low Water. It consists all of arable and low Pasture Land, but is greatly infested with Sand Drift. It contains about 3,840 Acres and 100 Inhabitants.[2]

Valay is a pleasant fertile Island lying upon the Northwest Coast of Wist, and separated from it also by a fordable Channel of the Sea. It is almost all arable and the Pasture upon it very rich. It is about 20 Miles long and one broad, and contains about 1,280 Acres with 40 Inhabitants.

Borera lies North from Wist, and is cut off from it by a Sound two Miles broad. It contains also about 1,280 Acres and 60 Inhabitants.

Heisker is situate 3 Leagues to the Westward of North Wist, is about 2 Miles long and two broad, and contains 2,500 Acres and 70 People. The Soil of this Island is almost wholly Sand, yet yeilds a considerable Produce in Corn and Cattle, by means of Sea Wrack. It contains no Moss nor Turf, and the Inhabitants have no Fewel, but what they bring from Wist. Besides these, there are four smaller inhabited Islands lying adjacent to North Wist; Grimsay, Rona, Oransay and Kirkabost which together contain 85 Inhabitants, and about 3,000 Acres.

All these Islands of North Wist together contain then 68,900 Acres, and afford of Rent at present 1,300£ which comes nearly to 4½d. p. Acre; but as the Value of the kelp is included in this Rental, which is a great Proportion, perhaps near on half the whole, the Lands exclusive of the Sea Weeds can scarce be supposed to be let at above 2½[d.] p. Acre. These Islands are the property of Sir James MackDonald[3] and are all Inhabited by the People of his Family and Clan.

Number of People

The Islands of North Wist compose one Parish, which by an accurate account lately taken by the Minister contains 2,465 Inhabitants, who are all Protestants excepting one Person. Of this great Number, there are only about 100 Persons who can understand an English Sermon, but the English is now making greater Progress than formerly, by means of two Schools lately erected in the Country: the one is upon the Royal Bounty, with a Salary of 25£ yearly, and the other is supported by the Society for propogating Christian Knowledge, with a Salary of 10£. This [island] sent to the Army during the late War, above 60 Men.

Soil

The above Islands adjacent to North Wist consist wholly of low Land and of a sandy Soil of the very lightest kind, intermixed with som Spots of Heath and Moss. The Soil upon all the west Coast of the main Island is of the same Nature, but the interior parts consist chiefly of Moss and Heath, and the east Coast is occupied by a Tract of Mountains running South and North, the highest of which reaches about 1,300 Feet above the Sea. Of all the Land in these Islands, there is not above an eight Part, that is 8,500 Acres, that have at any time been cultivate by the Plough or Spade. There are not above 3 eights, that is, 25,500 Acres that can be deemed irreclaimable, which consist chiefly of Mountains, deep Mosses, large Tracts of Rocks, and Fields of Sand. The remaining 34,000 Acres appear mostly capable of being brought into Culture, and consist chiefly of Heaths, Morasses and sandy Downs. A considerable Quantity of this reclaimable part of Wist, consists also in fresh Water Lakes, which are of great Extent and extremely shallow and might be easily drained. Their Bottom is always a deep heavy Mud, mixed with Sand which is no sooner made dry, than it becomes the richest Soil that is known. Very considerable Tracts of Land also, might be gained off the Sea in several parts of this Island to great advantage, but this is too laborious and expensive an Undertaking, and too precarious to begin Improvement within such a Country. The Draining of the Lakes and Morasses, and the Cultivation of the Heaths and Downs, are more easy and certain Meliorations, and should therefore be preferred.

The sand Drift has made great Devastation in many parts of North Wist, and continues yearly to be more and more formidable. Several parts of the Country which are but little raised above the ordinary Level of the Sea, have also suffered greatly by extraordinary Tides, which are frequently occasioned by the great Violence of the South West Winds, combined at the full or Change with the heavy Swell of the Atlantick. Such a Tide, in the year 1756 broke over an extensive Isthmus, and turned it into a Heap of Sand which before would have pastured 100 Cows in Summer for a Fortnight or three Weeks. By this Irruption, the Peninsula of Inchemish,[4] which is two Miles long and a Mile and a half broad, was disunited from North Wist and turned into an Island, and by the breaking of the Isthmus a Deluge of Sand has been poured in upon the Farm Town of Ballyshar. The Houses in this Village are now blown up to the Roofs, so that there will soon be a necessity of having it removed further into the Country. Near this place the Sand Drift has also choaked up a Canal, which had been dug 7 or 8 Feet deep and half a Mile long in order to drain two Lakes which are now by that means destitute of Level.

Agriculture

The Quantity of cultivated Land in North Wist, is extremely small, compared to the number of the Inhabitants. They never therefore have Grain to serve themselves, but are always oblidged to other Countries, and in the year 1760 imported no less than 1,200 Bolls of Meal. They consume a much greater Quantity of Grain, since the Kelp Manufacture was introduced than before. The Sustenance of the labouring Servants formerly consisted chiefly in Fowl, Fish and Milk, with little or no Bread, but they require and consume a great deal of Bread and Meal ever since they have been employed as Manufacturers.

There is no Grain sown in North Wist, but Bear and grey Oats; formerly, there was a great deal of Rye raised in this Country, but the Farmers becoming sensible of its hurtfull Effects upon their light Sandy Soil, have given it entirely up. Though their Popish Neighbours however in South Wist have the same sort of Soil, they still adhere strictly to this old but pernicious Custom.

The only Manure used in North Wist is Sea Wrack and when this is employed upon the few Spots of deep black Land, which are in the Country, it has a good Effect upon 4 or 5 Crops; but when laid upon the light sandy Grounds, its Effects are scarcely perceptible after one year.

This Island exports annually 400 black Cattle, about 300 alive, and 100 salted. Those which are Salted, are the Refuse of their Cattle, which the Drovers will not take out of the Country, and which would not live through the Winter. They salt them about Martinmass, and carry them to Glasgow in April, for the use of the Shipping. Some of them are put up in Barrels, and others are Salted and put up in the Hides, in a particular manner, which it is thought preserves the meat, as well as any Cask whatever.

This Island also exports yearly 300 Stone of Butter and 200 of Cheese. The Stone is 16lb. Trone Weight or 22lb. English, and the Butter sells at 6sh. p. Stone, and the Cheese at three shillings, so that the produce of these two Articles amounts to 120£.

A good Cow usually produces to the Value of a Guinea in Butter and Cheese from Whitsunday to Martinmass, but the common Practice, is to raise only one Calf upon the Milk of two Cows. These, besides the Milk required to support the Calf, generally produce 3 Stone of Butter, and 6 Stone of Cheese between Whitesunday and Martinmass, which amounts to £1 16sh.

Manufacture

There is not any species of Manufacture carried on in this Island, except that of Kelp, which is indeed a very important Article. North Wist can afford every year 500 Ton of Kelp, which at 3£ 5sh. p. Ton, amounts to 1,625£, and in the year 1762 it afforded 800 Ton, but the Leases were then expiring, and the Season was peculiarly favourable. This Product of Kelp was at least three times more than the Land Rent of the whole Island, which shews the vast importance of this Article, and the Advantage of cultivating such a valuable Branch of Manufacture and Commerce.

The Linen Manufacture is not any where in the British Dominions in a more imperfect state, than in this Country. The Inhabitants have neither foreign Lint nor foreign Lintseed; and of the Lintseed of their own Growth, there are not above two Hogheads sown yearly in all the Island; from which, they make a little coarse Linen but the most part of that they consume and all their fine Linen is brought from Ireland. Their most general Soil which is a light Sand, is indeed an improper one for raising Lint, but some places they have a deep black Mold, which would produce Lint of an excellent Quality, and by draining the fresh Water Lakes in this Island, considerable Tracts of Land would be obtained, which would be the richest and best for raising Flax, of any in Scotland.

Fishery

There is plenty of large Cod upon several parts of the Coasts of North Wist, and its Lochs receive a regular annual Visit from the Herring Shoals; yet there is no Fish of any kind taken and cured, nor is there a long Line, nor a Herring net in all the Island. In the last Century, the spacious Bay, and fine Harbour of Loch Maddy in this Island, used to be the chief Seat of the Herring Fishery where 400 Vessels have been known to be loaded with Herrings in one Season. At this place, Charles the first, designed a Settlement and encouraged a Company of English Merchants to erect a fishing Magazine, the Ruins of which are still to be seen, and which had probably by this Time been a place of Note, had not the Civil Wars intervened, which rendered the Design abortive.[5] The Herring Fishery here, so far as can be learnt, is the same as formerly, and may still be prosecute with great success.

BENBECULA

BENBECULA

This Island is situate due South from North Wist, and is separated from it by a Strand or Channel of the Sea, three miles broad, which is fordable at low Water. The Island is nearly 6 Miles long from east to west and 5 Miles broad from South to North, and according to these measures, contains 19,200 Acres. Clanranald,[1] is the chief Proprietor, whose Land Rent in the Island amounts to 222£. Macdonel of Boysdale[2] has also Property in it to the Extent of 70£ a year. So that the Lands in this Island, including the fresh Water Lakes in it, are set at present at about 5d. p. Acre. Old Clanranald has his Seat in this Island,[3] and it is wholly Inhabited by Macdonnels, the People of his Clan. Besides the above Land Rent, Benbecula affords annually from 170-200 Ton of Kelp, from which Clanranald draws 166£ a Year, which makes the whole Rental of the Island amount to 458£.

Benbecula contains 600 Inhabitants, so that there are 32 Acres in the Island to each Person. Of this Number of People, there are only 90 Protestants and of these, only 6 or 8 who understand English. They have no School in the Island, nor any access to publick Worship except one in 5 or 6 weeks, when the Minister of South Wist comes to preach in the Island. From this Island there went 28 Men to the Army during the late War.

This Island is the lowest, and most level of all the Western Islands. It has not an Eminence in it except one Hill, towards the east, called Benbecula, from whence the Island has its Name,[4] which is of a round shape and easy Ascent, and not above 300 feet above the level of the Sea. There will be 8,000 Acres of arable Land in the Island, and not above 2,000 irreclaimable, which consist mostly of fields of blowing Sand. The remaining 9,200 Acres are capable of being easily brought into Culture. Of these not less than 4,000 Acres, that is, a quantity of Land equal to one half of all the arable Ground at present in the Island might be obtained from fresh Water Lakes, that can be drained at a small expence. The other 5,200 Acres consist of dry Heaths, some boggy Grounds and Sandy Downs.

The Soil of the Arable Land in Benbecula is of the same sandy nature, with that of the low Lands in North and South Wist, and affords of Bear, Grey Oats and Rye in such Plenty, in a wet Summer, as is sufficient to maintain the Inhabitants; but they are oblidged to import a good deal of Meal, if the Season is dry. They sow little or no Lint, and have hardly a Vestage of the Linen Manufacture among them. The Shores and Sounds about the Island abound greatly with Mullet; there is Cod also to be caught upon the east Shore, and in the Season, the Bay of Viskarvay[5] upon the east Coast, is frequently filled with Herrings; yet through the year there is not a Fish taken and cured by the Inhabitants.

SOUTH UIST

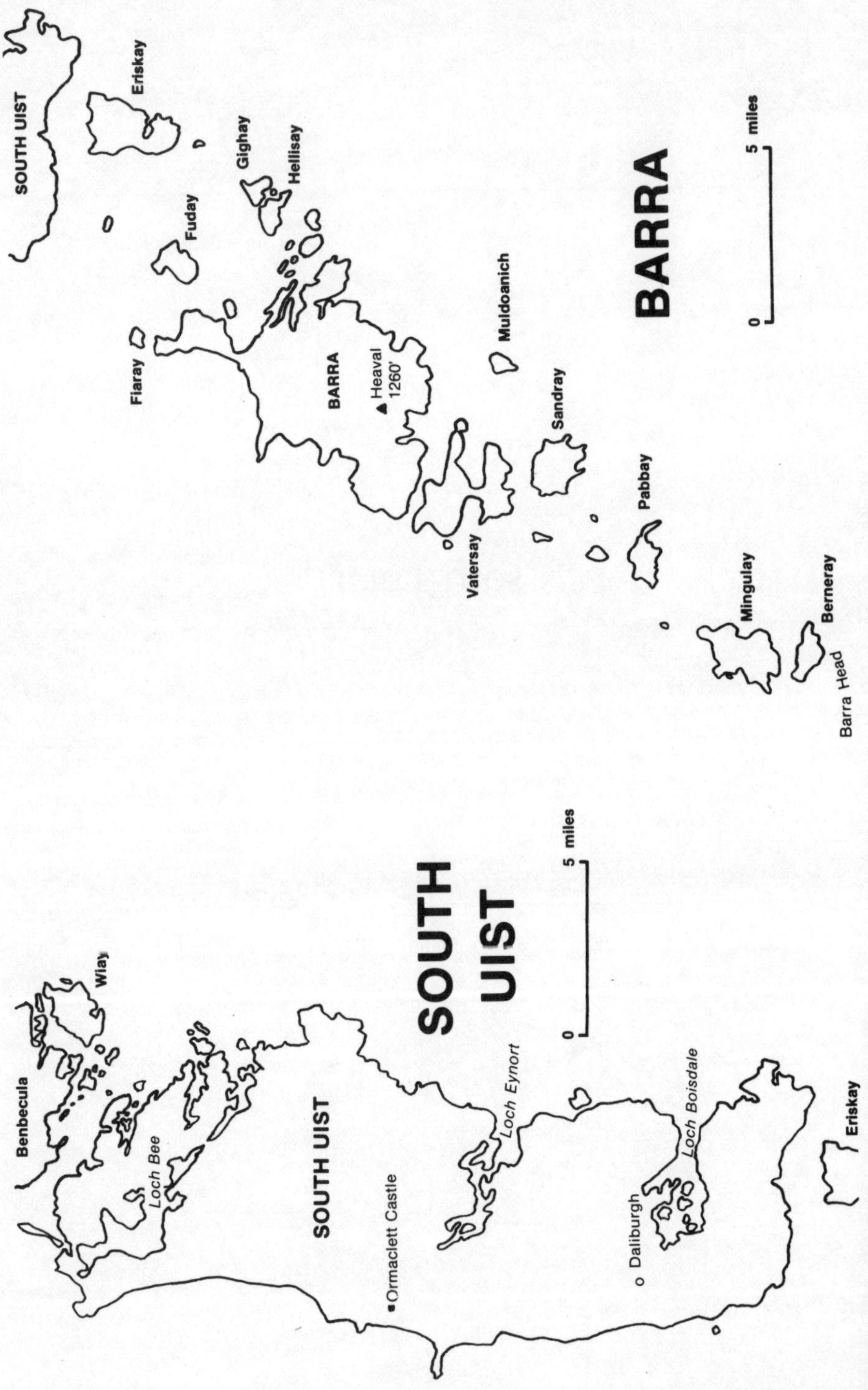
SOUTH UIST
Eriskay
Fuday
Gighay
Hellisay
Fiaray
BARRA
Heaval
1260'
Muldoanich
Sandray
Pabbay
Vatersay
Mingulay
Berneray
Barra Head
BARRA
0
5 miles
Benbecula
Wiay
Loch Bee
SOUTH UIST
Ormaclett Castle
Loch Eynort
Loch Boisdale
Daliburgh
Eriskay
SOUTH
UIST
0
5 miles

S. WIST

Extent and Rental

This Island lies directly South from Benbecula, and is divided from it by an extensive Strand or Channel of the Sea, 3 Miles over, which is fordable at low Water. It extends streight South and North, 33 Miles in length, and at a medium, is full 6 Miles in breadth, from East to West, so that it contains 126,720 Acres, but the Ground covered by the fresh Water Lakes upon the Island, is included in this Computation, which are at least 15,000 Acres. The whole Land Rent of the Island, amounts only to about 500£ by which it appears to be an average, at little more than one Penny Sterling p. Acre. Clanranald is the Sole Proprietor of this extensive Country, which is all inhabited by the Macdonnels of his Clan, or their Followers; which are People of other names, but who are attached to that Gentleman, as their Head or Chieftain.

Number of People

In this Island there are upwards of 1,580 Inhabitants, and about 70 Acres to each Person. Of this Number of People, there are only 160 Protestants, and of these, there are not above 14, who understand an English Sermon. This Island, with those of Benbecula and Erisca, compose one Parish, at least 40 Miles long and 6 broad, in which, neither the English Language nor the Protestant Religion, have ever made any considerable Progress. These Islands have very little Intercourse with any other People, and it is judged, the Galic Language subsists in them in greater Purity, than in any other parts of the Highlands. The Inhabitants are a strong healthy People, troubled with few or no Chronical Diseases, and with few acute Distempers, except Fevers and Fluxes which indeed carry off great numbers of them. The small Pox also, when they visit these Islands occasion great Mortality, but as young Clanranald[1] did last year set an excellent example by inoculating his Children, the practice it is to be hoped, will become general, which in a very short Period of Years, would fill these Islands with more Inhabitants than they can at present support. South Wist sent 72 Men to the Army during the late War, and besides those from Benbecula, there went 100 more from Clanranalds Estate in Moydart and Arisaig upon the main Land.

Soil

Of the 111,720 Acres in South Wist, there will be 20,000, that have been cultivate with the Plough or Spade, which consist wholly of light Sandy Soil, run to Decay, with Rye and Oaten Crops and want of manure. There may be about double that Quantity, or 40,000 Acres, capable of being reduced to Culture, which consist chiefly of low dry Heaths, and Sandy Pasturage. The remaining 51,720 Acres maybe deemed irreclaimable, being composed of steep rocky Mountains, and extensive Tracts of moving Sand.

There are besides, full 15,000 Acres covered by a Chain of fresh water Lakes, which runs lengthways through the Island. These Lakes are all extremely shallow, with a fine sleechy Bottom, and might be easily drained, though their Surface is lower by seven feet, than the Level of the Sea at Spring Tides. The largest of these is Lochvi, towards the north End of the Island: it is above 4 miles long and 2 broad, contains at least 5,100 Acres, and is not any where above 7 feet deep. Loch Dalbrog[2] in the South part of the Island, has been lately drained by Mr McDonnel of Boysdale, though immediately adjacent to the Sea, and its Bed 6 feet below high Water Mark. This is the first experiment that has been made in the Island, and by draining this Lake, about 2 square Miles have been gained, which is now the richest Land in Wist, and indeed as rich as any Land Whatever.

The East Coast of South Wist, is occupied by a Range of Mountains running south and north, the highest of which is about 1,800 Feet above the Level of the Sea. They are full of ragged Rocks, and are mostly covered with Heath, yet afford a very good Pasture for Sheep. The Sheep are of the lowest Size, and their wool of a very indifferent Quality, and are singular in this, that many of them have four or six, and some of them even eight Horns.[3] In September, 1763 a Score of the largest sized Sheep in Annandale were brought to Wist, by Clanranald, and put to Pasture upon these Mountains. In August last, after their Lambs were weaned, they were in as good Order, as any Sheep in the South of Scotland, and not one of them had suffered in any Shape by the Winter, though they had not been smeared.[4]

The West Coast of South Wist for the Extent of 33 Miles is a dead Plain; in most places, about 2 Miles broad, and of so deep a Sand, that there are no Springs in it, but what rise in the Lakes to which the Inhabitants must have Recourse for their Water. The Shore is fenced with vast banks of blowing Sand, with which the whole Country is flooded in Time of Storms. This Sandy Deluge is of the utmost Detriment here, as it is indeed along all the West Coasts of the long Island, and no effectual means have ever been used to restrain its Devestation. In this Island, it has come with such Violence upon many Houses and Villages, that they have been oblidged to be removed, to escape being overwhelmed. It has choaked up Rivulets, and made the Waters of the Lakes from whence they issued, advance upon the Land, and overflow some of the best fields in the Island. The Crops also, are in the greatest Danger from it, and it was indeed Melancholy in the beginning of last August, after a

Tract of high Winds, to see some excellent Fields of Bear, turned in a few Days into Fields of Sand, in some places a yard deep. This immense Mass of Sand which overspreads the Western Shores of the long Island, is owing to the Nature of the Coast: for from Barra head to the Harris, which is a Tract of about 100 Miles, the water does not deepen to 20 Fathoms, till you get 10 Leagues from Land. The Violent Surge of the western Ocean in this Shallow Water, both forms and pushes on the Sand to the Shore. When it arrives there, the west Winds being predominant, and of great Strength, it is hurried forward upon the Flat Country. As it leaves the Shore, the Sea advances and accordingly has made great Incroachments in many Places. In South Wist the Foundations of Stone Walls are to be seen at the lowest Ebb, above half a Mile from the present Floodmark.

The Mountains upon the east side of South Wist, have about 200 head of Red Deer upon them, but they are kept from increasing by the Eagles which haunt the Country and destroy the Fauns. The whole Island is full of Otters, which the Inhabitants Kill in great Numbers, and sell their Skins for 5 or 6 Shillings a piece.

Plants

It is observable, that many plants abound in great Quantities, and with a very luxuriant Growth upon the blowing Sand of the Western Islands, which in other places inhabit the richest black Soils. Such are the Senecio Jacoboa. Linn. Ragwort. Lolium perenne. Linn. Rye Grass. Carduus lanceolatus. Linn. Spear Thistle. Trifolium pratense. Linn. Red Clover. Serratula arvensis. Linn. Way Thistle. Trifolium repens Linn. White Clover. Artemisia vulgaris Linn. Mugwort. Artium Lappa. Linn. Burdock. The Sandy Downs of South and North Wist and Benbecula, are covered with a fine Carpet of the most excellent Plants for Pasturage. Such as the Plantago lanceolata Linn. or Ribwort Plantain, Red and White Clover, the Anthyllis vulneraria. Linn. or Kidney Vetch and especially with the Vicia cracca. Linn. or Tufted Vetch, which covers entire Fields with its rich and copious purple Flowers, and affords a thick Weighty Crop, of which the Farmers make the best Hay that these Islands afford. They esteem it also highly for Pasture, as it has the remarkable Property of making the Cows who feed plentifully upon it, to take the Bull Readily, and early in the Season, which is a matter of great Consequence in a breeding Country, where they have great Difficulty to support and preserve their Calves in the Winter. They take this Vetch to be the true Lucern, but though it is widely different from that Plant, it is of great Value as a natural Grass, and might still be of greater Consequence, if it was raised by Art.

In a Country abounding with such Herbage, a great produce of Honey might be reasonably expected, but the two first Bee Hives that have ever been in the long Island, were brought but last year from the Isle of Sky, to Clanranalds Seat of Ormoclait in South Wist.

These Islands however of North and South Wist and Benbecula abound at the same time, with several useless and pernicious Plants.

The Polygonum amphibium, Linn. or Perennial Willow-leaved Lakeweed covers with a luxuriant Growth many extensive Tracts of moist Sandy Grounds capable of the most easy and profitable Cultivation, but are thereby rendered entirely useless. The Leaves of this plant are of an acid Taste, and no Cattle will touch them, either green or in Hay.

Many of the Arable Fields in these Islands, as also in Barra, Harris and Lewes, when they are left Ley, instead of bearing Grass, bear nothing but the Daucus officinarum Casp. Bauk. pin.[5] or Birdsnest which all the different kinds of Cattle refuse for Pasture. The yellow, white and red rooted Garden Carrots are judged by Linnaeus to be all derived from this Plant by Culture. The Roots of it are eaten by the Inhabitants of the Long Island and have been raised for Use in some of their Gardens.

The Oenanthe crocata, Linn. or Hemlock Dropwort grows in many of the western Islands, but most plentifully in North and South Wist, by the Sides of the Lakes and Rivulets, and seems to be the most virulent Plant that grows in Brittain. In preparing a Sprig of it for a Hortus siccus, the very Effluvia of it, will affect a Person with a considerable Degree of Megrim; and there are many Instances of People being killed by eating the Roots of it, having mistaken them for Parsnips. Mr Macdonnel Younger of Boysdale in South Wist, has every year 3 or 4 Cows killed by this Plant in the Month of April, when it begins to spring and when there is little to be had in the Fields, the Cattle browse upon it, and as it comes easily up by the Roots, being pressed with Hunger, they eat them without Reluctance, but it soon affects them with great Delirium and Dissorder, which terminates in Convulsions and Death. The Farmers know of no Remedy for it, but Milk, Butter or Greasy things put down their Throats, which they think cures them when taken in Time.

Great Numbers of Cattle are certainly killed by this Plant, in the Western Islands, and along all the West Coast of Scotland where it is not known, nor suspected to be the Cause of their Death. The Extirpation of it should be the Care of Gentlemen and Farmers, wherever it grows, which would not be a very Difficult Matter, as it is a very large Plant, and resides only in Watery Places.

Price of Labour

The Wages of a labouring man Servant, in South Wist, during the year, consists of 13 Shillings in Money, Grain sown to the Extent of 16 Shillings and two Pair of Brogues, the whole amounting to about 1£ 11sh. The Women Servants have 5 or 6 shillings in Money, a little Wool with Time allowed them to spin it, and some other small Perquisites, which alltogether cannot be valued at above 10.sh. yearly.

The Maintenance of a Man Servant in a Family stands not above 2£ 10sh. per annum and that of a Woman Servant scarce 1£ 10sh.

The whole expence of making a Ton of Kelp amounts to a Guinea and it is sold this year at 3£ 5sh. p. Ton.

Price of Commodities

	£	s	d
The Grass of a Cow, or of 8 Sheep during the Year in the finest grass	0	6	8
The Cows sell from 1£ 5sh. to 1£ 15sh. At a medium	1	10	0
The Oxen sell usually 3sh. cheaper than the Cows - At a medium	1	7	0
The best Wedders sell in October from 2sh. 6d. to 3sh. At a medium, each	0	2	9
The Stone of Cheese which is 21 lb: English	0	3	0
A Stone of Butter of the same Weight	0	6	0
Dried Ling per Hundred	2	18	4
But they were sold last Year at Glasgow p. hundred, at	4	10	0

Exports

	£	s	d
South Wist and Benbecula exports annually 700 black Cattle which at an Average of 1£ 8sh. each, amount to	980	0	0
South Wist exported last Year 5,000 dried Ling, which yeilded near	225	0	0
Benbecula affords annually 200 Ton of Kelp and South Wist 100, which at 3£ 5sh. p. Ton yeilds	975	0	0

South Wist sends a considerable Quantity of Butter and Cheese to the Ports in the Clyde. After a Wet Summer it exports some Grain, but is obligded to import, if the Summer has been dry. There is but little Grain destroyed with Aqua Vitae as there is but one Distillery in the Island, which is in a private Family; the Spirits which the Inhabitants consume being mostly brought from other places.

State of Agriculture

Bear, Grey Oats and Rye are the only Grains sown in South Wist, which are raised both by the Plough and the Spade. From the light sandy Soils, the Farmers after covering them with Sea Wrack take a Crop of Bear, and then two Crops of Rye, after which they are thrown out Ley, and at the end of 5, 6 or 7 years are croped again in the same manner. The rich black Soil, which is frequent in the Island, has afforded crops of Grain immemorially, without any respite. They take alternately from it a Crop of Bear and Oats, and all the assistance it gets, is a Covering of Sea Wrack to the Bear Crop. Yet notwithstanding this impoverishing method, the Land appears to be in good Heart and affords rank Crops.

There is a remarkable Difference in the Quality of the Grain, raised upon these two different Soils. The Boll of Bear, consisting of 20 Pecks, which is produced upon the high sandy Soil above mentioned will afford 25 or 26 Pecks of Meal; whereas the same Boll of Bear, growing on the deep black Soil, kept constantly in Tillage yeilds usually but 14 Pecks of Meal and sometimes only 12.

They do not account their Bear Crop good if it is not above 10 fold. It is usually between that and 15, and 20, 25 and even 30 fold, and has been often known to be produced upon their richest Sandy Grounds. Their Oats are seldom above 4 fold, and their Rye as much, but they account the Rye Crop the most valuable of the two.

There might be as early Crops in South and North Wist and Benbecula, as in most parts of Scotland, but though they have seldom any considerable Degree of Frost or Snow, and though the Soil in general, is sandy and dry, yet they sow no Grain till about the beginning of April. The Rye and Oats are then sown, and the Bear is not put into the Ground, till towards the End of May, they usually begin to reap it on or about the 15 of August.

Though black Cattle is the Staple Produce of the Western Islands yet it is but of late years that the Inhabitants have ever made any Hay to support them in Winter, and the most that is still made anywhere, serves only to support some of the young Cattle, which stand in greatest need of it. None of Tenants in South Wist ever made any Hay, till the year 1756, but now, there are very few of them but what make some. They began last year to cut their Meadow Hay on the 20th of July, which was twenty Days later than usual.

Potatoes were first Introduced in South Wist 25 years ago, and by planting them in uncultivate Ground, there are now full 900 Acres, under the Spade and Plough Culture, more than there was at the Time. The Quantity of Corn, Grass and Cattle upon several Farms in the Island being thereby increased one third during that Period.

The Culture of Potatoes has also a visible Effect upon the Population of the Country. As the Potatoes have spread all the Highlands, have from this Cause, become sensibly more populous.

Though there is a vast extent of Champaign Country in the Islands of South and North Wist and Benbecula yet wherever the Sandy Soil prevails, which is over the greatest part of it, inclosing is impracticable because of the Sand Drift, for the Surface could not be broke by Ditches, without endangering the whole Country. Neither is there any Rock near the Surface for building Walls and though there was, they would be inevitably blown up and rendered unserviceable. Upon the East side of those Islands however, and in some of the more inland places, there are Tracts of black Land, and of Moorish Grounds which might be beneficially inclosed.

The Crops in North Wist and Benbecula, but especially South Wist, are exposed to a very singular Missfortune; being sometimes entirely destroyed by the vast Flocks of Wild Geese, which haunt these Islands. This Bird is never seen in the South of Scotland except in Winter but in these Islands it hatches and resides all the year round, as they are peculiarly adapted for its Reception, by the numerous and extensive fresh Water Lakes they contain, which are filled with Islets and their Shores covered with the finest Grass. These Birds are most numerous from the 1st of July to the 1st of October during which Time it is the principal Employment of the Inhabitants to defend the Corns from their Depredations and for this Purpose make use of a Variety of Expedients. It is remarkable in the Wild Geese that it never alights in a Field of Grain, but always in the neighbouring Grass Field and from thence walks in to the Corn: the Farmers therefore totally surround their Corn Fields with a Heather Rope two or three Inches thick, laid upon the Ground and this the Birds do not venture to walk over, unless much pressed with Hunger. They are remarkable for being of a very shy suspicious Nature and are extremely cautious against all Gins and Decoys, so that their Fear of this weak Defence, seems to be occasioned by their Suspicion of a Snare.

Sometimes however it is insufficient to prevent their entring the Corn, and the Farmers are oblidged to surround the Field with small Pillars of Turf, two Feet high, by these the Heather Rope which is led round the Field is suspended six or eight Inches from the Ground, which renders it a more effectual Fence, yet notwithstanding these Precautions, when the Corns are near ripe the Owners are forced to watch them all the Night over, and to kindle Fires in many places, which frequently upon the rising or shifting of the Wind communicate themselves to the Crop and make great Devastation.

To these very great Hardships the People of those Islands have been subjected, only since the disarming Act took place.[6] But since that Period, these Birds have increased to such a Degree, that they threaten in a little Time to deprive the Inhabitants of Bread. To allow them a few Arms for the Preservation of their Crops, would be a piece of Humanity which their Necessity and their Distress loudly call for.

Manufacture

There is no kind of Manufacture in this Island whatever, and the greater Part of the Inhabitants, especially of the Women, are absolutely unemployed. The Spinning has never yet been introduced, though there is no Country where it would be more beneficial, as the Wages and Maintenance of a Woman Servant throughout the year do not amount to above Forty Shillings. Cheaper Labour than this, does not exist certainly in any part of Europe.

The Inhabitants get no foreign Flax nor Flax seed, but sow a little of their own, in order to provide themselves with coarse Linen Cloth.

There is one piece of Encouragement, which needs be no very expensive one, by which the Linen Manufacture would make considerable Progress in the Islands. That is, to furnish the Inhabitants with foreign Lintseed at prime Cost. They are anxious to sow it and to pay for it, but cannot procure it, and this oblidges them to sow their own Lintseed, which is sometimes the Produce of above 100 Generations in the same Island, and degenerate to such a Degree, that one would scarce take the Crops to be Lint. After pulling, they hang it up to dry in Bunches, which are scarce longer than those of Sparrow Grass, and when they are fully dry, they beat and bruise them between two Stones, without any watering, till they make good a Seperation of the Lint from the Reed.

In South Wist they have great plenty of a rich moist black Soil, capable of producing as fine Flax as any in the World. By an Experiment which Clanranald had made, I saw Lint in the same Field, sown at the same Time and Managed every way in the same manner, but one part of it raised from America Lintseed, and the other from the Lintseed of the Country. The Crop of the former was 3 feet 6 inches long, and in the Bolls ready to pull on the 2nd of August, while the Crop of the latter was but 13 Inches long and only in Flower. Which shows, that with the same Culture, foreign Flax seed is capable to produce Lint near four times higher and at least five or six times more crop, than the Lintseed of this Country can do, and capable to produce it, also, at least a Fortnight more early. A remarkable Circumstance, and an additional Advantage which is very considerable.

Sheep

In this Island, there are a great Number of Sheep, but the Breed degenerated to the last Degree. It is remarkable, that as Sheep increase in Size, their Wool increases in Finess, and this improvement is always attended with the lengthening of their Tails, and the Loss of their Horns. In the English Flocks, few Horns are to be seen, but in Scotland where the Sheep are of a less Size, and the Wool coarser, none of the Sheep have long Tails, or are without Horns but such as partake of the English Breeds. In South Wist, where the Sheep are still smaller than in the main Land of Scotland, the Wool accordingly is still coarse in Proportion and attended with a still further Diminution of their Tails, and Increase of Horns; for here, the Sheep Diminutive as they are, have generally two Pair, and frequently three Pair of Horns.[7]

Such Degeneracy in the Sheep of this and the other Islands is not owing to the Climate or Pasture, but to the want of Skill in their Management, the want of proper Precautions necessary to preserve them of a just Size, and especially to their being too numerous for their Pasture, and to the immemorial Continuance of the same Breed in an Island, without ever being crossed. This last Dissadvantage, Clanronald is endeavouring to rectify in South Wist by bringing Sheep of a better Breed from the South of Scotland. I saw a great Number of them which he had brought from Anandale and which had been above a Year upon the Island. They were all in excellent Order, had afforded a Crop of exceeding good Wool, and not one of them had died either upon the Journey or during the Winter, and without smearing, though they had all been smeared, the year before they came into his Possession.

A great deal of Advantage may be expected from improving the Breed of Sheep in this manner in the Islands, as also by increasing their Number, and diminishing that of Black Cattle. For there is Reason to think, that the Sheep are capable of being made the most profitable of the Two, to the Farmer, and they are undoubtedly so, to the Country in general. The raising of Black Cattle promotes no Species of Industry among these people, but on the contrary is the very Nursery of Idleness; whereas a large Quantity of superplus Wool, would support great Numbers of them in one of the most useful Branches of Industry.

Fishery

The East Shore of South Wist is remarkable for one of the finest Ling Fisheries in all the Highlands, but though it might be carried on to a very great Extent, it is not pursued by any of the Inhabitants of the Island excepting by Mr Mcdonald of Boysdale.

As this Fishery deserves particular Attention, I made all the Enquiry I could, to obtain an idea of the most proper manner of carrying it on, and of the Expence attending it.

The Fishing Ground lying within two Leagues of the Shore the Vessel necessary, is a four oard Boat, with 5 Hands, furnished with 12 long Lines: each Line being 360 Fathoms long, with 100 Hooks on it. Besides these, Six small Lines are required, each 100 Fathoms long, with 100 Hooks, for catching Bait, which are Flounders, Conger Eel, and small Cod. And the 12 long Lines, require 4 Buoys, and as many Buoy Lines, each 150 Fathoms Long.

ESTIMATE of the Prime Cost of this Vessel, and of the Expence in keeping it employed during the three Months of the Ling Fishery, at S.Wist.

	£	s	d
Boat with Sails and Oars	5	0	0
For 12 long Lines	12	0	0
For 6 Small Lines	1	4	0
For 4 Buoy Lines	2	0	0
For 4 Buoys	0	4	0
	20	8	0
Wages to the Headsman of the Boat during the three Months of the Fishery	1	13	4
To the 4 other Men	4	0	0
To the Dyet of the 5 Men during the three Months	3	0	0
To 8 Barrels of Salt at 12sh. each	4	16	0
TOTAL	33	17	4

The Barrel of Salt will cure 100 Ling and if well Managed, 8 Barrels will even cure 1,000.

A Boat of the above kind may be reckoned to make a good Fishing if she cures 7 or 800 Ling, but cannot make less than 1,000 if constantly employed, nay Boysdale has cured 2,000 in the Season with one Boat.

These Ling sell in the Ports of Clyde for 4£ 10sh. p. hundred upwards, so that supposing a Boat to cure 1,000, the value amounts to 45£, and the whole Expence of curing them only to 13£ 9sh. 4d.

At the most moderate Computation therefore, there is to be Made by such a Boat, during the three Months, 31£ 10sh. 8d of neat Profit exclusive of the Tear and Wear of the Boat and Tackling which cannot be reckoned much; as they may be of use throughout the greatest part of the Year.

From the above Computation it must appear that this Fishery by due Attention might be highly advantageous, both to Undertakers and the Publick, and yet at present it is almost totally neglected.

In the Year 1764 there were only 10 Yauls in South Wist, that fished any Ling, and though not in a constant or regular Manner, yet they cured above 5,000 Fish, which were made on Account of Mr McDonald of Boysdale.

Though many of the Poorer sort of the Inhabitants, are very expert in Fishing, perfectly well skilled in curing the Fish, and abundantly sensible of the Profits upon the Fishery: yet their Poverty and distant situation renders the Difficulty of acquiring Boats, Salt and Tackling insurmountable, though it is by them only that the Fishery can ever be carried to a considerable Extent.

BARRA

BARRA

Situation and Extent

Barra with its smaller adjacent Islands compose the Southern Extremety of that great Chain known by the name of the long Island, and is seperated from S. Wist by a Channel 7 Miles broad, full of small Islands.

The Island is of a very unequal Figure, but in general computed at 8 Miles in length and four in Breadth, comprehending 20,480 Acres, the Rental of which being about 200£, the whole is let for little above 2d. per Acre. This, with the smaller Islands contiguous to it, composes the Estate of the chief of the Mcneils, who have been in Possession of it, from very remote Antiquity, the family being in possession of Vouchers for about 30 Descents.

Adjacent Islands

Bernera or Bara head is the most southerly Island, a Mile long and a quarter of a mile broad. It contains 20 Persons and Rents for 6£.

Mingula, the next to it, is three miles long, and above one broad. It contains 52 Persons upon it and Rents at 12£.

Pabay is above a Mile long and above half a Mile broad. Contains 16 Persons and lets for 5£. This Island is greatly spoiled by the Sand Drift.

Sandera is the next Island, North of the former, above a Mile and a half long, and above a Mile Broad. Contains 40 Persons. Rental 12£.

Vatersay, a very fertile Spot, is three Miles long and three broad. Has 104 Inhabitants, and lets at 35£.

Fuda,[1] on the North of Barra, is a Mile and a half long, and of equal Breadth. Contains 56 Inhabitants. Rental 22£.

Feala, likewise on the North of Barra is near a Mile in length and Breadth, has 10 Persons upon it and Rents for 6£.

These 7 Islands, with a great many smaller ones, belonging to them, uninhabited, but used for Pasturage, appear to contain about 15,000 Acres, and being let for about 100£ a year, are rented for less than 2d. per Acre.

Inhabitants

These Barra Isles, which compose a Parish contain 1,285 Persons, and about 27 Acres for each Inhabitant. They are all Papists, except 50 who are Protestants, and none of them understand any thing of English, except a few of the young People, who have been lately taught, at the School kept there by the Society for propogating Christian Knowledge.

The present Barra is a Minor,[2] upon whose Behavior, the Continuation of these People in the Popish Religion, or their Conversion from it, will very much depend. Though under the Direction of his Grandfather and Tutor, old Mcneil of Vatersay,[3] a man of excellent Principles, and the chief Support of the Protestant Interest in that part of the World, yet his incumbered Circumstances, and the Inclinations and influence of his Clan, will probably prevail over the Endeavours that are used to breed him a Protestant. His Father raised a Company with which he went to America, and was killed at the Battle of Quebec. His Mother, Grandmother & Aunt have Annuities of the Estate, which, with the Debts, leave only 30£ a year, clear, to support & educate the Boy and Sister. Being unable to bear the Expence of an Education at Edinburgh or Glasgow, he was sent to School at Aberdeen where he resides without any Tutor, and where Mr Grant the Popish Bishop lives, who was formerly the residing Priest in Barra.[4]

From the Island of Barra 31 Men were sent to the late War, which all died, or were killed in America, except 6 who have returned.

Of the 1,285 Inhabitants, in the Year 1764, there were only two Persons among the Males above 80 years of Age. They are in general extremely healthy, and suffer little from any Diseases, but those that are epidemical. In the year 1758 the Small Pox swept away above 80 of them, but they had not been known in the Island for 12 years before, and Inoculation has never yet been practised among them. And in the year 1762 an Epidemical Fever, with which they are sometimes visited carried off 70 of them.

Soil

The inland parts of Barra consist of one Mass of Mountains, the highest of which is about 1,600 Feet above the level of the Sea.

They descend with a very steep declivity to the East Coast and are covered to the Beach, with deep black Moss and rank Heath. On this side of the Island however, the Excursions of these Mountains form several excellent Creeks for the Reception of small Vessels.

The west side of the Island lies fully exposed to the Atlantick, and affords no Harbour. The Coast is high & bold, and the Sea urged by a strong Wind, united with the western Swell, rises and rages upon the Rocks in a very frightfull manner.

On this west shore however, there are several Tracts of very good light Soil, which affords crops of Bear and Oats, but greatly prejudiced by the extensive Fields of blowing Sand, which turn and wheel, and move over the Country, in a very hurtfull way. This Sand Drift, against which they have no Defence, has oblidged them to remove Houses, and even entire Villages, in several parts of the Island.

The Barra Isles do not contain above 8,000 Acres, that have ever been cultivated: there may be about 8,000 more, capable of being reclaimed; but the remaining 19,480 consist of steep Mountains, deep Mosses, and places so embarrassed with Rocks, as cannot be turned to any use, but Pasture for low sized Cattle.

Climate

This Island being very remote from the main Land both of Scotland and Ireland, full of Mountains, and surrounded by a raging Ocean, its Climate is rather Boisterous than cold. It never suffers any considerable Degree of Frost, nor any that ever continues so long, as is common in Scotland and England. But the Winds, and Rains are impetuous, and the Heat in Summer, never so great as in these Countries. Yet the Soil of their cultivated Fields is friendly and forward, though the Climate is forbidding, and generally affords them Bear Harvest on or about the 15th of August.

On 31st of July at noon and the two preceding Days, Fahrenheits Thermometer stood in the Sun at 96, and in St Barrs well at 46, which is the finest Spring in the Island.

From the first of September, to the first of March the Wind seldom varies above two or three from S.W. On the 19th February 1749, a Hurricane from that Quarter, with a high Tide, broke over for the first Time, an Isthmus which divides the Island into two parts.

The Isthmus was very extensive, and consisted of excellent Land, but ever since that Inundation has been a blowing Sand, though the Sea has never again forced its way over it. The same Tide, made also great Devastation in [the] Clyde, and at Greenock and Inverary flowed into Houses.

Exports

Barra exports annually about 140 head of Black Cattle, and about 160 Salted. For want of Cask, they have a very singular Method of Salting and packing them up in the Hides, which preserves them very well, and in which they are carried to the Ports in the Clyde, where they are disposed of to the Shipping.

They cure annually in Barra 6,000 Ling, which usually sell at Glasgow for between 4 and 5£ per Hundred. But they may be purchased in the Island for 6d. or 7[d.] a Piece. Such is the Danger and Difficulty of the Exportation by the Inhabitants, in their small Boats, to the Clyde.

In the Year 1763 they began for the first Time, to make Kelp in Barra, and manufactured 40 Ton. In the year 1764, they made above 60 Ton, and as they advance in the Knowledge of making it, will probably produce a greater Quantity.

They commonly export a little Bear, and always had a large Quantity to spare, till a great deal of their best Land, came of late years, to be overrun with the Sand Drift. Their Bear is a Grain remarkably good of its Kind, having a full Body, and a thin Husk, owing to the light Sandy Soil in which it grows.

There are two Stills in the Island, which furnish the Inhabitants with Malt Spirits.

There is not twelve hundred People, in any part of the British Dominions that live so entirely upon the Product of their Soil, as those of Barra. The above Exports bring them as much money as enables them to pay their Rents, and for the rest, they live wholly upon what their Fishing and their Farms afford them, having little or no Demand, for the Productions of any other Country whatever.

The Prices of Labour and of Commodities, are much the same here, as in South Wist.

Agriculture

In this Island, as many other parts of the Highlands, the cultivated Land bearing so small a proportion to the number of Inhabitants, a great part of it comes thereby to be manufactured with the Spade. In this way, they plant their Bear here, as they do their Potatoes, in lazy Beds. They lay either Dung or Sea Ware upon the Green Sward in Winter. In February they dig Trenches, and cast out the Earth on each Side upon the Beds. When it is perfectly dry, in the End of April or beginning of May, they sow their Bear, and then Harrow it with a Hand Harrow, which is an Instrument like a Garden Rake, with Wooden Teeth. In this way they obtain exceeding good Crops of that Grain, and as they sow extremely thin, they have a very large Increase, compared with the Quantity of Seed.

This Spade culture is also greatly promoted by the Smallness of the Farms, which prevents the Possessors from employing the Plough. Many of their Possessions being under 5£ Rent, and not a few, even under 30sh.

It is but 12 Years, since Potatoes were first cultivate in Barra, and without them, they would not now be able to support themselves in Grain, since a great deal of their best Soil, has been of late years rendered unserviceable by the Progress of the Sand Drift. They serve as Sustenance to the whole Inhabitants, above a Quarter of the Year.

The People of Barra suffer great Inconveniency in their Houses, in their Fishery, and in their Agriculture, from the want of Wood. They have not a Stick growing in the Island, and must hazard a long and dangerous Voyage in their little open Boats, to the Isle of Mull or to the main Land, before they provide themselves in an Oar or a Spade Shaft. Though there is no doubt but wood might be raised in several places upon the East side of the Island, if it was defended from the Cattle.

They have in this Island, an inexhaustible Quantity of Sea Shells, of the finest kind, with which, they might raise their Land to any Degree of Fertility they please, but are wholly unacquainted with the use of them. The Labour they employ in covering an Acre of Ground, with Sea Weeds, which last only for a single Crop, if laid out upon Shells would communicate a much greater Degree of Fertility to the Soil, for 20 or 30 years.

In the extensive Sand, called the Craymore of Kilbarra[5] there are several Square Miles, which in other Countries would be obtained from the Sea but here perhaps it would be too expensive an undertaking.

There is not in Barra anything that can be called a Manufacture, excepting Kelp.

Fishery

Upon the East Coast of Barra, there subsists a very valuable Fishery, though very little pursued. This may be easily conceived, when 8 yauls belonging to the Island, in less than three Months, in the year 1764, cured 6,000 Ling, which sold at Glasgow for about 270£.

It is remarkable, that Cod and Ling always abound most, where there is the greatest Plenty of Shell Fish, especially of Cockles, Clams, Mussels and Razor Fish. These Shell Fish are a principal Article of their Sustenance, always found in their Stomachs, and frequently quite entire. And as no Coast can be more fertile in these Shell fish than the east Shore of Barra, they are therefore to be looked upon as the chief Reason, why it is so much frequented by Cod and Ling. The same observation holds in the Ling Fishery off the Lewes, and in the Cod Fishery at Gairloch in Ross-Shire.

Cod and Ling, like most other Fishes, have their Migrations, and frequently change their Residence.

For many years before and after the year 1720, there were usually cured and sent from Barra about 14,000 dried Cod. This Fish was then in such abundance upon the Coast, that a single Boat, in two or three Hours, would have caught 140 large Cod fit for curing, besides small ones. But since the year 1730, few or no Cod have been seen about the Island.

While the Cod were thus plentiful at Barra, there were no Ling to be found: but ever since they deserted the Coast, the Ling have subsisted in that great abundance, in which they are found at present.

The Ground which they occupy, consists of two Banks, which stretch along the east Coast of the Island: the one near it, but the other at a greater Distance. The nearest one, is only a Mile from the Shore, and to this, their present Fishing is mostly confined, but the other is 6 Miles off. Their Boats are so small, and so ill found in Tackle, that it is seldom they can venture to the distant Bank, though it is much more extensive, and the Fish upon it larger and more numerous than upon the other.

Their Lines being set over Night, they go out in the morning and draw them, when they take off the Fish, and with the Bait, which they carry along with them, reset the Lines. When they bring the Fish ashore, they split and wash them and cleanse off the Blood and Slime with Heather Brushes. They then lay them in small Heaps, upon the Rocks with a Layer of Salt between each two Layers of Fish. They are allowed to ly in this manner for two or three Days, when they are again washed in Sea Water, and laid out on the Rocks to dry: and in good Weather, they will be sufficiently cured in eight or ten Days. They have learnt from the Irish Fishers to turn up the Back of the Fish, whenever the Sun is hot, which prevents their turning yellow, and preserves upon them, that Bloom which is a certain Sign of their being well cured.

The great disadvantage at present in the Fishery at Barra, is the smallness and insufficiency of their Boats, by which they are kept idle during a great part of the fishing Season, as they dare not venture abroad in them but when the

Weather is very moderate; and they are likewise extremely defective in Lines and fishing Tackle. The Rusche Fishers[6] in Ireland, which are the most expert of any in the Cod Fishery, fish in small Wherries, half decked from 6 to 10 Tons Burden, which are the proper Vessels to be used upon this Barra Fishery.

The Mackrel are to be found on the Coasts of Barra only in the Month of August. They are much larger, but not so fat as those in the Sound of Mull and on the Shores of the main Land.

Natural Productions

There is a Plant grows in this Island, of the Root of which the Natives make an exceeding fine red Dye. It is the Galium verum, Linn. The yellow Ladies Bedstraw, or Cheese rening, which, though a Plant that grows universally over Scotland, it is not anywhere known to be of use as a Dye, excepting in some places in the Western Islands. It grows most luxuriantly and affords the largest Roots upon sandy Downs, so that it is found in Barra in the greatest Perfection; but in these Places, the People are prohibited from digging it up, for as there is nothing but blowing Sand under the Grass, when once the Surface is broke a Sand Drift commence, which will soon destroy a whole Field. As this Plant is of the same natural Class with the Madder, appearing to be little if anything inferior to it in Quality, and as it would be best raised upon those sandy Fields and Shores, that are at present unprofitable, its Cultivation therefore, is a thing that promises some Emolument.

In the Island they have a greater Quantity of several kinds of Shell Fish, than is to be found perhaps anywhere else in Britain, and if they could be pickled or preserved like Oysters, their Abundance is such, that they might afford a Branch of Trade. They serve as a principle Article, in the Sustenance of the whole Inhabitants, for at one time may be seen above 100 People, with as many Horses, upon that extensive Sand called the Craymore, carrying off Loads of Cockles and Razor Fish, which though not the best, are the most easily purchased.

The Ostrea maxima, Linn. which by many is preferred to the common Oyster, and might no doubt be pickled in the same way is to be found in great Quantities, and is reckoned one of the greatest Delicacies that the Sea produces, by the Inhabitants of the Western Isles. They ly upon a clear channely Bottom, in water 6 or 8 Feet deep at low water, where the People take them up with long fine Spears, which they strike through the thin or flat Shell of the Fish. They are not only agreeable eating, but exceeding wholesome, and so large, that three or four of them will dine a Person. The concave Shell of this Fish, which will sometimes hold near half an English Pint, was antiently the usual Cup in the Highlands, so much signalized in the Poems of Oscian, and in many places it is still in use for the same Purpose.

The Mya lutraria Linn. is also another large Shell Fish, equally good with the former, and found on the Shores of this Island in great Quantities.

ROCKALL

ROCCA

About 45 or 50 Leagues West and by North of Barra, lies a high Rock, called by Sailors Rokol or Rocca, but by the Inhabitants of the long Island Rocco-Barra, who have an old Traditional account of it. About the middle, it is very high above Water, with a great many Breakers, at a considerable Distance round it. It is white with the Dung of Sea Fowl, and has the appearance at a Distance of a lofty Ship. It is in none of our Sea Charts, though the Dutch have it in theirs, and though the Vessels passing to and from the West Indies by the Orkneys come frequently in sight of it. A Ship was lost in the Year 1686 with French and Spaniards on board who made their way from it in their Boat to St. Kilda.

The Existence of this small Rock amidst such a World of Waters make it probable, that there are Soundings and Cod Banks in its Neighbourhood especially, as it is crouded with Water Fowl, and as some of the Newfoundland Banks are known to reach within 200 Leagues of it.

ISLAY

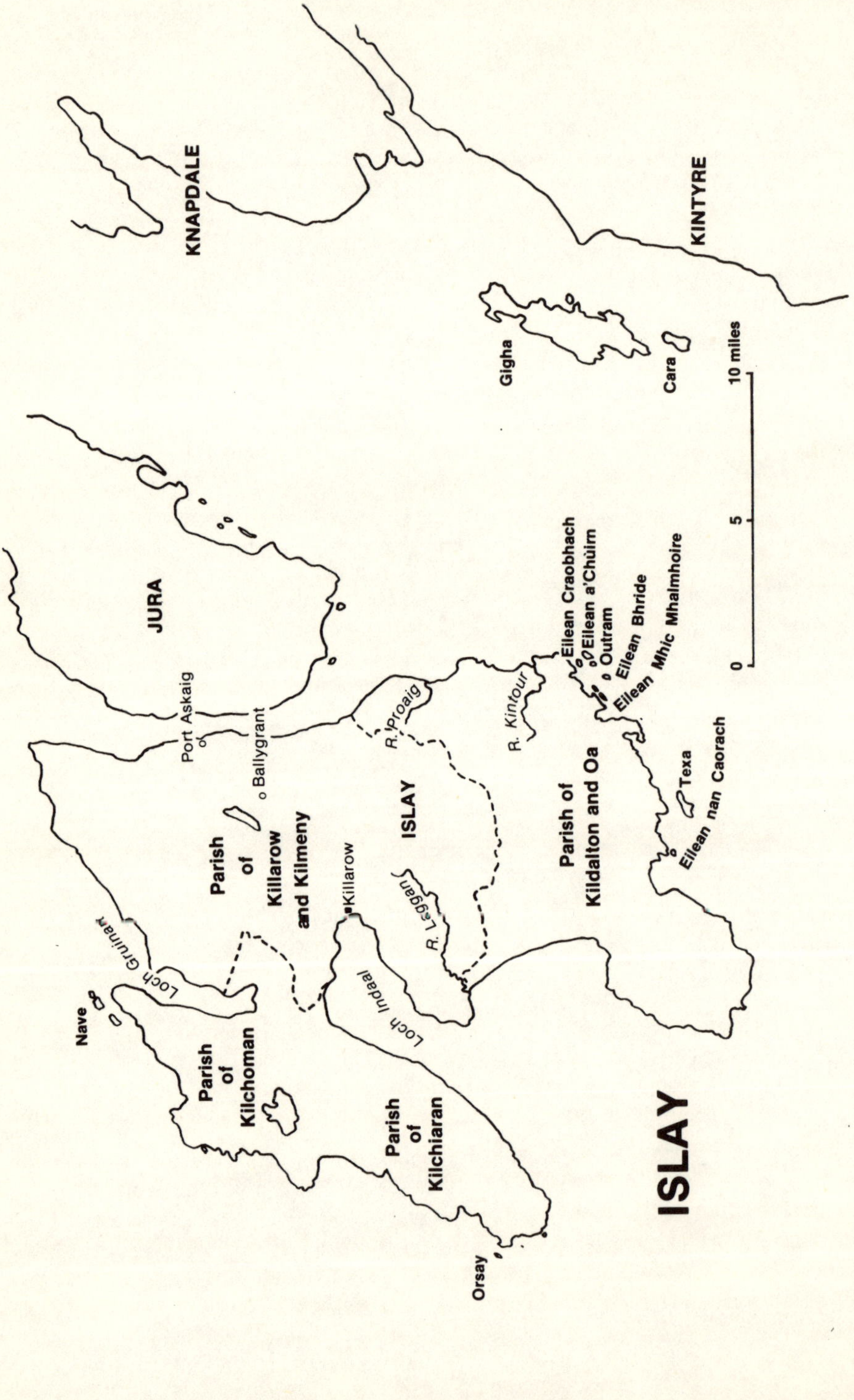
KNAPDALE
KINTYRE
JURA
Gigha
Cara
0
5
10 miles
Eilean Craobhach
Eilean a'Chuirn
Outram
Eilean Bhride
Eilean Mhic Mhalmhoire
R. Kintour
R. Proaig
Port Askaig
Ballygrant
ISLAY
Parish of Killarow and Kilmeny
Killarow
R. Laggan
Parish of Kildalton and Oa
Texa
Eilean nan Caorach
Loch Gruinar
Loch Indaal
Nave
Parish of Kilchoman
Parish of Kilchiaran
Orsay
ISLAY

ILA

Situation and Extent

The Island of Ila is situate about 15 Leagues from the Coast of Ireland, and about 8 from the west Shore of Cantire. There are 9 small adjacent Islands which belong it, Otrim, Cravey, Achume, Vride, Machilvrie, Oarsa, Chunich, Neave and Texa.[1] These are from half a Mile to two Miles in Circumference each: they are all stocked with Cattle, but the Isle of Texa, which is the largest, is the only one that is inhabited. Mr Campbell of Shawfield is Proprietor of the whole, excepting about 300 a year [*sic*] which belongs to two or three other Heritors.[2]

This Island at the lowest Computation is reckoned 20 Miles long, and 16 broad, and if we allow for the two Lakes, which run into the Island and the other irregularities in its Form, by considering these only as measured Miles, the Superficial Contents amount to 211,200 Acres.

Number of People

Ila formerly comprehended four Parishes, which are now joined into two. The one consists of the united Parishes of Killiren and Kilchoman; and contains upwards of 4,000 Inhabitants. The other is composed of the united Parishes of Kilmany and Kildalton,[3] which together make a Parish 20 Miles long and 8 broad, and contains about 3,000 People.

Ila sent to the Army and Navy, during the late War 500 Men, which was nearly a fourteenth of its whole Inhabitants. Yet this great Proportion it could spare perhaps every 10 years without Detriment, was it not for several Causes, which conspire to prevent its Population. Among the Children, the Measles are peculiarly Mortal. The small Pox are less hurtfull than in the other Islands, because the Disease generally visits Ila once a year; yet of those who are seized with it a much larger Proportion die, than in any district upon the main Land where this is the Case, and Inoculation has not as yet been introduced. The Bloody Flux also is a prevailing and fatal Distemper.

The Migration of the People of Ila, and indeed of all the southerly Islands to Ireland, is more detrimental however to their Population, than all their Diseases. These Emigrants are generally the young Men and Women, who either are induced to leave their Country for want of Employment, or enticed by the Hopes of reaping more by their Labour in another Kingdom. And as these Islands raise a greater Number of People than are requisite for their present System of Agriculture and Labour, this Emigration must continue till they can be allured to remain at Home, by being profitably Employed.

On the 1st of August 1764 about 80 Young Men and Women embarked from Ila, in one Vessel for Ireland. They usually go about that Season of the Year, to the Harvest, but scarce any of them ever return. Nor do they even continue long there, but generally join the Emigrants which now go annually in great Shoals from the North of Ireland to America.

Soil and Climate

The Island of Ila differs remarkably in its Structure and the Nature of its Fossils, from the Coast of Ireland on the one Hand, and that of Cantire on the other. There is not the smallest Appearance of Coal in Ila, though it abounds on the Cantire Coast immediately opposite to it.

Two remarkable Fossils extend along the whole Irish Coast, that looks to Ila. The Rock of which the Giants Causeway is composed, and the white sort of Limestone which is so prevalent in Ireland and is frequently brought to many parts of the west of Scotland. Yet there is not a Vestage of either of these Stones in Ila.

Its Mountains consist of a Rock composed chiefly of a coarse debased Crystal, of a white Colour, that their Summits which are mostly bare both of Earth and Herbage appear at Sea, as if covered with Snow.

The Champaign parts of the Island are Intersected with Dykes of a coarse whitestone. They are of various Degrees of thickness from 10 Inches to 20 or 30 Feet. In some places they are not above 100 Feet distant from one another and in others above a Mile. In many places they rise entire, several Feet above the Surface of the Grounds, and never intersect one another, running always parallel. In this way they look like the Foundations of old Walls and Buildings and give the face of the Country a very odd Appearance.

The highest Mountains in Isla are scarce more than 1,600 Feet above the Level of the Sea. They are not abrupt, nor of a very steep ascent, and the worst of them afford an excellent Pasture for Sheep. It possesses most kinds of Soil, except Stiff Clay. The most general, is a thin, light, rich Loam, bottomed with Rocks which very much resembles that in the low parts of Galloway, and indeed the face of both Countries is very similar. In some Places, Sand or Gravel predominate in the Soil, in others, it is pretty stiff and adhaesive, and there are many large Tracts of Heathy and Mossy Ground extremely improvable.

Towards the North and South Extremeties of the Country, there is stretched along the Sea Shore, a great Extent of Downs covered with the finest Verdure, which indeed wear more the appearance of the Southerly parts of England, than of the North of Scotland. In some places also the Land is so low, especially about Lochondaal and Loch Grunard, that it is overflowed by the Sea, at Spring Tides. This creates a great Extent of Salt Marsh, the most valuable Pasture that is known, both for black Cattle and Sheep.

As the greatest part of the Island lies within 3 or 400 feet of the Level of the Sea, and as the Mountains are neither numerous nor of an extraordinary Height, it enjoys a very mild and favourable Climate, much the same with that of the opposite Coasts of Ireland and Cantire. The Soil also, being generally light, warm and forward, its Crops are therefore to be expected as early as those of any other part of Scotland. On the 11th June 1764, a field of full grown Ray Grass, was here cut for Hay.

After this Account of the Soil and Climate of Ila, it cannot but occasion some Surprize, to know, that the whole Island is at present let for little more than 3d p. Acre.

Supposing the Island to contain 211,200 Acres there are 31 Acres for each Inhabitant. There does not appear to be less than one fourth of it, that is, above 50,000 Acres, that have at some period or other been wrought by the Plough or Spade, nor above one eight of it, that is, 26,400 Acres utterly incapable of Culture. So that there remains above 100,000 Acres in this extensive Island capable of being reclaimed. On supposing the above Computation of its Extent to approach to the Truth.

Price of Commodities raised by Agriculture

The Grass for a Horse, throughout the Year, or 2 Soams, is from 12sh. to 1£.
The Grass of a Cow, or one Soam, from 6 to 10sh.
A fat Sheep sells at 6 or 7sh.
A Goat for 3s. 6d. or 4sh.
A Dozen of Eggs 1d.
The Pound of Butter 22oz p. lb 6d. Twenty years ago, it was only 3½d p. lb; but the Farmers now raise Oxen and fewer Cows than formerly, which has augmented its Price.
The Cheese is always half the Price of the Butter. When the Stone of Butter gives 8sh., the same Quantity of Cheese sells for 4sh.
The Sheep are not smeared, and their Wool, though it is lower priced, is of a much finer Staple, than any that the Sheep Countries in the South of Scotland afford.

Price of Labour

The wages of a Labourer are 6d. and even 8d. a Day. This article was never so high till of late, occasioned by the great number of Men sent to the War, and the Removal of so many of the labouring People to Ireland.

A Man Servant or Ploughman gets from 2£ to 2£ 10sh. p. Ann. besides Maintainance.

A Woman Servant from 16 to 20 sh. p. Ann.

Exports and Imports

The chief Export of Ila is black Cattle, of which, 2,800 were sent last year out of the Country, at 1£ 16sh. a Head, which amounts to 4,140£. The Grain raised in the Island is sufficient to serve the Inhabitants, and in good Seasons, they spare a considerable Quantity.

It exports likewise some Kelp, and a considerable Quantity of Butter and Cheese.

About 80 Dozen of Rabbit Skins at 5sh. p. Dozen, are sent annually to Glasgow.

As there are no Foxes, Badgers, Weazels nor Fumarts[4] in Ila, it abounds in Poultry of all kinds, especially in Geese, of which there are between 4 and 5,000 in the Island, whose Quills and Feathers might be rendered an Article of some Profit, but are at present neglected.

The great Extent of rich Flowry Pasture, with which this Island abounds, especially upon the Sea Shore, renders it capable of furnishing a very great Quantity of Honey and Wax for the supply of other Places. But though Bees are found to thrive vigorously, there are not as yet above a Dozen of Hives in the Island.

There are at present, above 50 Hogheads of American Flaxseed brought yearly into Ila from Ireland, and beside this the Inhabitants sow a considerable Quantity of their own Growth. They use no Flax but what is produced in the Island, and from this, exclusive of what they consume themselves, they export Linen yarn annually to the Extent of about 1,000£ but no Cloth.

Agriculture

The greatest Defect in the Agriculture of Ila, is the want of sown Grasses, for which, the Soil and Climate are extremely favourable. Ray Grass and Clover were sown for the first time in the Island, three years ago, and an exceeding good Crop was this year cut at Shawfield's Seat of Killerew on the 11th of June, which was as early as in most parts of Scotland, though the Soil was only twice ploughed without receiving any Manure. Four other Gentlemen had this year a crop of Ray Grass, and it is to be hoped the Example will have its proper Effect, by rendring the Practice general, which will soon change the whole System of Agriculture, and give the Country a new Appearance. In raising artificial Grasses here, fallowing is not necessary, as in many other Places, because the Soil generally is neither deep nor strong, and there is everywhere such Command of rich and cheap Manures.

The Grains in Ila require much to be altered. The small grey Oat, which is the grain of the Country, ought to be extirpate and the white Oat introduced in its Stead. The Rye likewise should be dismissed, being a most impoverishing and unprofitable Grain, in such a Soil as that of Ila. The two rowed Barley[5] which is yet unknown, should be brought into use. And above all, Pease and Beans, which have never hitherto been sown, should be cultivate with the utmost assiduity, as, there can be no right Agriculture without green Crops. By an Experiment made ann. 1764 at Killirew, it is evident, that Wheat, may be raised in Ila, in great Plenty and Perfection, where there was as fine a Crop of that Grain Horsehoed as could any where be seen in the South of Scotland.

Old Shawfield lett all his Estate in Ila in 3 nineteen year Leases, of which, there are now only about 11 years to run, with the unlucky Power of subsetting given to the Tacksmen; which they have continued to do by letting out Houses and Grounds to the lower People, from year to year. This unfavourable Circumstance, has defeated the Intention of these long leases and effectually prevented the Improvement of the Island, as these poor People, if they improve their Grounds, must next year pay more Rent or be turned out of their Possessions. Some of the Farms are lett for four times the Rent payed by the original Tacksmen, and the whole, upon an Average, are subsett for three times more Rent than is payed to the Landlord. Such immoderate and unreasonable Profits acquired by these Tacksmen without any Industry, makes them careless about any Improvement, and accordingly, the Lands ly much in the same Situation they were in when the Leases commenced. This is a remarkable Instance to show, that long Leases will always be of little avail in the Improvement of the Country, unless they contain Prestations and Improvements obligatory upon the Tenants. The only Prestation in these long Leases in Ila was the sowing of Lint, and that accordingly has been the Source of much Industry and great Advantage to the Island.

Potatoes

Potatoes are now cultivate over all the Islands, but to a greater Extent in Ila, than any where else, where many Fields of them are to be seen of 10, 12 or even 15 Acres each; all planted in lazy Beds with the Spade.

It has been questioned whether the Cultivation of Potatoes, is in fact advantageous to the Highlands, or ought to be encouraged, as they tend to discountenance Industry, by affording so great a Quantity of Sustenance with so little Labour. But there are some strong Reasons for thinking that they cannot be too extensively cultivate, especially in the Islands, provided, they be confined to waste Land.

In Ila there is a greater Quantity of Potatoes raised, than what is consumed by the Inhabitants, the Overplus being transported to the Ports in the Clyde and other Places. This Abundance is not only of great use in reclaiming the Soil, but has also a very friendly Influence upon the Progress of the Linen Manufacture in the Island and must certainly have the same Effect in every other Country. For where the Manufacturing People depend entirely for their Sustenance upon Grain, the Train of Labour necessary for that Purpose, becomes almost their Constant occupation throughout the Year; but when chiefly supported by Potatoes, their Sustenance not only comes cheaper, but leaves them more time to employ in Manufacture.

Potatoes were first introduced into the Island of South Wist about 25 years ago, and there are now above 900 Acres of Land under Spade and Plough Culture, in that Island, more than there was at that Time. The Quantity of Corn, Grass and Cattle upon several Farms, being thereby increased one third during that Period.

In like manner, there is not a Possession in the Isle of Skye of 20£ a year, but during 20 years past, has not had at least 20 Acres of Corn Field added to it, by planting Potatoes, in Ground never formerly cultivate.

These, and a great number of Facts of the same kind, make it questionable, whether any single Rule in agriculture can be established of greater Utility in the Islands, or perhaps in all Scotland, than this: That in every Lease of Grounds, it should be expressly Stipulated, that no Potatoes should be planted upon any Land, wherever the Plough or Spade have formerly been.

Woods

As a Country civilizes and increases in Inhabitants, its Woods must give way to Fields and Pastures. Though Ila has formerly been well stocked with Timber, it is now almost entirely destroyed by the Cattle, and the Consumption of the Inhabitants. The Wood they at present require for their Houses, Mills, Boats, Instruments of Husbandry and other Purposes, must either be of foreign Growth, or brought with great Trouble and Expense from the main Land. To remedy this, would be a matter of great moment, and of no great Difficulty, for there might still be plenty of Natural Wood in the Island, was it permitted to grow. In many parts, there are Spots of Coppice from 5 to 30 Acres, and in one place, there is a Tract which extends above 100 Acres. These Coppices consist of Oak, Ash, Birch, Grey Willow, Lawrel leaved Willow, Osier, White Thorn, Black Thorn, Rowan and Hazel which are all the arboreous Plants that are Natives in the Island. But though they grow vigorously, there are few of them much above the Height of a Man, for what they shoot forth in Summer, is eat down by the Cattle in Winter. Of all these, the Ash seems to thrive best, and in different parts of the Island, there are Trees of this sort to be seen, of 20 or 25 feet in Height, which are young, fresh and vigorous. It is imagined that if these Coppices were inclosed, and their Vacuities planted with Oak, Ash and Fir, the three most useful and profitable Trees in Scotland, they might soon become extremely beneficial and be capable to supply most of the purposes for which Wood is required in the Country.

All other Islands, and indeed most parts of Scotland are but too much in the same Situation, with Respect to Wood, as Ila. And was there a Premium granted by the Public for inclosing Coppices, of which there is great Plenty every where, it would be followed with very many advantages in the Improvement of the Country, especially in the Business of Inclosing, which in many places is prevented, for the want of dead Fences to protect the Hedges.

Manufacture

No Country can be better adapted, both for the raising and the manufacturing of Flax, than Ila. The Goodness of the Soil and Climate, the great Aboundance of enriching Manures, the cheapness of Labour, the general Vacancy of the People and the neighbourhood of Ireland, all conspire to render it one of the most [*sic*] Seats for the Linen Manufacture to be found in North Britain.

Mr Campbells Tenants in Ila are bound by their Tacks to sow half a Boll of Foreign Lintseed for each Quarter Land they Possess. His Estate in the Island comprehends 135 of these Quarter Lands, upon which 67½ Bolls of foreign Lintseed are sown annually, and about 8 Bolls more, are sown upon the Lands belonging to other Proprietors. This Lintseed is all of American Growth, and imported from Ireland, but besides this, the Inhabitants sow a very considerable Quantity of their own Growth, from which, they ought, if possible, to be restrained, for the Difference in the Price is a mere Triffle to the Difference between the Crops that are raised from the foreign and the Home Lintseed, yet the saving a little money upon the Price of the Seed, prevails with the Short sighted Farmer, over the future advantage to accrue from the Enlargement of his Crop.

This Importation of Lintseed and the Exportation of yarn mentioned above, show, that Ila has already made considerable Progress in the Linen Branch, which has arisen entirely from that salutary Stipulation in their Leases, whereby they are oblidged to sow a certain Quantity of foreign Lintseed upon every Farm. The Inhabitants have been very little aided in their Prosecution of the Manufacture, and therefore it still subsists among them in a very rude State, though with proper attention and Encouragement, it might be brought to great Perfection. The Difficulties to be encountered here, are not such as prevail in a Country, where the Manufacture has hitherto been unknown. The People have for many years been engaged in it, and though they pursue it in a very awkward way, yet they feel the Advantage of it, and are anxious to embrace any Improvement that may be offered.

They are still greatly at a Loss in many things relative to the Manufacture. They have never been properly instructed in the raising and dressing of Lint; their whole management in those articles is defective, and the want of Standard Reels is a great Drawback upon the sale of their yarn. The Establishment of Weavers among them, would be a matter of great Utility, for which, by the Quantity of yarn they now produce, they are fully prepared. That instead of exporting yarn which is only a material, the Island might reap the full advantage of a finished Manufacture.

Fishery

Ila had last year four Herring Busses, and was this year to have a Fifth, which go to the Fishery, from the Rendevouze at Campbelton. These Vessels are employed for several Months before they repair to the Fishery, in carrying Kelp from the Highlands to Liverpool, Belfast, Derry and other ports in Ireland.

The five following Rivers in Ila, Kintoure, Lagan, Grunard, Killerew, and Proaig, do each of them contain a considerable Quantity of Salmon, and were they fished with sufficient Care and Skill, might certainly afford many Lasts for Exportation.

Lochindaal and Loch Grunard, two extensive Arms of the Sea, abound greatly in Mullet, a Fish approaching to the Size of a Salmon, and justly esteemed the finest, that our Seas produce. A Man who was sent out to catch some of them, returned with about a Dozen, and said if he had been sufficiently provided with Nets, he could, in a few Hours, have taken several hundreds. As it appears to be a Fish perfectly well calculated for being preserved, either wet or dry, it were worth while to make Trial whether it could not furnish another Article of Export to the Island. If such a Trial answered it would strike out a considerable Branch of Employment in the way of Fishery, to the Inhabitants of several other Islands, in which this Fish may be caught in great Quantities. There is very good Cod Fishing upon the North side of the Island, towards Oransay, and also on the East Coast opposite to Cantire, but it has never been followed. There are neither Nets nor Long Lines, in the Island, nor any of the People who make Fishing their Employment.

NATURAL PRODUCTIONS

Manures

Ila abounds in a Variety of the most valuable natural Manures. Sea Sleech[6] is to be had in many Places, and in great Perfection and Sea Wrack every where upon the Shores, in the utmost abundance. The former of these has never been used, and the latter is applied only to the Lands that ly contiguous to the Sea Shore, but the whole Island except some of its most interior parts, may be cultivate with these Manures. The Sleech particularly, is exactly adapted for the improvement of the Soil that generally lies contiguous to the Sea in this Island, which is extremely light, either with Sand or Gravel.

Sea Shells abound in Lochindaal in an inexhaustible Quantity, where there are Banks of them quite pure and without any Mixture. The whole Island is so deeply cut by this extensive Loch, that by Land or water Carriage, more than half of it maybe shelled at a very moderate Rate.

Limestone also, is found many Places, in great Plenty, and of a very good Quality. There is a Tract of it, which runs through the Heart of the Island for above 10 Miles, upon which Quarries have been opened in several places. There is Peat everywhere at Hand for burning it, and a great Extent of Soil, precisely adapted for receiving the utmost Benefit from that Manure.

Rock Marle which is rather a rare Production in Scotland abounds in Ila, in an inexhaustible Quantity. The Center of the Island, is a dale Country, where there is a fine Valley about 6 Miles long, and three or four in Breadth, extending from Lochindaal to the Sound of Ila, which is all arable and well inhabited. Besides abundance of Limestone, this Tract contains a great Number of little Hills, which are composed from Top to bottom of Rock Marle of an excellent Quality. It is so soft as to be easily dug, is richly impregnate with calcarious Earth, and falls to Powder, upon Exposure to the Air, Properties which render it extremely valuable. Though this part of the Country is naturally very fertile both in Grass and Corn, there is no doubt, but a proper application of this Manure, will produce a very great and sudden Change upon it for the better.

Shell Marle also has been found in some parts of the Island, in flat mossy Grounds from 3 to 6 Feet deep, and in a considerable Body. It has the appearance of Rock Marle; reduced to soft Earth and mixed with Shells. This Marle has been applied to some Pasture Grounds, over run with Heath and having had its ordinary Effect of extirpating the Heath, and producing a rich Growth of white Clover in its Place, this Success is encouraging the Farmers to pursue the Practice of it to a greater Extent.

Crystalline Sand

Upon the South east Shore of Ila, opposite to the small Isle of Texa, is covered with a fine white Sand, which is wholly composed of Crystal [*sic*]. All the maritime Rocks thereabouts, consist of a crystalline Stone, which by the Motion of the Waves, is worn down into Sand, and thrown up in great Banks upon the Shore. This Sand is the principal Ingredient in the Manufacture of Crystal Glass, and is the same with that of the Isle of Wight, from which place, most of the white Glass Works in England are supplied. Though this Sand in Ila is extremely pure, when taken up upon the Shore, yet it is capable of being much further purified by washing which is always done to the Isle of Wight Sand, before it is committed to the Furnace.

From this Place it is probable that the Manufacture of white Glass upon the west Coasts of England, could be better supplied with their Material, and at a cheaper Rate, than they are at present. But the Advantage of having this Sand in such Plenty, and at such an easy Rate, and the low Price of Fewel and Labour, certainly give to some places upon the Clyde a great advantage over all the other parts in Britain, in carrying on the white Glass Manufacture, which has never yet been attempted in Scotland. Upon the North coast of Cantire, immediately opposite to Ila and about four Miles from Campleton, there are Coal Works at present wrought upon the Property of the Duke of Argyll, where Coal is to be had at the very lowest Rate, and where the Crystall Manufacture might certainly be successfully established.

Mines

About 80 or 90 years ago, there were Lead Mines discovered at Ballygrant in Ila, which were then wroght for some time and given up. About 3 years since, they were again opened and are at present pursued with a Prospect of considerable Success.

The Disposition of the metallick Veins at this Place, is very singular; widely different from every thing that has hitherto been discovered in Scotland, and such as at first View, might disconcert the most experienced Miner. They are all lodged in Limestone, which in Derbyshire, and in other Countries, is frequently the Matrix of Metals, but except at this Place, there has never been metallick Veins in Scotland, found in Limestone. Coal, Limestone and Freestone, generally accompany each other in Scotland, and are very much confined to the low Countries, nor has there ever almost been any metallick Substance discovered in them, except the Pyrites. The Appearance therefore of these strata may be generally accounted unfavourable to metals. All the considerable metallick Veins, hitherto discovered, are in the mountainous parts of the Country, and lodged in Fossils of a quite different Class, from the above Strata, and especially in the Whinrock, which is the general Matrix of Metals in Scotland.

These Veins in Ila however, are a singular Exception and the Limestone in which they are Lodged consists of extensive Strata, of great Breadth, and which run for several miles in Length. The streek of this Limestone is nearly South and North, and it dips to the East, not as Limestone generally does, at a small Angle, but precisely like Whinrock, in Edge Seams at an Angle of between 70 and 80 Degrees to the Horison. This great Body of Limestone, is intersected by Whinstone Dykes, from 6 Inches to 50 Feet thick, which run across that part of the Island, East and West, at right Angles to the Limestone; and the Course of each is regularly continued even after the Intersection.

The Limestone, like all Whinrock disposed in the same manner, contains Veins which run South to North in the same Direction with the Streek of the Strata, but these Veins are all barron and contain no Metal. The only metallick Veins hitherto discovered at this place, are what may be more properly called Intersectors, which are Fissures that intersect the true Veins, nearly at right Angles. These Intersectors do here run east and west and some of them been found [*sic*] of a very large Size and very rich, both in Lead and Copper, but they run in length, only a small way, being checked out at both extremities, by a solid opposing Wall of Limestone.

There has likewise been found in these Intersectors, mixed with the Lead, some small parcels of a remarkable Variety of the white Ore of Silver, which from its Structure and Appearance, may be called the Tinsel Ore of Silver.

Mercury

A great many years since, there was some native Quick silver, near Kilbranan in Ila. It was found among the Peat Earth in a Moss, and taking it up up in Quills, there was then a Quantity of it collected. Though I made a very particular Search in quest of that valuable Fossile, no marks of it could at present be discovered in the Place, where it was formerly found. As this Moss could not be the Place of its Production, the higher Grounds were likewise examined, and especially the Course of a small Brook which runs into it, upon whose Banks, the Strata of Earth, are in many Places exposed to View. From these Strata, Several kinds of minerals were collected, which will perhaps be subjected to Trial, though none of them indeed give great hopes of their being the Ores of Matrices of Quicksilver.

Isthmus of Cantire

To the Improvements which Ila demands, it may not be amiss here, to take notice of a very obvious one, which lies in its neighbourhood; in which all the Islands and west Highlands are equally concerned.

The Industry of these Countries is greatly damped by their remote Situation, from a proper Market for their Commodities. The Ports upon the Clyde are their usual places of Resort for this Purpose, but to these they can only have accesss in the Summer time. For having nothing but open Boats, their Navigation round the mule of Cantire is impracticable at any other Season, and is even tedious and dangerous in Summer. This Obstacle would be effectually removed was there a Navigable Communication cut across the Tarbert or Isthmus of Cantire.[7] This would open to the Islanders and to all their neighbouring Coasts upon the main Land, a safe and expedicious Passage into the Clyde, even in their open Boats at all Seasons of the year. Their Intercourse with the Ports upon the Clyde being rendered easier would become much more frequent; and the Advantages resulting from this, to those remote unimproved parts are too obvious to be insisted on. It is at present a frequent Practice with the Islanders, to draw their largest 6 Oar Boats, over the Isthmus, and to pay 3d. a Horse Load, for carrying over their Goods, rather than venture to circumnavigate the Mule.

This Isthmus is not above a Mile over the Ground is no where very high, and the Soil generally soft and deep. Notwithstanding these advantages, a Canal though Navigable only for open Boats of the largest Size, would be an Undertaking of great Expence, if it can be called great, when compared with the beneficial Consequences it would produce. In this Undertaking, the Public is evidently concerned, so are most of the Towns and Countries upon the Clyde, but it still more deeply interests all the Proprietors of the Islands, and of the West Coast north of Cantire, of whom some of the most considerable, sensible of its great Advantage, are willing to contribute largely for carrying it into Execution.

JURA

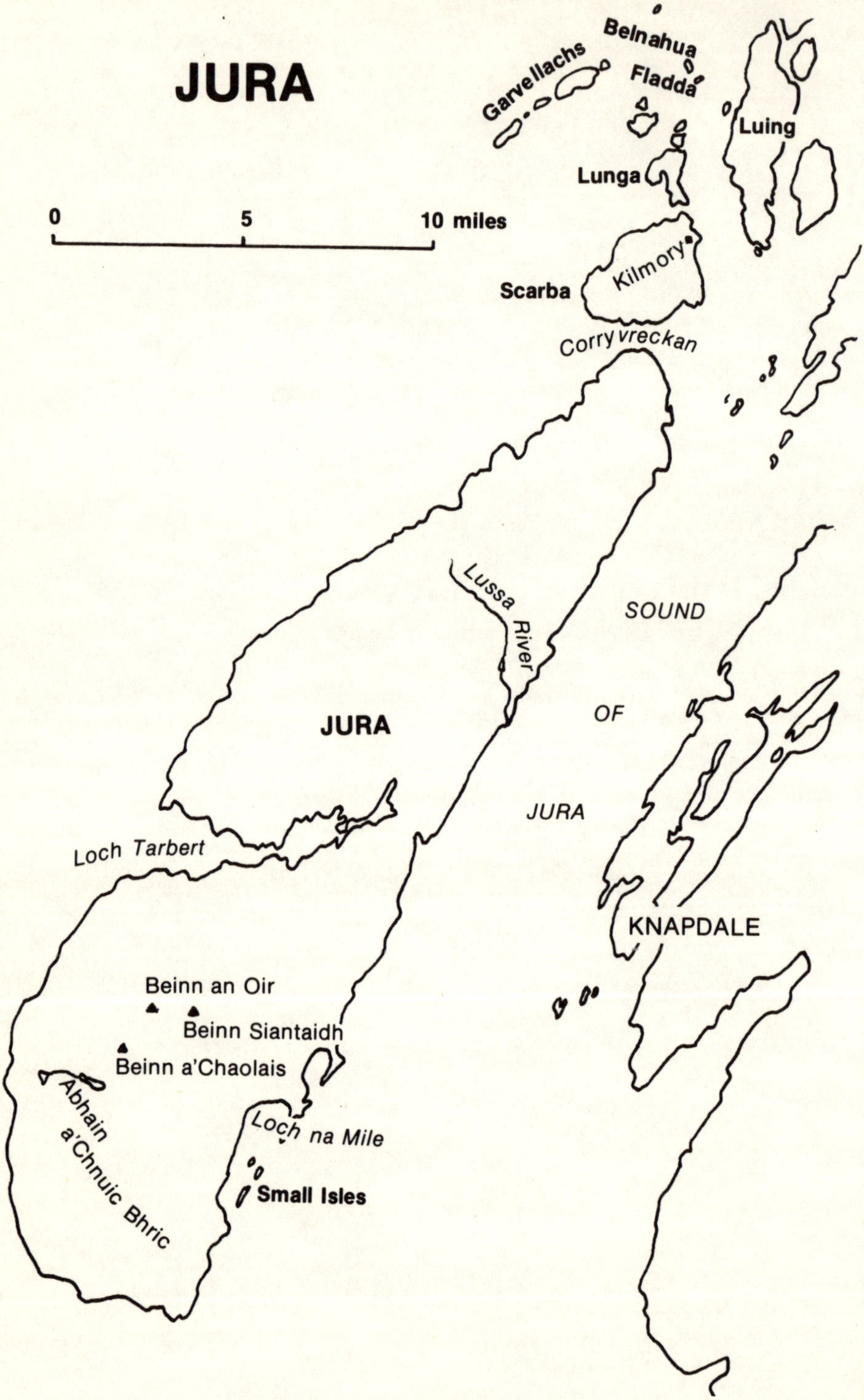
JURA
0
5
10 miles
Belnahua
Garvellachs
Fladda
Luing
Lunga
Kilmory
Scarba
Corry vreckan
Lussa River
SOUND
OF
JURA
JURA
Loch Tarbert
KNAPDALE
Beinn an Oir
Beinn Siantaidh
Beinn a'Chaolais
Abhain a'Chnuic Bhric
Loch na Mile
Small Isles

JURA[1]

Situation

Adjacent to Ila, lies the long extended ridgy Island of Jura, remarkable over many Countries for the Height of its Mountains. It stretches 24 computed Miles in length, nearly from South West to North East, and is in most places, about 6 or 7 Miles broad. But supposing it only to be 30 measured Miles long, and 6 broad, which is surely a very low Computation it then contains 115,200 English Statute Acres. The Proprietors are Campbell of Jura, McNeil of Colonsay, the Duke of Argyll and Campbell of Shawfield.

Mountains

The Mountainous Ridges occupy the middle of the Island, and run from End to End, rising still higher and higher, as they run from the North East, till at last, they terminate in four Peaked Mountains, of a great Height and of a similar shape. Two of these stand close together, and bound the westerly part of the Island. They are much higher than the others, and are well known to the Sailors who frequent the Deucaledonian Sea, by the name of the Paps of Jura.[2]

It is remarcable, that the Islands of Ila and Jura stand cross, in their Direction, to most of [the] other Hebrides. The chain that composes the long Island, the Isles of Sky, Mull and most of the others, stretch out, South and North as does also the Ridges of their Mountains, the same Direction with the Coast of Scotland, that is next adjacent. But Ila and Jura with their Mountains, observe an Opposite Direction, and extend lengthways, only two or three points from East and West. Their Position however is still the same, with respect to the neighbouring Coast of the Main Land, as they run nearly parallel with the great Promontory of Knapdale and Cantire, which like these Islands, stands cross to the general Direction of the Coast of Scotland. The Direction therefore of Ila and Jura, though contrary to that of the other Hebrides, appears to be the Effect of the same Cause. Of that Cause, which made Britain itself run parallel with the Coast of Scandinavia; and stretched out Macagascar [*sic*] in a Line with Africa. Of that great Law, which seems to have subsisted at the Formation of the Earth by which all the Islands upon the Globe in general, are extended in length in the same Direction with the Coast of the next adjacent Continent.

Rocks

The Rock of which the Mountains of Jura are composed is so full of fissures that it is brought easily to Pieces by the Force of Water. This is the Reason, why they are sometimes covered from Top to Bottom with one continual Shoal of loose Rocks and Stones and entirely destitute of Herbage of any kind, for a great Extent; and the Rock itself, being of a whitish Colour, these parts of the Mountains appear at a great Distance, as if covered with Snow. This Property of the Rock, is likewise the Reason, why the Sides Mountains [*sic*] are so deeply cut in many Places with frightfull Gullies, by the Torrents. In other Places, it is worn out into Caves, especially upon the Sea Shore, where there are severals of very large Dimensions. Though the Rock of these Mountains, however, is thus frequently found full of Veins and Fissures, yet in many places, it is to be seen piled up in vast solid Beds, without any Cracks, and its Substance is extremely hard and durable. It is of a very singular Species, seldom to be met with in other Countries and is of the same Stone with the great Blocks, of which the famous Stonehenge in Wiltshire is constructed.

Waters

The Island abounds greatly in Springs, and in Rugged steep descending Rivulets, falling from Rock to Rock, from their Source to the Sea. They are numerous indeed, but none of them are large, as the mountainous Ridge that runs lengthways through the Island, determines their Course upon its Sides, to a Run but of three or four miles. Two of them however, the Rivers of Crackbreac,[3] Nissa,[4] are of a larger Size and of a gentler Course, than the Rest, and are plentifully stored with Salmon. As for Lakes there are none that are considerable, nor is there indeed any Room for them, the whole Country being almost one Congines of steep Declivities. Water is no where permitted to loiter, being scarce sooner sprung from the Earth, or fallen from the Heavens, than it is rapidly precipitated into the Sea.

Harbours

Though the Country is high, and its Shores bold, it is not remarkable for the Goodness of its Harbours. Besides the Sound of Ila, it has no safe Retreat for a Vessel of any Burden, except the Bay of Meill[5] on the South east part of the [Island] where there is a very safe Anchorage, but the Entry to it is a little ticklish, through a Cluster of Isles, called the small Isles of Jura. The Coast of the Island being generally Streight, forms no other considerable Bay, except Loch Tarbat on the Northwest side, which is large indeed, and well sheltered, but so filled with Rocks both above and below Water, that no Vessel can enter it with safety.

Sound of Ila

The Channel which seperates the islands of Ila and Jura, is about ten miles long, and two broad, but in some places, is not above half a mile over and is called the Sound of Ila. It affords a very favourable Opportunity of Communication and Trade, to both Islands, from other Countries. It is greatly frequented by shipping, especially by the Vessels from Ireland, and from, most of the Ports on the west Coast of Britain, which Trade to Norway and the Baltick. This narrow Channel is the only passage they have, going either South or North through the Hebrides. For between the North East extremity of Jura and the Country of Lorn, there is nothing but Danger from the Currents and the broken Land. And from the Extremity of Ila, on the other hand, to Barra Head, though an extent of sea of above a hundred Miles, yet it is every where so embarassed with Shoals and Sunken Rocks, that no Passage that way can be safely attempted.

The Sound of Ila is in most places about 27 Fathoms deep at mid Channel, quite free of Rocks, and its Coasts, so bold, that a Vessel of Burden may run anywhere within Pistol Shot of the Shore. In a Bay upon the Jura side, there is a very commodious Road for Ships, opposite to Portaskig in Ila. The Tide runs through this Sound at the Rate of 6 Miles an Hour, but so fair, that in two Hours, it will carry a Vessel clear through without either Sail or Direction.

Whirl Pool of Coryvrekan

The Island of Scarba lies at the North East End of Jura and the Sound between the two Islands, is remarkable, for a furious Commotion in the Sea, at certain Times of the Tide. It is called the Gulph or Whirlpool of Coirachreaggan, commonly pronounced Coryvrekan, the Sound is about a Mile broad, and the Whirlpool is upon the Scarba Side, not far from the Shore.

Soon after the Flood has entered the Sound, the Sea, at the Place appears in great Dissorder. It boils, foams, and passes away in successive Whirls. The Commotion increases till near the fourth Hour of the Flood, when it becomes most impetuous. It then boils.from the Bottom, and throws up everything that is moveable by Water. The Waves are tossed up with a loud Roar, and to such a Height, that they fly broken from it and white for two Leagues, before they are dispelled.

Soon after the fourth Hour of the Flood these violent motions gradually abate, and for near an Hour before the Tide ceases to flow, their place is not to be known but becomes as smooth as the rest of the Sound. Soon after the Return of the Ebb however, they are again repeated, increasing and diminishing at the same Times, and in the same manner till the last Hour of Ebb quiets their Dissorders.

The Inhabitants [say] that when the Whirlpool is in its Fury its Attraction extends to a great Distance, which renders it dangerous for any Vessel to enter the Sound. But for above an Hour at High and Low Water, any Boat may pass near it, and even over it, with Safety.

Climate

The Climate of Jura is very different from that of Ila, and not near so mild, though in its immediate neighbourhood. The Lofty Mountains with which Jura is crouded from End to End, occasion this remarkable Difference. Upon these the Snow resides, till Summer is far advanced and in all Seasons of the year distress the Island with boisterous Winds and impetuous Floods.

Experiments[6]

1st

In Order to ascertain the Height of the Paps of Jura, I filled a Barometer on the 27th June, on the Shore of the Sound of Ila, at 7 O'clock in the morning, when the Mercury stood at 29 Inches and 7 Tenths. We set off at 10 O'Clock; and it cost us Seven Hours of excessive Fatigue, to get to the Summit of the highest Mountain. Here, at 5 in the afternoon, I again filled the same Barometer, when the Mercury stood at 27 Inches and 1 Tenth: a Column of Air therefore, of the Height of this Mountain, is equal to two Inches and six Tenths of Mercury. And assuming Dr. Halley's calculation of 90 Feet to each Tenth,[7] the Perpendicular Height of the Mountain turns out to be 2,340 English Feet above the Level of the Sea. This is just 300 Feet less than half a measured Mile.

2nd

Several years ago, M. Marain[8] and other French Academicians discovered by Experiments, that boiling water is not of the same Degree of Heat, at the Top of a Mountain, that it is at the Bottom: but by the Thermometer, is visibly colder upon the Mountain than upon the Plain. An additional and Important Question however, remained still to be discovered. What is the Height of the Column of Air, that corresponds to the fall of one Degree of the Thermometer in boiling Water. The great Height of this Mountain in Jura, and our Mensuration of it, in the exactest manner by the Barometer, at the same time that the Thermometrical Experiment was performed gave some hopes of solving this curious Question, with some Degree of Precision.

At 6 O'clock in the afternoon, Fahrenheits Mercurial Thermometer,[9] after repeated Immersions in boiling Water upon the Summit of Jura, was found to stand constantly at 207 Degrees. We left the Top of the Mountain at 7 O'clock, and it was about midnight, before we reached the Shore of the Sound of Ila. Here the Experiments were again repeated. The Barometer stood as in the Morning at 29 Inches and 7 Tenths, the Weather during the whole day having been perfectly steady and serene. The Thermometer, at the same time was committed to boiling water, when it stood constantly at 213 Degrees. The Water carried to the Top of the Mountain was from a pure perennial Spring on the shore of Jura and the Water of the same Fountain was employed in the Repetition of the Experiment.

The Difference therefore in the Heat of boiling Water, at the Summit and at the Bottom of the Mountain, appears from these Experiments to be equal to 6 Degrees in Fahrenheits Thermometer. And the Height of the Mountain, divided by this Number, gives 390 Feet for each Degree.

Inhabitants

The Island of Jura contains about 466 Inhabitants so that upon the above supposition of its consisting of 115,000 Acres, it contains 246 Acres for each Inhabitant. A most melancholy Proportion. To find a Parallel to it, we must go to the Wastes of America.

The People live mostly on Milk, Butter, Cheese, Fish, Mutton, Venison and us[e] very little vegetable Aliment. Notwithstanding this they appear to be rather longer lived than many of their neighbours. The Accounts of one Macraen who died here in the last Century at the age it is said of 140, are still fresh among the Inhabitants. The last Baillie of Jura was 87 and his father is said to have been 110. Several such remarkable Instances of Longevity I heard related but have not the Opportunity to find them sufficiently verified. We will not be far wrong however, in concluding from them that the Inhabitants of Jura, are in general a long lived People.

Diseases

They are not remarkable however, for a greater Proportion of Health than their Neighbours.[10] Diarrheas and Inflammatory Fevers are rather more frequent here, than in the Islands, where the Inhabitants live more upon vegetable Food, and the small Pox is no where attended with greater Mortality. The Soil of Jura is extremely dry, especially in all the Inhabited Places near the Sea; nothing can be purer than its Air, which is kept in perpetual Motion, by the Mountainous Nature of the Country. Its Waters likewise are most Salubrious, and the manner of Life among the Inhabitants the same as in the other Islands. In their Dyet alone they differ and to this Difference, may be ascribed any greater Prevalence, or any greater Degree of Mortality in the above Diseases. Grain is here in greater scarcity, than in the other Islands, and the People want Gardens to supply them with Vegetables. Of late years indeed the Cultivation of Potatoes, has greatly enlarged the proportion of their vegetable Aliment, and by pretty certain Observation, has added greatly to the Health of the People.

Fillun

Over the Highlands in General, there are fewer People to be observed either lame or Decrepit, than in any other Country perhaps in Europe. But in the Island of Jura, the Cripples are remarkably numerous; owing to a very singular Disease with which this Island is peculiarly infected.

This Disease arises from a Worm lodged under the Skin, that penetrates with exquisite Pain, the interior parts of the Limbs. It is termed in the Galic Language, Fillun, and is Generally lodged either in the Knees or Ancles.

It is first discernible very deep, as the Patients themselves say, at the Bones. Whether it really affects, or penetrates the Bones, I could not positively learn, though it is not unlikely, from the extreme Pain, which it occasions. But in a little Time, it makes way, through the Cartilages, Tendons and Muscles and penetrates the Skin, with several small ichorous Orifices.

The Worm dissappears, soon after this Stage of the Disease, but when it is suffered to come this length, it never fails to cripple the Patient for Life. Both men and women, children and Adults, are equally subject to it. And the intense Pain with which it is accompanied, sometimes destroys the Appetite and Spirits and occasions Death.

The Worm itself is about half an Inch long. It has a white Head, with a sharp bony Rostrum. And the Body is of a reddish Colour, and of a compressed Shape, with a Row of feet on each Side.

The only Cure known for this Disease is the Root of a Plant and the marrow Corld [*sic*] of Beef Bones or if they can not be had, they make use of Goat Tallow in its Place. The Root is pounded and mixed with the oleaginous Substance and the Mixture applied in the Form of a Poultice, as hot as the Patient can bear it. The application of this Remedy before the Worm breaks the Skin, kills it within and cures the Patient. Yet even those who are thus recovered most of them have their Limbs in some Degree lamed or distorted, and the Disease is so frequent, that there is not a Farm upon Jura but there are two or three Persons to be found, who have suffered by it.[11]

The Plant whose Root is used for the Cure of this Disease is the Pedicularis Palustris of Linnaeus, or Great Marsh Red Rattle, which has been long known as an officinal Plant, but this remarkable Virtue, which seems to reside in it, has been discovered and known only by the Inhabitants of the Hebrides.[12]

There does not seem to be any account recorded, either of the animal here described or the Disease which it occasions.

Parish

This extensive Island makes only a part of the Parish of Jura, which also comprehends Scarba and a number of small adjacent Islands, and those of Colonsay and Oransay, which are six or seven Leagues distant. The common People are extremely ignorant nor is it possible they can be otherwise in their present Situation. Most of the Children grow up without being taught to read, which was not the Case formerly, when there was a School supported here, upon the royal Bounty. But some years ago it was withdrawn without any Reason given, though there are few Places where it could be of more importance.

The utmost assiduity of a Minister is here altogether insufficient for the Instruction of the People. There are two places in Jura, where they assemble for public Worship, which are ten Miles distant from each other by a Road which can not be travelled on horseback but the Minister has neither Church, Manse nor Glebe. The Islands of Colonsay and Oransay he can only visit twice a year, and the other smaller Isles are cut off from one another by very hazardous Channels. In a Parish of such Extent so much dispersed and all the Parts of such difficult and dangerous access, it is not to be expected, that Religion can subsist in a very prosperous State. These and many other Inconveniences to which the Minister of Jura has always been subjected, have occasioned this melancholy Circumstance, that the Sacrament of the Supper, has never been but once dispensed in this Parish, during the present Century. Few such instances, it is to be hoped, are to be found in Christendom.

Agriculture

The Inhabitants sow as much Barley and Oats and plant as many Potatoes as serve to Support them. These Crops they have upon the little Plains by the Sea Side, but the whole of the Arable Land is very inconsiderable for of the 115,000 Acres which the Island contains, there does not seem to be above 15,000 that have ever been cultivated, or that are capable of Cultivation.

There is a particular Product for every Country, which its Soil and Climate, and the Situation with Respect to a Market point out. This however, is frequently overlooked or neglected by the Inhabitants, and another Product adopted than what nature dictates. This is remarkably the Case in the Island of Jura. The Capital Product is black Cattle, but they are low in Size and few in Number, nor do they yeild the Profit that might be otherwise reaped from the Island. In the low Valleys there is indeed Pasture for black Cattle, but three fourths of the Island consist of Mountains and Declivities, too steep and abrupt for any black Cattle to feed upon, and the Grass they produce is too short and fine to afford them a tollerable Pasture except in the Height of Summer. In Winter, the Pasture is insufficient to support them and by the want of dry Forage, a great part of the Produce of the Island is lost in that Season by the Death of the Cattle.

What the Inhabitants of Jura should therefore wholly betake themselves to, is Raising of Sheep. These Cattle will thrive, where Cows and Oxen must starve, and being far more hardy will go at all Seasons of the year to such Heights as are innaccessible to black Cattle. The Mountains of Jura are generally dry and Green, with such a Proportion of Heath as is beneficial upon Sheep Grounds. The Sheep of this Island may be driven to the Markets in Stirlingshire and Clydesdale at a small Expence; and was the Island fully stocked with them, under the management of skillfull Sheep farmers, I am persuaded, that their Wool alone, would amount to more than the whole Product of the Island at present both in Corn and Cattle.

Manufacture

The People in Jura have borrowed a little of the Linen Manufacture from their Neighbours in Ila. They have as yet sown little or no Lintseed, but are furnished with their Lint from Ila, and the yarn they Manufacture from it is exported to the Clyde. They send to Ila in exchange for the Lint, as also to some places in the main Land a considerable Quantity of Wool, some of which is of an exceeding good Quality, and of a snow white Colour, as the Sheep are never smeared nor housed. But they Manufacture no more of it than what serves for their own Cloathing.

We have found above, that the Inhabitants of Jura are mistaken in the Product of their Island, and they are, no less so, in the Manufacture they ought to pursue. Neither their Soil nor Climate are well adapted for the Production of Flax, and the Manufacture of it they ought entirely to resign to the Neighbours in Ila. Their Wool is what nature points out as the Object of their Industry. It is in sufficient Plenty to employ all the Labour in the Island, and were they once trained to dress and spin it, they would find their Labour much more profitably employed, than it can possibly be in any Branch of Linen Manufacture. In short there cannot be a greater Solecism in Manufacture, than their present Practice of exporting Wool and importing Lint.

Natural Productions

The Shores of Jura afford a considerable Quantity of Sea Weeds, which are annually manufactured into Kelp. The Mountains abound with Red Deer, and upon every Farm there are large Flocks of Geese, which live almost entirely upon what they pick up in the Fields. No Limestone, Marle, nor Freestone have hitherto been discovered. Iron Ore abounds in many Places, and Sir Alexander Murray mentions his having discovered several Veins both of Lead and Copper but these are at present unknown to the Inhabitants of Jura.

There are large Rocks of the Hone or Whetstone upon the Shore of the Island of Jura, lying on the Sound of Ila, about three Miles South from the Passage at Portaskig. It is situated in Plates or Layers of different Thickness. Some of them are Coarse, and Fit only for common Tools, but others of them are capable of serving as Whetstones for the finest Razors and chirurgical Instruments, and may be cut with a Saw into any shape like Wood. If Quarries at this place were opened the importation of Hones from abroad might certainly be superceded.

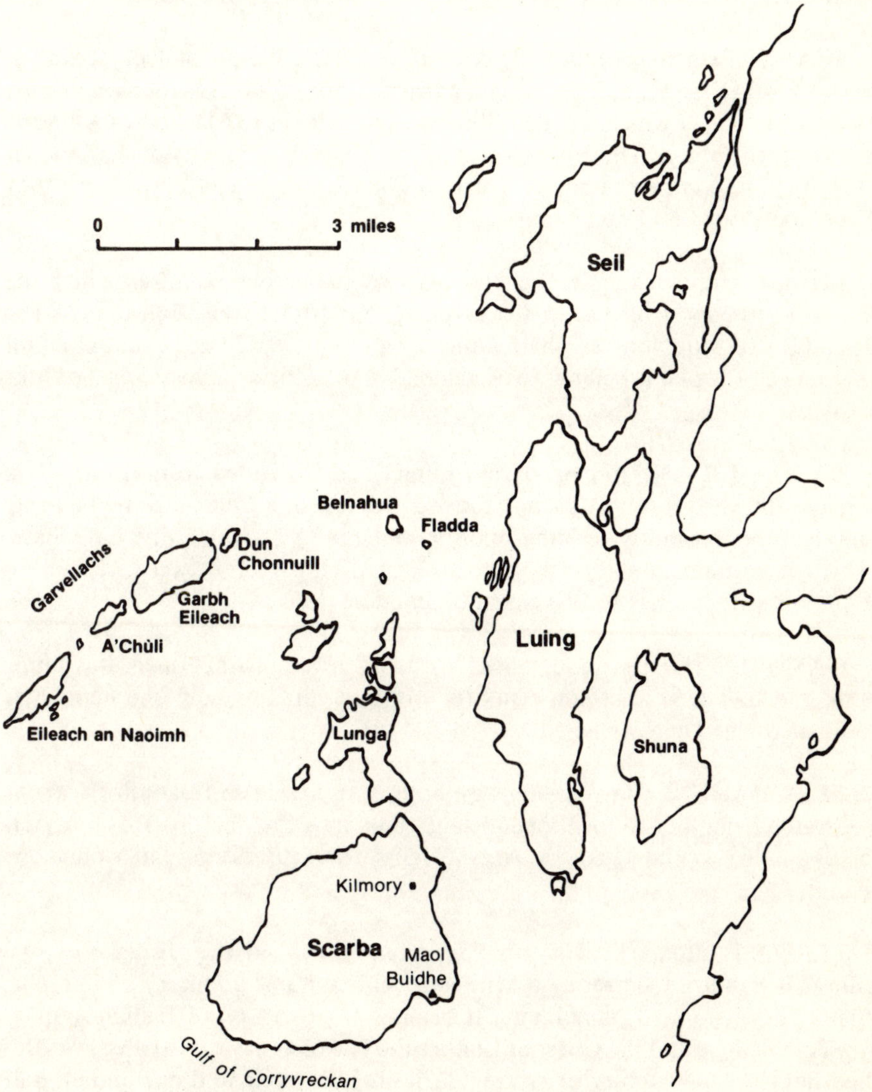

Smaller Islands adjacent to Jura

Smaller islands adjacent to Jura

The following Isles are contained in the Parish of Jura, and are mostly separated from that island only by narrow Channels of the Sea.

SCARBA which is separated from Jura by the Gulph of Coryvrekan is about 2 Miles long and 2 broad being nearly a round Figure. It contains only two Farms one of which is called Kilmorie and belongs to Maclean of Kilmorie who resides upon it. The other named Milbuie,[13] is the Property of the Duke of Argyll.[14] The Rent of these two Farms amounts only to £44 sterling, yet they have upon them 60 Inhabitants.

LUNGA is divided from Scarba by a very dangerous Sound in which the Current runs as strong as in Coryvrekan, but without any Whirlpool. The Island is two Miles long and half a mile broad, rents at £24 and contains about a Dozen of People. It belongs to Maclaughlan of Kilbride a Vassal of the Duke of Argyll.

BALNAHEUAN[15] lies East from Lunga and is divided from it only by a Chanel 200 yards broad. It is not above a Quarter of a Mile long and has only one Family constantly residing upon it, but the Quarries of fine blue Slate, which it contains employ for a great Part of the year between 12 and 16 Labourers. It belongs to Stevenson of Balnaheuan.

GARIVILOCH[16] lies about a Mile West North West from Lunga. It is a mile long and half a Mile broad, rents for £10 and contains only one Family. It belongs to the Duke of Argyll.

ELUCHANUVE[17] lies directly west both from Lunga and Gariviloch, and is seperated from the last mentioned Island, only by a Channel 50 yards broad. It belongs also to the Duke of Argyll, rents for £10 and contains only one Family.

FLADA is situate East North East from Lunga, at the Distance of two Miles. It is but a Quarter of a Mile long and contains a Quarry of fine blue Slate, but has only 6 Inhabitants. It belongs to Stevenson of Balnaheuan.

Between Jura and the Coast of Cantire the Isle of Gigay[18] is situated, which I had not the Opportunity of visiting. It is six miles long and one and an half broad and with the Adjacent Island of Caray, composes a Parish which contains 463 Inhabitants. Caray is about half a mile long and lies about a quarter of a Mile South from Gigay. Both Islands are very fertile and mostly arable and belong in Property to Mr Macneil of Tainish.[19]

COLONSAY AND ORONSA

COLONSAY

Situation and Extent

The Island of Colonsay, or as it was antiently written by Adamnanus[1] Coloso, though in the Parish of Jura is situated at the Distance of about Six or Seven Leagues to the westward of that Island. It is reckoned to be 8 measured Miles long and 3 broad and allowing for the Inequalities upon its Coasts, may consist of about 12,000 English Statute Acres. It was formerly supposed to contain between 4 and 500 People; but by a List taken by the Minister of Jura Anno 1766 their Number was found to amount to 760, and according to this Computation, there are 15 Acres in the Island for each Inhabitant. The whole Island belongs to Mr Macneil of Colonsay,[2] and the People are mostly of his Name or Family.

Face of the Country

The Island abounds both in Corn and Cattle and is all either arable Land or Rich Pasture, excepting the Hills which may contain perhaps 2,000 Acres, and mild Soil which may be all reclaimed however, and will probably be so in Time, by the Cultivation of Potatoes. The Hills are numerous, but not of a great Height or of a steep ascent, they not being above 600 Feet above the Level of the Sea. They are covered in many Places with rank Heath, which is mixed and interwoven with immense Quantities of the Uva Ursi.[3] The styptick Nature of this Plant gives some Ground to think, that it might be applied for tanning some of the finer sorts of Leather. If it was found valuable for this Purpose, it might be procured from Colonsay, and from several others of the Islands in Quantities sufficient for the Purpose.

The Soil of the Island is very fertile, and the Fields of Corn exceedingly pleasent intermixed every where, with small Meadows and Pastures of a fine Verdure. The whole Island is perfectly dry, for the Soil, though fertile, is extremely thin, and every where stretched out upon a Rock. It abounds however in Springs, has a few small Rivulets, and there is a fine fresh water Lake in the Heart of the Island. It has no Land Locked Harbour, but about the middle of the Island, on the East Side, there is a small Bay, which affords very good Anchorage in the Summer Season.

Wood

In several of the Meadows and Pastures in this Island, there are considerable Spots of Coppice Wood, very fresh and vigorous, which would undoubtedly rise to very good Timber, was it not perpetually cut down by the Inhabitants or Cropt by the Cattle.

There is nothing like Wood, in any of the western Islands, except on Mull and Sky. In most of them it would be difficult to find so much, as is necessary to make a Wicker Basket. In some of the Islands, they must undertake a dangerous Voyage in open Boats of 60 or 70 Miles, before they can make a Plough or build a Barn. Hence they are entirely destitute of Proper Houses, Boats and Instruments of Agriculture. Nor can Industry flourish; it can scarce even subsist, where there is such a Famine of Wood.

Though the Inhabitants are all strongly convinced that no Wood will grow in their Islands, yet there is no doubt, that in every one of them useful Timber might be raised. They have been formerly well wooded, as appears from the remaining Coppice, in several Places, and from their numerous Peat Mosses, in many of which are found Trees of a considerable Size. But the Woods are long ago extirpate by time, by the Cattle, and the Consumption of the Inhabitants. They might still have natural Wood, were their Coppices permitted to grow, as there is as little Doubt but they might have good Planted Timber; though of this, I saw indeed but two Instances in all the Islands. The one at Armadil in Sky, where both the Fruit and Forest Trees, have grown to as large a Size as in most parts of Scotland. The other, in this Island of Colonsay, where a Plantation of Ash Trees near the Harbour, not 30 Years old have grown above 40 Feet High and are thriving and Vigorous.

The violent Winds to which the Hebrides are subjected would render the planting of single Trees or even entire Plantations in exposed Places very unsuccessful. But this objection is to be obviated, by crouding them thick together for a considerable Space of Ground in a sheltered Situation which is every where to be had. The Trees to be planted are the Oak, Ash, Birch, Plan Tree and Scots Fir.

The Coppice Wood in Colonsay is intermixed with the Hypericum and – rosemum Lin. or Tutsan,[4] and is greatly ornamented by it. That Plant being of a more picturisque and beautiful Appearance in its wild State, than when cultivated in Gardens.

Animals

There are neither Muirfowl, Black Cock nor Partridges in Colonsay, nor any Adders, but it has a particular Sort of Snake, sometimes a yard long, of which I could nor be any further satisfied by the Discription than that it seems to be a distinct Species from the other three Serpents we have common in Scotland.

There is also a large Fish frequent upon the Shores of this Island called by the Inhabitants a Conger. It is not the Conger Eel nor could I be certain of what Species it is from the Description given of it, but it is of an excellent Quality, and seems capable of Furnishing a profitable Article of Fishing.

Eider Duck

Upon the Sea Rocks on the Shore of this Island we fell upon a considerable Number of Nests of Eider Duck, the Anas Mollissima of Linnaeus. The Plumage of this Bird, which is much used, and the most costly that is known is at present furnished to Europe only by the Danes who have it from Iceland and the Isles of Norway. The Bird abounds in several of the Western Islands and the great Value of its Feathers was known, even in Buchanan's[5] Time, who particularly describes it by the name of Colca,[6] in his Account of the Hebrides. It is larger than a Duck and lays five Eggs which are very large compared to the Size of the Bird and of a green Colour. It builds in the most distant and Solitary Islands and is never observed to approach Land except in the hatching Season, living all the rest of the year in the Ocean. Its Down, which are so highly valued, are light and elastick to a surprising Degree, and afford the most Heat with the least Weight of any Substance known. Of these fine Downs the Bird divests itself, in order to line and perfect its Nest, and the Nest from which alone they are collected, affords a Surprising Quantity. A very considerable number of these Birds now build in Colonsay, though several of the most intelligent of the Inhabitants agree in observing, that it is only Eight or Nine Years since they first [took] up their Residence in this Island.[7]

Rabbits

Upon the North side of Colonsay, there are several Hills of Sand, and an Extent of Sandy Downs, which are planted with Rabbits, that appear to yeild more profit, than could otherwise be obtained from that Barren Tract. It affords annually 130 Dozen of Skins which sell at Glasgow for 5 sh. p. Dozen.

Kelp

In the year 1762 an Irish Manufacturer paid £10 for the Liberty of the Sea Weeds in the Island of Jura, from which he made 40 Tun of Kelp; but the Inhabitants becoming sensible that this was too advantageous a bargain have since chosen to Manufacture it themselves. The Island of Colonsay does now also afford 40 Tun of Kelp which at £4 p. Tun amounts to £160, a considerable and newly acquired Article in the Produce of the Island.

There is made also in Jura, about 100 Bolls of Fern Ashes, which are sent yearly to Ireland, where they are sold at 12 sh.p. Boll. Each Peck weighs 10lb and the Boll contains 16 Pecks.

Mr Macneil the Proprietor, has a very genteel Seat towards the North side of the Island called Kiloran, at which place, there was antiently a Church dedicated to St Oran. There is a School maintained in the Island by the Society for propogating Christian Knowledge, which was attended when I was there, by 39 Boys and only six Girls, learning Reading, Writing and Arithmetick. The great Difference between the Children of the two Sexes, is very remarkable; but the same is the Case over all the Highlands. Wherever there is access to a School, the Boys are carefully put to it; but the Parents consider Learning of any kind as of little Moment to the Girls, on which Account, great Numbers of them never go to any School.

ORONSAY

ORANSAY

ORANSAY is an Island or rather a Peninsula, adjacent to the South End of Colonsay, being seperated from it by a Channel of the Sea, about a Quarter of a Mile broad, which is left dry at low water. There are several other small Isles among the Hebrides of the same Name, and they are remarkable for being all situated in the same manner, being only Islands at high Water. Oransay however seems to have derived its name from St Oran, the famous Disciple of Columba, and contains the Remains of an extensive Monastery, with a Church, Chapel and Cloysters dedicate to his Memory.

It is a small pleasent Island about 4 Miles in Circumference, and contains about 900 Acres. Of these, there are about 700 stretched out in a fine Plain of a light sandy Soil, extremely fertile both in Grass and Corn; no part of the Island is above 100 Feet above the Level of the Sea, so that this low Situation with the Sandy Soil, procures a very early Crop. Here, the Rye which was only sown in the Spring, was fully shot into the Ear, the 22nd June. The whole Island has been cultivate except about 100 Acres of Rocky Shore, lying on the west Side, which can never serve for any thing but Pasturage. A Brother of Mr Macneil, the Proprietor possesses the Island in Tack and has 5 Familys upon it which contain 30 People.

Wool

The most remarkable thing in this small Island, is the Wool it produces, which appears to be the best in Scotland. It is long, fine and as white as Snow. The Sheep which produces it were originally brought from Ireland, and both in their Bone and Wool do far exceed the Sheep of the other Islands. The Quality of Wool depends in a great Measure on the Quality of the Pasture, and no Soil is found to raise finer Wool than Sandy Downs on the Sea Shore, such as this Island of Oransay does mostly consist of, where the Grass is short and fine and at the same time dry, firm and salutary. Even in such fine Pasture however, great attention must be paid to the Breed, otherwise it will even here run wild and degenerate. In the Islands of Tirey, Coll, South and North Wist, Benbecula and others, there are as rich Sandy Downs as any in Oransay, and much more extensive, yet in none of these Places are there any Sheep or Wool comparable to what this small Island produces. In these other Islands, the aboriginal Race of Sheep still subsists, without any mixture or alteration from abroad and without any care to improve it at Home. Whereas upon a Pasture perfectly similar, the foreign Strain introduced into Oransay, has raised a Race of Sheep of a larger Size, with Wool of a much finer Quality. This Fact points out a very great Improvement to be made in the above Islands and in several others of the Hebrides, the Importation of a Breed of Sheep from the North of Ireland.

Monastery

The Monastery here is built in a more rude and simple manner than is any where else to be seen, and is evidently the Workmanship of a very remote Age.[8] It appears to be of a more antient date than any of the present Remains at Icolumbkil, and older perhaps than any other Church Building in Scotland. It is a Square of low Buildings, the East side of which measures 105 Feet. The East Wall of the Church still remains entire about 40 Feet high, having the large alter Window in the middle of a Stone Cross of about 3 Feet in the Top of the Wall. There is a Square Court within these Buildings, three Sides of which have been occupied, with Cloysters of a very small size and simple Construction. They are open to the Court and the Pillars, which support the Roof consist each of two erect Stones about 4 Feet high, vaulted above with two Flag Stones which meet at Top. On two of these Pillars, on the South side there are Inscriptions in an antient Gothick Character but much obliterate. The inside of the Church is filled with the Sepulchral Stones of the Macdufies who were formerly the Lords of Colonsay[9] and of the other Cheftons of the neighbouring Isles. Each of them has a rude human Figure upon it in Armour, as large as the Life with an Inscription. Upon one of them, which besides the human Figure, has a Deer and a Sword engraven upon it, there is the following Inscription, Hic jacet Murdardus Macdufie an D. 1539.[10]

GIGHA

GIGHA

The Island of Gigha which I had not an opportunity to visit lies between Ila and the Promontary of Cantire, being Separated from Cantire by a Channel of the Sea about a League over. The Island is about 6 Miles long and a Mile and an half in Breadth. The small Isle of Cara lies about a Quarter of a Mile from it on the South side, and is about a Mile in Circumference. The two Islands compose a Parish which contains 463 Inhabitants.

The greater Part of these Islands belong in Property to Mr Macneil of Taynish. Their Rental amounts to about £500 a year. They are almost all arable and are remarkable for their Fertility. Of Mr Macneils Property there are 1,512 Acres which have been surveyed and Measured, that yeild 277£ sterling of Rent which is above three shillings p. Acre, and is by far the highest Rented Land of any in the Western Islands.

Gigha contains several good Harbours, and great abundance of Shell sand upon their Shores. It has also plenty of Limestone and Coal at hand upon the opposite Shore of Cantire, by which means, all the Lands of the Island, might be highly improved. The People are begun to sow a good deal of Lint, which they manufacture like the People of Ila into coarse yarn for Exportation.

IONA

ICOLUMBKIL[1]

Situation

The Island of Icolumbkil is situated at the South West Extremity of the Isle of Mull, and distant about 30 computed Miles from the nearest part of the main Land, which is the Country of Morven. It is seperated from Mull by a narrow Sound, about half a Mile over, and three Miles in length. In this Strait, there is Depth of Water for any Vessel and Ships of War have sometimes passed through it; but the narrowness of its Channel and the Sunk Rocks with which it is embarassed render it a very dangerous Passage.

Name

This small Island has been famous 1,200 years for having been the Residence of Columba, the Person who first propagated the Knowledge of Christianity in the most Northern parts of Britain. But it has been known by several different Names.

It was first called by the name of Y, that is, by way of Eminence, the Island, which is the meaning of that Letter in the antient Language. This Name it seems to have acquired upon Columba's arrival and it is so written in some of the old Inscriptions that are yet extant upon the Island. This name is still expressed in the Galic Language by the seperated Sound of this single Letter,[2] which is the same with the names of Hy and Hii given by Bede[3] and other Authors. Its latin name was Iona, being thus termed by Adamnanus,[4] the most early Writer we have concerning it; and it is so styled on some of the Monuments in the Island, erected but a little before the Reformation. By some of the old Irish and Danish Writers it is called the Insula sancta or Holy Island.

Dimensions

The Island extends in length about 3 computed Miles in the Direction of the opposite Coast of Mull, and of the Sound that runs between them. It is near two Miles over where broadest, and belongs in Property to the Duke of Argyll. It seems to contain about 3,840 English Statute Acres, of which a large Proportion, perhaps 2,500 have at some period or other been cultivated. There may be still about 500 capable of being reduced to Culture, comprehending some Tracts of Heathy Soil and of sandy Downs. The remaining 840 Acres may be the Amount of the irreclaimable part, which consists of the rocky Summits of the Hills, the steep Declivities, and the blowing Sand on the Sea Shore.

Hills

It contains no Mountain, but is full of small Hills. The highest, which does not exceed 400 Feet above the Level of the Sea, and the boldest Shore, lies upon the South West side.[5] The Ridges of these Hills run in the Direction of the length of the Island and shoot out at its Extremities into many small rocky Heads, which form a Number of rugged inaccessible Creeks. But the Coast along the two sides of the Island, lies more in a streight Line. It forms in most places a low sandy Beach and where it is interrupted with Rock, the Rocks do not shoot out into the Sea as at the Extremities of the Island, but run along Shore.

Springs

The Island is supplied with Plenty of the finest Springs and though they are very small, yet a number of them collected form a pleasent Rivulet, that runs past the Ruins of the antient Nunnery. There is no standing Water upon any part of the Island, but in a Plain adjoining to the Gardens of the Abbey and surrounded with small Hills, there are Vestiges of a large piece of artificial Water, which has consisted of several Acres, and been contrived both for pleasure and utility. Its Banks have been formed by Art into Walks, and though now a Bog, you may perceive the Remains of a broad green Terrace passing through the middle of it, which has been raise considerably above the water. At the Place where it had been damed up, and where are Marks of a Sluice, the Ruins of a Mill are Still to be seen, which served the Inhabitants of the Monastery for grinding their Corn. Pleasure grounds of this kind, and a method of dressing Grain still unpractised in these Remote Islands must no doubt have been considered in such early Times as matters of very high Improvement.

Harbour

There is properly no Harbour belonging to the Island, but in a small sandy Bay, below the antient Abbey we found very good anchoring Ground in five Fathom water, within two Cables length of the Shore. There is another landing place for Boats, but a very dangerous one except in quiet weather upon the South West part of the Island. It is a Creek lined with perpendicular Rocks of Serpentine Marble and fully exposed to the western Swell. It was here that Columba first landed from Ireland and the Place has ever since had the Name of Port i curach,[6] that is, the Harbour of the Boat, by way of Distinction. The word 'curach' signifies that sort of Boat which the antient Irish and Caledonians constructed with Ribs of Wood covered with Skins and such it seems was the Structure of the Vessel, in which Columba made his Voyage from Ireland.

Soil

A light sandy Soil prevails over the whole Island, which in some places however is very fertile. Upon the Sea Shore especially, there are some small Plains, exceedingly pleasent that afford good Crops of Bear and Oats. The Hills are covered with a fine Verdure and afford a very rich dry Pasture, for Black Cattle and Sheep. Some of the Hills are arable to the Top, but those on the South End of the Island are over run with Heath; yet the small Valleys interspersed among them are filled with Grass of the finest Quality.

Climate

Being detatched from any considerable Tract of Land, and surrounded by the Ocean, this small Island enjoys a very temperate Climate remote from the Extremes both of Heat and Cold. It is but seldom in a Winter that the freezing Degree takes place and if there happens to be a little Snow, which is a rare thing, by the lowness of the Land, by the warmth of the Ocean and of the sandy Soil, it is quickly dissolved. As in all other Islands however, of the like Situation, the Winter is comparatively warmer than the Summer. The worst part of the Climate proceeds from Winds and Rains, which are very frequent and heavy all the year round; and produce a great deal of broken Weather even in the midst of Summer. In this Season therefore the Heat is always less here, though it is greater in Winter, than in any part of the Island of Britain. And for the same Reasons, the same Observation holds with Respect to Britain when compared with the European Continent.

During Summer however there are Intervals here of very fine Weather, and considerable Warmth. Upon the second and third of July Fahrenheits Thermometer stood here at midday in the Shade at 67° the one Day, and at 69° the other, and each night in our Tent it stood at 66° at midnight, being hung in a free Air, between the Tent and Marque.

The Heat of the Summer, with the warm nature of the Soil, proves sufficient to produce more early Crops, than in most parts of Britain. For though the People are very late in sowing their Grain, they have always Harvest early in August.

Adamnanus the Successor of Columba, and the Writer of his Life, relates that the old man having ordered a Quantity of Bear to be given to a Person, in compensation for a Damage he had sustained. He ordered him at the same Time, to sow it, though it was then about midsummer, assuring him, contrary to his Expection [*sic*], that he would the same Season reap from it a plentiful Harvest. In obedience to this Mandate, the man committed the Grain to the Soil, on the 12th of June, and reaped a Crop from it in the beginning of August. The Fact is not surprising to have happened here, though it is regarded by the Author with admiration and recorded as one of Columba's Miracles. A very common Appearance in the Production of Grain, might at that Period be a matter of great Surprize to the People of the Hebrides: for I find no certain Account of their having sown Corn of any kind previous to Columba's Settlement among them, which was after the middle of the Sixth Century.

Number

The present number of People upon Icolumbkil amounts to about 200, so that the Island contains 19 Acres for each Inhabitant. But in the year 1688 when it was visited by Mr Sacheverell, then Governor of the Isle of Man, he found upon it 80 Families.[7] These, at 6 Persons to each Family, the nearest Computation for the Highlands, amounted to 480 Persons, which is more than double their present number. This great Diminution of the People, which unhappily is not confined to this Spot, but is general over all the adjacent parts, has been caused by the great Consumption of the Men in frequent Wars, and a constant Emigration both of Men and Women to Ireland and other Countries.

Religion

The Island belongs to the Parish of Ross in Mull. But the Minister's Residence is so distant, that they are quite cut off from his Instructions, unless when he visits their Island, which can happen but seldom, because of the vast Extent of his Parish. They are Professed Protestants, but being entirely destitute of the means of Knowledge, and having no School they are left in such a State of Ignorance, as in a Christian Country is really deplorable. For of the 200 Inhabitants, there is not one, who can either speak English or read the Scriptures, though their little Island was for many Centuries one of the chief Seats of Religion and Learning in Britain.

They are all of the lowest Rank, under a Gentleman of the name of Campbell who rents the Island,[8] but they are a civil inoffensive People. They are apparently in great Poverty, and yet are happy in having to supply all the wants with which they are acquainted. Entirely excluded from all Intercourse with the Rest of Mankind, they enjoy the mere necessaries of Life, with Peace and Contentment, and have always been remarked, as being of a soft and gentle disposition.

Superstition

They have all of them a remarkable Propensity to whatever is marvelous and supernatural. Every Person has the traditional History of Columba, with numberless Legends, which have been handed down from his monkish Seminary. They are famous for the second Sight; full of Visions seen either by themselves or others; and have many wild and romantick notions concerning Religion and invisible things. Though they know not what Popery is, the Vestages of it they suck in with their Milk, which appear in many of their Opinions and Practices. Having no opportunity of Publick Worship above three or four times a year, when visited by their Minister, it is their Custom to repair on the Sabbath to their Devotions in the ruinous Abbey, to Columba's Tomb, and to the Chapells of several different Saints.

Their Regard is so great for these antient Monuments that it has always been the Custom, before any Person was buried in Icolumbkill to carry the Corpse with great Reverence, round the whole Buildings, which occupy a great Space of Ground. This Practice was for the first time abolished, but a little before I was there, by the Reverend Mr Neil Macleod their present Minister.[9] Having accompanied a Funeral from the Isle of Mull, he insisted with great Resolution, for it required not a little, that the Corpse should be interred, without this previous superstitious Ceremony.

It is not at all surprising however, that the Inhabitants of Iona should be remarkable for Superstition, beyond their neighbours, where are mankind otherwise, in a State of Ignorance, Solitude and inactivity. But besides these general Causes, there are others more peculiar to their situation. They are a People, whose Imagination is evidently the most lively of all their Faculties. The huge Fabrick of artificial Superstition, erected on the Spot in which they live, has rendered the very Air of their Island infectious. Their un-limited Veneration for Antiquity, supplies the Place of Truth, in the most marvelous and frightfull Legends, and their Slender Acquaintance with Religion, is but the Parent of that Superstition, which can only be remedied, by a more perfect Knowledge of divine Things.

Columba

By all Accounts, the famous Columba arrived at Icolumbkil accompanied by a considerable number of Priests in or about the year 564. Being zealous to the Highest Degree, in the Propagation of Christianity his chief Design was the Conversion of the Picts, who then inhabited some of the most northern parts of Scotland. The extraordinary Veneration in which he seems justly to have been held and his high Reputation for Sanctity, were communicated to his Island. So that a Sepulchre in it, became generally coveted, by the great Familys in Scotland, and even by the Grandees of Norway and Ireland.

Columba's Institution by this means, was soon richly endowed, and became the first, as it was for several ages, the only, University, in this part of the World. Being famed for all the Philosophy and Theology of the times, and for the severe manners and Discipline of its Founder, which were long kept up; it became a general place of Education, not only for the Scots, but for the British and Irish Churches.

For several Centuries, the Inhabitants of the Monastery of Iona continued under the absolute Authority of their Abbot, exclusive of any others not subjected to Vows, but governed by the Laws of Columba. During this Period, they were what are called Culdees and all accounts agree in their being renowned for their Learning, for their high contemplative Piety and Austerity of Life. But the Establishment of the Papal Power was accompanied with a great alteration, and Monachism having soon after made its way into Scotland, they became an Abbey of Benedictines, which was of balefull Consequence both to their Learning and Virtue.

Amidst the fierce Conflicts of surrounding nations of the Picts, Norwegians, Britons, Irish and Scots, the veneration with which Columba's Institution was regarded by all Parties upheld it in Safety. It grew and flourished amidst all the rough Vicissitudes of these barbarous Times. Even Magnus nudipes the Norwegian Conqueror of the Hebrides, notwithstanding all the Cruelties of his Incursions in the year 1,098, moved by the reputed Sanctity of the Place, spared the Island of Iona and its Inhabitants from the Devestations, that in all other parts attended his Progress.[10] But,

Quod non fecerunt Barbari, fecere Barberini.

The Learning of Ages, which had been treasured up in this little Island, the Records of Nations, and the valuable Archives of remote Antiquity, which had been safe under the Fury of Barbarians; fell at once a Sacrifice to an ill judged Decree of the Sinod of Argyll. Authorised by this, the zealous Mob at the Time of the Reformation, fell upon Iona, as the most valuable and venerated Seat of the Popish Clergy, and nothing escaped Destruction, but those parts of the Buildings, and such solid Monuments, as were Proof against the Hands of Rage, and even the Teeth of devouring Time.

It is doubtful if any of the present Buildings are of so old a Date as the Age of Columba. For we are informed by our Historians, that the Abbacy having fallen to Decay, was rebuilt and consecrated to Christ and Columba, by Mulduinus King of Scotland about the year 664. It is not unlikely that some of the present Buildings may belong to this Aera from the smallness of their Size and the Simplicity of their Structure. But it is evident that others of them have been the Work of subsequent Times. Though the whole appears to be of a more rude workmanship and of a more simple sort of Gothic Architecture, and it is probable, of a more remote Date than that of any other of our Church Buildings now extant in Scotland.[11]

Cathedral

St Marys Church which was the Cathedral of the Bishop of the Isles, though inferior to many other Gothic Cathedrals and Abbeys of a more recent Date in Scotland, has been very magnificent for the remote Period in which it was built, and considering the Want of Materials, and the Difficulty of Building in this remote part of the World.

It is extremely remarkable for the Materials of which it is constructed. It is built of the Red antique Egyptian Granite; the very same Stone which the Romans brought from the East and with which they erected their most superb Monuments. There are Rocks of it in Icolumbkil, but that of which the Cathedral is built, has been all brought from the adjacent Coast of the Isle of Mull. There the stone can be more easily purchased, and is of a finer Quality, equal indeed to the finest that the Romans ever brought from upper Egypt. It is no where polished in any part of the Cathedral, but every where painfully formed by hammering to a plain Face, and there are many fine Blocks of it, 5 or 6 Feet long, both in the Walls and in the Rubbish. The Labour of Quarrying and forming such a Quantity of this Stone, as so great a Building required, is a piece of Work, like the Egyptian Obelisks of which we have no Idea in modern Times. The Rock is solid, the stone of almost impenetrable Hardness; but Time itself cannot impair and where it can be overcome, is the fittest Material in the World for Monuments that are to last for Ages.

The Windows, Doors, Corners, Arches, Pillars and other Ornaments of the Church, many of which have been exquisitely carved, are all of a fine Free stone, brought from Quarries at a great Distance in the Isle of Mull. The Cement of the Building like that of other Structures, is so strong, that it is easier to break the Stones than to tear them asunder. It is of Lime that has been calcined from Sea Shells, and formed into a very gross Mortar, with coarse Gravel in a large Proportion; and a great Quantity of the Fragments of white Coral, the Corallium album pumilum nostras. Ray syn; p. 32.n.1.[12] which abounds upon the Shores of the Island. The superior Strength of the Cement in antient Buildings, over that of our modern Structures is ascribed to its greater age. But till our Lime be used with a much greater Quantity of Water than at present, with a much larger Proportion of Sand, and that Sand of a much larger Size, no age, nor Time will ever render it a Cement of equal Power to that of the antients.

When this Structure was erected, the fine blue Slate in the neighbouring Islands of Lorn, was no doubt unknown. But it has been roofed with a Stone of a very peculiar and beautiful kind. It is of a rich talky Substance, resplended with the most vivid Colours, and used in the form of large Slates. It has been brought, no doubt, from some of the adjacent Islands, though I no where met with any natural Rock of it.

The Cathedral is built in Form of a Cross, and in most places, the Walls are Standing pretty entire, to where they joined the Roof. The South Front measures about 164 Feet in length, including the Walls, and is all along ornamented with Pillars and Arches of Freestone. The Body of the Church measures 60 Feet in length, and the two Cross Isles, are each 30 Feet in length and 18 in Breadth within the Walls.

The Cupulo is a Square of 22 Feet, which is the measure of each of the Arches that support it. Above this rises a Square Steeple of the same Size, which is decayed at the Top, but still remains between 70 and 80 Feet high. The ascent in it has been by a narrow winding Stair of hewn Stone to the Bellfrey. It is said, that there was here a remarkably fine Peal of Bells, which were carried to Glasgow, at the Time of the Reformation.

The Choir is 60 Feet in length within the walls and 34 Feet in Breadth over the Walls. It has two small Chapels adjoining to it, the one on the South, and the other on the North side ornamented with Pillars and Arches. The East Front of the Choir stands entire to the Top, about 50 Feet high, containing the great Window over the Alter, and a Cross of Freestone upon the Top of it three Feet high.

The Choir contains several pretty Pillars, carved in the Gothic way, with Figures, representing different parts of the Scripture History; and here are still some Fragments of the antient Alter Table, which was of white Marble. Mr Sacheverell who visited this Place in the year 1,688 relates, that it was then one of the finest pieces of white Marble he ever saw, about 6 foot long and 4 broad, curiously veined and polished, and then quite entire, except one Corner, which had been broke by accident. It has since however been gradually broke and carried off. For the Vulgar in the Highlands are all desirous of having a Bit of it as a Relick of Columba, and from the Superstitious Perswation, that the Possession of it preserves from Shipwreck.[13] There is a Bed of this Marble, but to Appearance an inconsiderable one in the Island, from which, it is said, the Alter Table was procured.

Upon the left hand of the Alter, the Fount still remains, and next to that, the Confessional, a Seat about 9 feet long, having a fluted Pillar at each End, and three Arches built into the Wall over it of fine Workmanship. Two stone Partitions come down in the Middle, in each of which there is a small Hole for Whispering the Confessions.

Near the Alter, and upon the north Wall of the Choir, there is a very fine Monument of one of the Abbots of Iona.[14] His Statue, larger than the Life, lies at full Length; with the Mitre, Crosier, Ring and Bishops Robes. It is all of one entire Stone finely polished, with four Lions at the Corners, and round the Edge an Inscription in the antient Galic Character. This Monument is usually thought to be of black Marble, but it is of the true Basaltes of Pliny,[15] a Stone incomparably harder than any Species of Marble. It is what the Columns of the Giants Causeway in Ireland consist of, and of which there are similar Columns in several parts of the Isle of Mull, from whence this Block has probably been brought. It is of the same Nature with our common Whin Rock, but is harder, blacker and of a finer Grain. The Hardness of it is such, as makes the Execution of this Monument really surprising, which has been the Workmanship of no inconsiderable Statuary. The Cushions on which the Head of the Statue rests, look as if they would feel soft; and the foldings of the Drapery, notwithstanding the obdurate nature of the Stone, are light, easy and natural. Being thus remarkably qualified to resist the Injuries of Time, we accordingly find it, as entire, and every slightest Touch of the Chizzel as sharp as the Day it was finished.

Before the Alter, in the middle of the Choir, lies another fine Monument Stone of the Basaltes. It has the Figure of a Man in armour upon it, as large as the Life, in Relievo, and is said to be that of one of the Macleans of Douart, who were for many Ages Lords of Mull. We were told, that it had been richly embossed and ornamented with Silver, though there is nothing but the Tradition of the precious metal now extant.

Library

Along the North side of the Cathedral, and immediately adjoining to it is the Monastery, consisting of a number of Buildings of different Sizes and built at different Times. Here were the Appartments and Cells of the Religious, but now so perfectly ruinous, that they convey no distinct Appearance. Upon the west side, there are the Remains of a very fine Cloyster, and adjoining to it, a large Building, consisting of two Floors, each of which, has contained only one large Hall. That upon the Ground is vaulted above, and paved with hewn Stone. This was the common Hall for the Publick Excercises and Disputations, and the upper one, which has likewise been paved with hewn Stone, above the Vault, was the Library, which it is said was a most extensive and valuable Collection of antient Records and antient Learning.

All that I could learn of its Fate, was, that the Reformers came so suddenly upon Icolumbkil, that the Inhabitants had Time to carry little or nothing away. Some of the Books and Papers however were conveyed to the Castle of Cairnburg, belonging to the chief of the Macleans, and then judged impregnable. Here they remained, till a Seige, in the Time of Cromwell, when they were mostly destroyed by Fire. Some of them however still escaped, of which I got notice of one Manuscript, and saw an old Gentleman in whose Hands it had been for some Time. But found, after hunting it through three or four Islands, that the last Leaves of it, as it was unhappily of Vellum had fallen a Sacrifice for Measures to a Taylor. It was a Latin Translation of an Arabian Work in Physick.

Kings Tomb

The Caemitory to the South West of the Cathedral, is the place where the antient Kings of Scotland were buried. Some of our Historians reckon their number 48, and account Icolumbkill the usuall Place of the Interment of our Kings, from the Death of Fergus the Second, or from about the year 430. But it is not probable, nor are there any Accounts sufficiently authentick to prove that this Island was the Sepuchre of any of the Scots Kings, previous to Columba's Settlement, which was not till the year 564. It is therefore most likely, that Eugenius the third, who died in the year 568, was, at the utmost, the first King, who was buried in Iona, and from that Period, what our Historians relate may be admitted, that there was a Series of 30 Kings intered in this Place, untill the Reign of Malcolm Canmore, when the Abbey of Dunfermline became the royal Sepulchre.

We have no Accounts in History of any remarkable Monument, that ever was erected in this place, to the memory of any of these Kings, and there is none at present indeed to be found. Buchanan relates, that in his Time, there were three small Shrines in this Caemitory, of which that in the middle bore this Inscription, Tumulus Regum Scotiae; that on the right Hand, Tumulus Regum Hiberniae, and the one on the Left Tumulus Regum Norvegiae. Upon the Spot which he points out, there still remains a small Building, which answers exactly to the Description he gives, and what renders it more certain, there is a ruinous Heap overgrown with Grass, at a little Distance from it, on each Side, which appears to be the Remains of the other two Buildings he mentions.

This Shrine, like all the Monuments over the Graves in this place, faces the East. It is not above 10 Feet long and 5 broad, within. Its Walls are only about 3 Feet high, and the Roof is arched, and built entirely up with Stone. These Dimensions show, that it could not serve for burying more than one Person at a Time, and yet in this small Space, the above 30 Kings seem to have been all entombed, during the Currency [of] 432 years.

Adjoining to this small Building, a considerable Space of Ground is covered with the monumental Stones of the Chiefs and Great Families in the Highlands. Each Stone lies flat on the Ground, and is seldom larger than the Dimensions of the Grave it covers. It was the antient Custom, as it still is in some Places, to bury a whole Family or at least the Heads of it, if they died at the necessary Intervals, in the same Grave, and under the same Stone. And this appears to have been the Case, with the Sepulchre of the Kings. It differs from all the other Monuments in this Caemitery, in being built, the rest being all such single Stones, as have been now described, and is thereby sufficiently distingwished to be the Shrine which Buchanan describes. It is now probably above 700 years old, and has been very rudely but strongly built. It is yet quite entire, except at one Corner, where part of the Roof has fallen in, or perhaps has been broke down, by the Curiosity of People to view the inside. But there is now no Vestage of an Inscription upon any part of it.

The Remains of thirty Kings, and some of them very great ones, reduced to such a span. The Dust of Achaius, of the Donalds, and of the Constantines; of Kenneth the Second, and Gregory the Great, each of them the Conqueror of a Potent Kingdom; all confind within the walls of this narrow House, is such a Curiosity, as is no where else perhaps to be met with in the World, and to a Contemplative mind, the Saddest Spectacle of Human Greatness.[16]

Crosses

In the Field upon the west side of the Church, there is a Cross which appears to be of very antient Date. It is of one Stone near 8 Feet high and 20 Inches broad; set in a Pedestal. It is of the hardest Whinrock, and though it wears the Appearance of great Age, it is but little impared except at the Top where a part of it has been broke off by Violence. Adamnanus seems to mean this Stone, where he informs us, that in Columba's Time, there was a Cross which stood midway between the Monastery and the Granary, which was afterwards, says he, fixed in a Pedestal. This is the precise Situation of the Cross we describe, for there is a very antient Ruin of the Granary, about the same distance, west from it, at the foot of the Hill, that the Church is distant from it to the East. This Cross is of a different Form, and apparently of a different Aera, from any others to be seen in the Highlands. And no Wonder, as it appears to be contemporary with Columba, and the oldest Monument extant in the Island of Iona, nay probably the most antient Christian Monument in Scotland.[17]

At some Distance from this Cross, to the South, there stands another of a much larger Size and more entire. It is one Solid Column of the hardest whin stone, fourteen Feet high, and yet only Eighteen Inches broad, and Six Inches thick. It is fixed in a Pedestal of one Stone, which is about three Feet high, and hewn quite round into three Steps. Though posterior to the former, it appears to be very antient.[18] The Labour and Art of quarrying such a Column, transporting it to the Island, and of polishing and erecting it when it was brought are Circumstances really surprising in those early times; when one considers how inadequate the Power of that part of the Country, would be at present to the Execution of such a Work.

Nunnery

All the Buildings and Monuments here mentioned, with the Gardens around the Monastery, have been surrounded by a strong Wall, which is now greatly demolished. And the whole Grounds within it are overgrown in the Summer Time with such Rampant Weeds, that it is difficult to wade through them.

From this Place, to another Antient Building, which was a Nunnery, there runs a Causeway about 300 Paces in length, and about 15 Feet broad; intersected at right Angles by another of the same kind which runs from the Harbour, to what is judged to have been the antient Village of Sodor. This Causeway consists entirely of large Blocks of the same red Granite, of which the Cathedral is built, and have been very artfully wrought and compacted together.

By the Side of it, on the left Hand, as you go from the Shore to the Church, there stands another Cross, and the only one that now remains besides the two above mentioned;[19] though it is said, there were above an Hundred of them upon the Island, before the Reformation. It is a grey Whinstone Ten feet High, and fourteen Inches broad, and only three Inches thick. It is perfectly entire, but has no Inscription upon it. It is finely shaped, and accurately carved, with a great many pretty gothick Ornaments, and is indeed a very genteel elegant Column.

The Nunnery is a plain Square Building. The Walls of it are pretty entire; and it has had a Court within, paved with hewn stone. The Building of it is erroneously refered to the Days of Columba. For as Nunneries were not known in Scotland, till the Introduction of the regular Popish Clergy, it must be of a much posterior Date. The Chapel has been a very neat Building, and is said to have been the burial place for the Ladies of high Rank, as the Chapels of St Mary and St Oran adjoining to the Monastery, were for the Men. There is in this Chapel a very fine Monument of the Basaltes, with the Statue of a Prioress upon it, in an Episcopel Habit with a Mitre upon her Head.

Mr John Frazer[20] who was Dean of the Isles before the Revolution, had a Book written by his Father, a learned man, who possessed the same Office con-taining the antiquities of Iona, and above 300 Inscriptions. This Book he lent to the Earl of Argyll, and it is supposed was lost among that great mans Effects. Most of the Inscriptions at Icolumbkil, and those too the most antient and interesting, are now either half covered with Earth and Rubbish, or so overgrown with weeds and moss, that it would require both Time and Labour to bring them to Light.

MULL

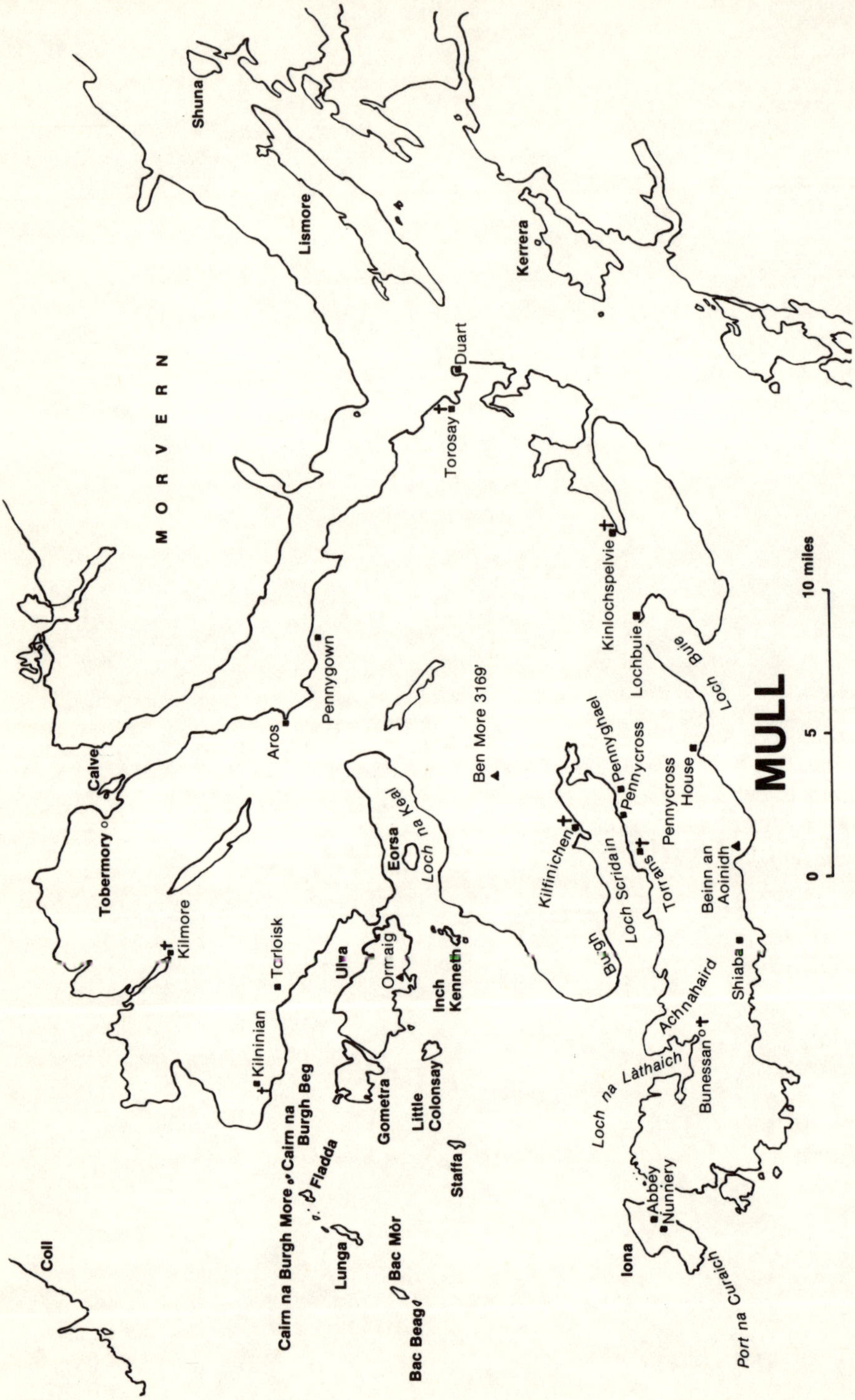
Shuna
Lismore
Kerrera
M O R V E R N
Duart
Torosay
Kinlochspelvie
Kinlochbuie
Lochbuie
Loch Buie
MULL
0
5
10 miles
Pennygown
Aros
Ben More 3169'
Loch na Keal
Eorsa
Pennyghael
Pennycross
Pennycross House
Beinn an Aoinidh
Kilfinichen
Loch Scridain
Torrans
Burgh
Calve
Tobermory
Kilmore
Tcrloisk
Ulva
Ormaig
Inch Kenneth
Kilninian
Little Colonsay
Gometra
Cairn na Burgh Beg
Cairn na Burgh More
Fladda
Lunga
Staffa
Bac Mòr
Bac Beag
Coll
Achnahaird
Shiaba
Bunessan
Loch na Làthaich
Abbey
Nunnery
Iona
Port na Curaich

MULL

Situation

The Isle of Mull called by Torffaeus[1] Milsea and by Adamnanus Malea, lies opposite to the Coast of Morven, and is seperated from it by a navigable Channel, called the Sound of Mull, which is not above half a League over; yet is the only safe Passage for all Vessels of Burden, that sail either to or from the North through the Western Islands. This Island, with the adjacent Counties of Kingarloch, Morven, Sunart, and Ardnamurchan upon the main Land, are all situate within the County of Argyll. The Point which terminates the great Promontary of Ardnamurchan, and which lies opposite to Mull, is the most westerly part of the main Land of Scotland, and by an exact Observation taken by Mr Cowley[2] was found to ly in 56 Degrees 58 Minutes of North Latitude.

Extent

The greatest Extent of Mull from South to North, is about 42 Statute Miles, and its greatest Breadth from East to West about 36; but at a medium, it will be 33 miles long and 27 Broad. According to these Dimensions, in streight Lines, it should contain of Land and Water, 570,240 statute Acres. But as the Island is cut in many places, with extensive Inlets and Arms of the Sea, if 378,640 Acres are allowed to be occupied by these, which is a large allowance, there remains 191,600 Acres of Land for the Contents of the Island.

Rental and Proprietors

The whole Rental of this extensive Island amounts not to above £2,395 so that it appears to be rented at present for about three pence p. Acre. The Duke of Argyll is the chief Proprietor, and is Patron of the three Parishes in the Island. The other Heritors are Maclean of Lochbuy, Maclean of Torluisk, Maclean of Coll, Maclean of Drimnin, Mackinnon of Mackinnon, Macquarry of Ulva, Macquarry of Ormaig, Macgilvra of Peninghail, and Beaton of Penincross.[3] Most of the Inhabitants are either Macleans or Campbells and their followers, or those lesser Tribes, which are strictly attatched to the Families of these names.

Inhabitants

Mull contains three very extensive Parishes.

The Parish of Ross, which contains all the South West part of the Island, on both sides of Loch Screedan, and consists of the two united Parishes of

Kilfinichen and Kilvickewin, is about 24 Statute Miles long and 12 broad, and contains 1,676 Inhabitants. The Island of Icolumbkil is in this Parish. There are four Places of publick Worship in it, Kilfinichin, Bunnessan, Torrin and Icolumbkil, but there is no Church at any of them. The Minister has no Manse, and only the Grass of a Legal Glebe.

The Parish of Torasay comprehending also the united Parish of Pennigown, lies on the South east part of the Island. It is 19 Miles long and 15 broad, and the number of People in it amounts to 1,200. There are 3 places of publick Worship, at which the Minister officiates, Pennigown, Torasay and Kinlochspelven, but he has no Church, Manse nor Glebe.

The united Parishes of Kilninian and Kilmore, comprehend all the north parts of the Island. These make a Parish 27 Statute miles long and 18 broad and contain 2,449 Inhabitants. The Island of Ulva is in this Parish. There are 4 Places of Worship in it far distant from each other, at which the Minister officiates by turns, Kilninian, Kilmore, Aros and the Island of Ulva, but he has neither Manse nor Glebe. At Aros there is kept one of the 4 Latin Schools which are supported in the Highlands upon the royal Bounty. The Schoolmaster has a Salary of £25 a year and has usually about 30 Scholars. Besides English and writing, he teaches Latin and Greek and the Elements of Mathematicks and Book-keeping.

The number of People then in Mull, amounts to 5,325, and by comparing this with the number of Acres it contains as above mentioned, it appears, that there are 54 Acres in the Island for each Inhabitant.

There went out of this Island to the Army during the late War, 350 Men, of which only 50 have returned. A great many of them were killed in America, and the rest are still in the Service.

There are only eight or ten Persons in Mull who are Papists, and these are not Natives of the Country. Of all the Inhabitants, only about 335 can understand a Discourse in English, so that the Ministers are obliged for the most part to deliver their Instructions in Galic. Though there is a legal parochial School in each of the three Parishes, and a Grammar School mentioned above supported by the Committee on the royal Bounty, yet the Country is so extensive, and the Inhabitants so much dispersed, that the greater part of the Children, by their distant Situation, have not access to these Schools, and so grow up without ever being instructed in the English Language, or the Principles of Religion.

Soil and Climate

The Island is full of very high Land, especially towards the Center, and upon the westerly Coast. There is one very lofty Mountain, at the Head of Loch Screedan, called Benmore, or the great Mountain, as it far surmounts all the others in its neighbourhood. Of all the Mountains in Argylshire, it is reckoned next in Height to Cruchan Ben and is juged higher than the Paps of Jura. Though many of the mountains of Jura are black with Heath and barren to the last Degree, yet there are others, that have a fine verdure and afford an excellent Sheep Pasture.

The Island appears to contain about 80,000 Acres that must be juged altogether irreclaimable, consisting chiefly of high Land, upon Mountains, steep Declivities, deep and extensive Mosses and large Tracts embarassed, and in some places almost entirely covered with loose Rocks. The Reclaimable part of the Island may amount to 70,000 Acres, and is for the most part composed of wide extended Heaths, where the Moss is not too deep to prevent Cultivation; of large Tracts of dry green Land upon the Skirts of the Mountains; of low swampy Grounds that might be profitably drained, and of Sandy Downs by the Sea Shore. The Remaining 41,600 acres in the Island, and in the small Isles adjacent to it, have undergone some sort of Culture, either with the Plough or Spade, though the Land at present under Cultivation does not come near to that Quantity. In former Times, Mull has been considerably more populus than it is at present.[4] The high martial Spirit of the People has drained the Country upon all warlike Occasions; the Vicinity of the Island also to the main Land of Scotland, and the easy access to the South, draws away its Inhabitants; and the pernicious Emigration of great Numbers to Ireland, have all conspired to render it less populous. This Depopulation is very remarkable from the extensive Fields that have evidently been in Tillage about 80 or 100 years ago, but have never since been opened, and are in many places quite overgrown with Heath.

Though some Tracts of the Island are extremely mountainous yet the parts upon the Sea Shore enjoy a very good Climate, where there are some woody Valleys warm and low, capable of bringing to Perfection all the common Species of Grain, and of affording very early Crops. Here the Fields of Bear on the 4th of July, seemed equal to any that are to be seen in Scotland, and were then come fully to the Ear. On that Day, Fahrenheits Thermometer exposed to the Sun in the open Air stood at 112, which is 14 Degrees above the Heat of the human Blood. The Crops of Oats, at that time likewise shewed the Soil to be fertile, and the Climate favourable and the large Spots of bright bleu Hyacinths, with which they were every where interspersed at that Season, gave them a very beautiful Appearance, which is no where else to be seen in our Corn Fields in Scotland.

The Island in general, is extremely destitute of Trees, yet in several places there are small Woods which are very convenient for the Inhabitants and of no less use to several of the more remote Islands, where there is no Timber to be found of any kind. In other parts of the Island, there are considerable Tracts of Coppice which would soon grow up into usefull Woods, were they but defended against the browzing of the Cattle. In the Woods upon this Island there is great Abundance of Holly growing naturally.

Harbours

There is a very good open Road in the Bay of Castle Duart, on the South East side of the Island, where Vessels may ride safe from strong Westerly Winds and the western Swell. There is likewise Anchorage in Lochbuy on the South side of the Island, but it is far from being a safe Place in hard weather.

Loch Screedan is an extensive Arm of the Sea which runs 12 Miles into the Island, upon the west side but affords no good Harbour, and is liable to most dangerous flans [*sic*] from the high Mountains which run along the north side of it. At the Entry to Loch Screedan upon the south side, there is a Harbour called Loch Lay[5] shut up by some small Islands, where there is very safe Anchorage. Here we lay two Days, and found great Plenty of Oysters and other Shell Fish.

To the north of Loch Screedan there is another deep Arm of the Sea called Loch na Gaul sometimes frequented by Vessels, but the finest Harbour in Mull or perhaps any where, is that of Tonbir Mory which lies upon the Sound opposite to the Land of Morven. This is a capital Retreat for all the Shipping which pass through the Hebrides. The Harbour is land locked at the Entry by a small woody Island called the Calve, about two Miles in Circumference. The opening to the South is passable only for small Boats at low Water, and that to the north, though clean and deep is little more than Musquet Shot over. The Mountains rise from the Harbour intermixed with Rocks, Woods and Cascades of Water and form a very beautifull Landscape. On the Top of one of the Hills, there is a little ruinous Chapel, dedicated formerly to the Virgin Mary, and hard by it a Spring of fine water which gives name to the Harbour, Tonbir Mory being the Well of Mary.

One of the Capital Ships of the Spanish Armada, called the Florida, was blown up in this Harbour of Tonbir Mory in the year 1588. The Inhabitants relate, that one Doctor Beaton Physician to the Family of Maclean was on board, sitting on the upper Deck when this accident happened, but was saved and lived for several years after. The Ship was supposed to have contained most part of the Treasure which was on board the Spanish Armament, which induced some adventurers to fish upon the wreck a hundred years afterwards, in the year 1,688. By diving in about ten Fathom Water they recovered some Plate and money but as it was not sufficient to defray the Expence, the Undertaking was given up.[6] The same Enterprize however was renewed by some Divers in the year 1752 who raised from the Wreck some Cannon, several Iron Balls and other things, but not of considerable Value. An eye Witness to this attempt related that the Balls of Iron when first raised out of the water, were so soft as to cut easily with a knife, but upon being exposed for some Time to the Air, they turned as hard as any other Iron. The same Fact is attested by many People who were present at the Recovery of some Iron Ordinance, from the Wreck of another Ship of the Armada, which was lost off the Promontory of Pencross[7] at the Mouth of the Clyde. Some of the Guns are still preserved, which are as hard and to Appearance as little impared as if they had never been in the Water, though they were more easily cut by a knife than Lead, when newly raised from the Wreck.

This singular Effect of Sea Water upon Iron lodged in the Bottom of the Ocean for 164 years, is a curious Fact in the History of that Metal, which has not perhaps any where else occurred.

Price of Commodities

	£	s	d
The Oxen 3 years old, at a Medium, each	1	14	0
Their Price and that of Cows, runs from 1£ 5sh. to 2£.			
The Horses, at a medium, each	3	0	0
Their Price runs from 1£ 10sh. to 4£.			
The Sheep at a Medium, each		6	0
Their Price runs from 5 to 7sh.			
Butter p. Stone		8	0
The Stone contains 22lb and the lb 16 oz.			
The Cheese p. Stone		4	0
The Stone contains 24lb and the lb 16 oz.			
Eggs each 14			1
Graidin Oat Meal, p. Boll, at a Medium		11	0
Ten Mutchkins or English Pints and a Gill or Quartern make a Cog, 8 Cogs make a Stone, and 5 Stones a Boll.			
The Price of Meal in this Country is surprisingly uniform never less than 10sh. nor more than 12sh. per Boll.			
Oatmeal of White Oats p. Boll at a Medium		13	9
The price runs always from 12sh. 6d. to 15sh.			
The Boll of Bear at a Medium		14	9
This is larger than the Meal Boll. The Price runs from 13sh. 6d. to 16sh. and when distilled yields 2 Scots Gallons of Aqua Vitae.			

Exports

Mull exports of Black Cattle annually about 2,000 at 1£ 14sh. p. head	3400	0	0
Of Horses, 500 at 3£ p. Head	1500	0	0
Of Kelp 100 Ton, at 3£ 10 sh. p. Ton	350	0	0
Of Fern Ashes 170 Bolls at 12sh. p. Boll	102	0	0

These are the chief Articles exported from the Island. The People send out of it no Wool, woolen yarn or Cloth; no Linen yarn nor Cloth, but buy from other places, almost all the Linen they wear. Their chief Article of Importation however is Oat Meal, which is brought every Year in great Quantities from Aberdeenshire, Bamfshire and Caithness. In the year 1762 there were 30,000 Bolls of Meal Imported into Argyllshire from these Counties. Their injudicious attatchment to Pasturage and the neglect of the Plough leaves the Country uncultivated, subjects them often to the want of Bread and runs away with the Profits of their Cattle.

Weights and Measures

Before the Reign of King James the first, every Shire and Town, and even every Barony and House, had its peculiar Weights and Measures. That Monarch first endeavoured to rectify the abuse, and many attempts have since been made to the same Purpose. A perplexing variety of Weights and Measures, does notwithstanding still prevail, over all Scotland, and hence arise numberless Frauds in vending the necessaries of Life. An abuse the more to be regretted, as the Persons who chiefly suffer by it are the Manufacturers and the Poor.

In most parts of the Highlands the Standard Weights and measures of Scotland are altogether unknown. The Inhabitants deal with one another according to certain local weights and measures of their own, which are unpractised and even unknown in their immediate neighbourhood. Nay in, many Places, as in the Isle of Mull, they have none that are in general use, and the People buy and sell almost quite by guess.

If different weights and measures must prevail in the different Countries, Shires and Towns of Scotland, it would be very usefull, if an exact account of them was taken, and published in a List, in the Scots Almanack, with their several values, compared with those of our Standard Weights and Measures. This would tend greatly to bring these Standards into more general use, and prove such a Direction, as would prevent many of the Fraudulent Impositions, that are frequently practise in the Sale of Commodities.

State of Agriculture

Husbandry is in the same unimproved State in Mull, as in the other Islands. A great deal of the Land is laboured with the Spade, as well as the Plough; and the greatest Improvement ever made in the Island has been of late years, by the Planting of Potatoes. Was their Cultivation confined to waste Ground, it would be a regulation of great advantage both to the Proprietors and Tenants as the Bulk of the reclaimable Land, is precisely adapted for being subdued and brought into Culture by Potatoes. The Minister of the Parish of Ross subset 4 years ago, about 15 Acres of his Farm at the Rent of 6sh. yearly. The Ground was extremely coarse, and had never been formerly cultivate, but the man who took it was industrious, and the first year planted above an Acre of it with Potatoes. He did the same, the three following years, and last Season, besides his annual Acre of Potatoes, he had upon four Acres formerly reclaimed, as plentiful a Crop of Corn, as was anywhere in the Neighbourhood upon Land that had been imemorially in Tillage. The Minister was offered this year 18sh. for the Subtenement, but very properly would neither disspossess the Poor man nor raise his Rent, who had thus tripled its value by his Industry in four years. Of the 70,000 Acres of reclaimable Land in the Isle of Mull there is very little but what is capable of the like Milioration.

They have no other Grain in the Island, but Bear and grey Oats, and though they have come to make some natural Hay upon most of the Farms, yet Rye Grass and Clover have never been sown, but in one Place, where they miss gave, undoubtedly through want of Skill which has made the Farmers however believe, that their Soil and Climate are incapable of producing these sown Grasses.

Sheep Farming

The Proportion in the Prices of Cattle is very different here from what it is in other Places. In the South of Scotland a Cow is equal in Value to 12 Sheep, and a Horse equal in Value to 2 Cows. This Proportion between the Cows and Horses is nearly the same as in the Isle of Mull, but the value of Sheep holds a very different Proportion, for there 5 Sheep are nearly equal in Value to a Cow. The high Value of Sheep in the Island, and in many adjacent Highland Countries upon the Main Land, seems to render Sheep Farming more lucrative and inviting than the Grazing of Black Cattle. This Prospect of turning their Pasture to more Account, has prevailed on many Gentlemen and Farmers in these Countries, to enter upon Sheep Farming and to bring Sheep from the South of Scotland for Stocking their Grounds. But while the Cause subsists, which has enhanced the Price of Sheep in these Parts, it will render their attempts very precarious, and if it should be removed, the Sheep will then fall to the same, or to a lower value than in other Places.

The Devestations made among the Sheep by the Eagles, but especially by the Fox is the great Cause of their high Value in the Isle of Mull and in most of the Highland Countries.[8] This destructive Animal prevails so much that no Farmer can pretend to keep more Sheep than what he is capable of housing, as it is exposing them to certain Destruction to suffer them to ly abroad, and notwithstanding all his Precaution he must meet with such Losses as a Sheep Farmer cannot possibly bear. In many of the western parts of Rosshire and Invernesshire, a Tenant thinks himself well off if the Fox has not destroyed one half of his Lambs before Christmas and frequently he will not have above one third remaining against that Time. By this, the Farmer is oblidged to keep no more Sheep than what are necessary to afford clothing to his Family, and there is seldom above two or three score to be found upon some of the largest Farms. This oblidges them also to breed a great number of Goats which are not near so profitable; but Goat is an animal better armed, of greater Strength and Courage than the Sheep, and lies at night among Rocks and Precipices, where the Fox dares not attack him. Accordingly, the small Farms in Kintail, Glenshiel, Glenelg, Knoidart and Lochaber keep often from 5 to 15 score of Goats, but few or no Sheep.

There was a Farm in the Country of Ardgour not far distant from Mull, turned this year into a Sheep ground. In the month of June 29 Score of Ewes and Wedders, were brought from Douglass in Clyddesdale and put upon it. Their price at Douglass upon an average was 6sh. 6d. each. Their driving from Douglass to Ardgour in twelve Days cost 5d p. head and only three of the whole Flock were lost upon the Journey.

At the above Rent of the Farm, the Grass of each Sheep stood only 6½d. Of the tarred Fleeces of the Sheep which were shorn in July, 7 went to the Stone, and the Stone which is 21 lb weight sold upon the Spot for 6sh. 6d. It may be safely therefore judged here, as is the Case through most parts of the Highlands that the Fleece is equal in Value to the Grass and herding. The Lambs of these Sheep will sell about the first of August for 2sh. a head. And the Ewes brought from the South after having 3 Lambs sell at Fort William for 9sh. a piece.

From this Account, it is easy to perceive that the Profits upon this Sheep Farm would be extremely high if no Accident intervened. But though the Country of Ardgour is better freed from the Fox than most parts of the Highlands, and though the above were carefully herded and watched yet between the month of June they were put upon the Farm and the End of November, there were near 40 of them destroyed by the Fox. This shows that notwithstanding the above advantages, this missfortune must render Sheep Farming in that Country a Vain attempt.

Fox

To attempt the Woolen Manufacture at present in the Highlands could be of no general Benefit, because the Quantity of Wool is inconsiderable, and scarce sufficient to supply the Inhabitants with Clothing, and consequently can afford no Export. No attempt therefore to carry on the Woolen Manufacture needs be made in the Highlands till the Number of Sheep, or rather till the Quantity of Wool be increased beyond the Home Consumption, and this we are not to expect till the number of Foxes be diminished.

Was the Country freed from this pernicious animal, Sheep Farming would be every where pursued to a great Extent, and a large Quantity of Superplus Wool would be raised for Manufacture. There would then be every where large Flocks of Sheep; they would be no longer housed, a practice only to be used with a Handfull; and a Method of Management very troublesome to the Farmer, which the Fox oblidges him to pursue. Nay, every Farm could then maintain a larger Number of Sheep over and above all the Cattle it at present supports; as they can subsist the year round, upon the Mountains and high Grounds, where the Black Cattle feed only a little in Summer. To compute the Sheep that might be thus kept over the Highlands in general, without diminishing the present Stock of Cattle, at 300,000 is not perhaps to exaggerate their number.

The Facts and Observations here made concerning the State of Sheep Farming in the Highlands, show, that the Extirpation of the Fox is a matter of high Concern to the Publick. Neither is it less so to Individuals, for the Farmers are subjected to great Losses by the Destruction of their Sheep, and even Proprietors have been oblidged to let down their Rents in several Places expressly upon this Account.

It is only of late years however, that this Grievance has become so intollerable, that is, since the dissarming of the Highlands, for before that Period, the People being very patient in Hunting and dextrous Marksmen, they kept the Country clear of all the pernicious wild Animals by their Fire Arms. If they are not to be allowed the Use [of] Arms for the same Purpose, some other Method should certainly be fallen upon to remedy the Evil. In making the attempt both the Publick and Proprietors ought to conspire, as both are equally interested, and so important does it appear, that upon a gross Calculation, the high Sum of £20,000 expended in the total Extirpation of the Fox over the Highlands in general, would not seem to be unprofitably employed, though a far less Sum would undoubtedly be sufficient to answer the Purpose.

The Country might soon be cleared by a Premium of 3sh. for every Fox that was destroyed, but the Premium behoved to be augmented as the Number of Foxes was diminished. To render this Method effectual, it would be likewise necessary to arm a certain number of the People, perhaps half a Dozen in each Parish, who might be induced by the Premium to make the killing of the Fox their principal Employment.

The only other Method of attaining the same End, is to hunt with Dogs, which in many parts of the Highlands would be very difficult by Reason of the Strength of the Country which would give the Fox great advantage. A numerous Pack of Dogs would not be necessary, and one consisting of three Grey hounds, three Terriers and two Couple of strong Beagles, is judged the best and cheapest of any for the Purpose. A considerable Number of these Packs however would be required in each of the Highland Counties in order to accomplish the Design.

The most effectual way to eradicate the Fox and Eagle out of the Highlands, would be to adopt both these Methods at the same Time. To appoint a Premium for every one of these Animals by whomsoever killed and to station a Pack of Dogs in each District of the Country, with a small Premium to the Huntsman, for every Fox destroyed to secure his Diligence. By these means, in three or four years, the Country might be effectually delivered from what is become a most intolerable Evil.

Leases

Long Leases are constantly affirmed to be absolutely necessary for the Improvement of the Country, and able of themselves without any further Encouragement given to the Farmer to advance its Progress. But the Principle, it would seem, cannot be safely assumed as general, but may be true or false, according to the Disposition and industry of the People, their Opportunities of Improvement, and the Progress it may have already made in the Country.

A great many years ago, the late Duke of Argyll[9] with an excellent Intention to excite some Persons upon his Estate in Mull to set a Pattern of Industry and Improvement, let out three considerable Farms in Leases of three Nineteen-years Duration. But the Attempt has not been rewarded with the Success it deserved for these Farms are to this day as little Improved as any others in the Island.

Subtenants

The Subsetting of Lands is one great Obstacle to the Improvement of the Highlands. A Relick of the old feudal System which it were well, was abolished, and that every Person who holds Land, should rent it of the Proprietor. The Profit of the Landlord, the Advantage of the Publick, the Progress of Improvement and the Liberty and Happiness of the People demand this. All the subtenants, which are the Body of the People in the Highlands are Tenants at the will of the Tacksmen, and are therefore his Slaves. It may be frequently observed, that the most oppressed Man in the South of Scotland is the Tenant of a Tenant, and it is not to be supposed that it is less so in the North.

The subtenants possess of Land generally from 15 to 40sh. of yearly Rent, and are very numerous in all parts of the Country and upon every Farm. Over the Highlands in general, there will be a Subtenant for every £4 sterling paid by a Tacksman. In some places every Farm of £30 Rent, has at least 10 Subtenants upon it. On the Lochiel Estate of £600 a year, the Tenants rent only about £5 each at an Average, and yet each of these, at an Average has two Subtenants. This is a Subtenant for every 50 shillings worth of Land rented by the Tacksman, and the like Proportion holds in many other parts of the Highlands.

Did the Subtenants hold these small Possessions by a more certain Tenure, and enjoyed them by a Lease from the Landlord, there would be a far greater appearance of Industry among them than there is at present, for their precarious Situation must continue as it has always been an effectual Discouragement to every Improvement of the Soil. Their Subjection also to the Farmer on whose Ground they live, leaves them no more Time than what is barely sufficient for supporting themselves and Families. The Tacksman generally has one Day of the week of the Subtenants Labour the year round, which, with the Spring and Harvest Work and other Occasions, will amount to more than a third of his whole Annual Labour. He can therefore have neither Time, nor Ability to move one step out of the common Road; or to attempt any Improvement, which many of them would undoubtedly do, were they but masters of their time and independent in their Possessions.

Steel Bow

There is another pernicious Method of subsetting of Lands which of late, is become a very frequent Practice in Mull and some of the other Islands, and also in the adjacent Countries upon the Main Land, that is, when a Tacksman subsets his Farm, with the whole Stock of Cattle upon it. This is called setting a Farm in Steel Bow, but why it is so called does not appear. In this case, the whole Stock upon the Farm is valued, and upon the Expiration of the Subtenants Lease, he must either produce the Stocking in the same Condition, or pay the Value of what is wanting. By this sort of Agreement, the Tacksman always draws from the Subtenants two Rents of the Farm, and sometimes three, and has generally from 12 to 18 p. Cent for the value of the Stock upon it. These high usurious Profits, have induced very many Tacksmen, to subset their Farms in this manner. But it is plain that all Improvement must be stopt upon a Farm in this State. The subtenants never make any thing by it, and yet for want of Land of their own, and opportunity of employing their Stock otherwise, are oblidged to submit to this strange sort of Tenure.

Manufacture

There is scarce an Appearance of Manufacture in this large and populous Island, except the Kelp which is made in Summer. A great Quantity of Aquavitae [is] distilled, which the People are at Liberty to do without Duty and without Restraint, which brings some money into the Island, but this instead of being an Advantage, is greatly prejudicial to the Country. Though it yeilded no Revenue it would be worthwhile to maintain Excisemen over all the Highlands and Islands, to prevent the Destruction of the Grain, and the Harm done to the People, by the excessive use of that spirituous Liquor.

There is no other Appearance of Labour in Mull except in the way of Husbandry, and this in the way it is at present conducted, is not half Employment for half of the Inhabitants. The want of Manufacture, among so large a number of People, and in such a State of Inactivity is much to be regretted, especially as they are a People capable of powerful Industry though entirely ignorant how to exert it. The Linen Manufacture is the most proper Species of Industry to be introduced into this Island, and the People are universally well disposed to pursue it. They are acquainted with the advantages that flow from it, to the Inhabitants of some neighbouring Countries on the main Land, and wish for nothing so much as an Opportunity of being initiated in the Manufacture. Their great Complaint is the want of foreign Lintseed which they seldom can procure, and never till the Season is too far advanced for sowing it. And yet even then, they are glad to purchase it at an extravagent Price, as it never costs them less than one Shilling p. Pint. Were they but properly furnished with this Article, they would of themselves, without any other Encouragement, make great Progress in the Manufacture of coarse yarn.

Fishery

Though the Isle of Mull is almost every year visited by the Hering Shoals, and though there is plenty of Cod and Ling upon many parts of its Coast, there is not a Net or Long Line in all the Island. None of the Inhabitants are acquainted with anykind of Fishing, but with the Rod, and in this way, they procure the most part of their Subsistance in Summer, by catching great Plenty and variety of Fish from the Sea Rocks. Within half a League of the Point of Burg, on the west side of the Island, the Sea is 80 Fathom deep, where it has been discovered to abound with Ling, for above a League, between that point, and the small Island called the Dutchmans Cap.

NATURAL PRODUCTIONS

Coal

There are some very strong Appearances of Coal, at three different places in the Parish of Ross in Mull.

At Achinahard,[10] at the mouth of Loch Screedan, in a Farm called Artunn, belonging to the Duke of Argyll, there is a Seam of Coal, one foot thick, which is nearly horizontal, and upon a Level with the Sea, extending in Length exposed to View about 35 Feet. The Pavement upon which it is situated, is a black Slate, the Roof consists of 2 Feet of irregular whinrock, over which there is a Stratum of regular Whinstone Pillars 10 Feet deep. These are covered with the Staple of the Earth, which is only 6 Inches thick.

At Chohinruagh,[11] that is, the Red Cave, upon the Farm of Seba,[12] belonging also to the Duke of Argyll, there are three Seams of Coal, nearly horizontal, in a high prominent Cliff on the Sea Shore. The lowest is one foot thick, and over it there are 20 Feet of solid whinrock; then a Second appears, 2 Feet thick, which is covered with 6 Feet of the whinrock, over which the third Seam is extended, which is one Foot thick, and is covered with 5 Feet more of the same Rock, and the Staple of the Earth.

On the north Side of the Mountain of Beninurigh[13] near the South Extremity of the Island and but half a Mile from the Sea Shore, there is another Appearance of Coal, of greater Consequence than either of the former. It is exposed to View, by a Breach, made into the Side of the Mountain, by a rapid Brook. The Seam extends along the Channel of the Brook 131 Feet, before it withdraws under Cover, and is inclined to the Horison, at a very small Angle. The Pavement is of black Slate, upon a Level with the Brook, but its Depth is unknown. The Seam itself, is in most places from 4 Feet to 4½ Feet thick, of pure Coal, of an exceeding good Quality, and of which the Inhabitants have dug ten or Twelve Horse Loads at a Time, for Fewel. The Roof of this Coal is likewise Whinrock, which is from 3 to 10 Feet thick, covered by the Staple of the Earth. The Farm in which this Coal lies, is in the Hands of the Creditors of Murray of Stanhope.[14]

These Appearances of Coal, are of a very singular Nature, as that Fossile has never been discovered in England, or in the South of Scotland, lodged in Whinstone. This would render the working of them extremely precarious, since no Person has any Experience of Coal situated in such a Manner. Yet the Discovery of Coal in any of the Western Islands, is a matter of such Importance to the Fisheries, as would justify a considerable Trial, at the last mentioned Place.

Limestone

There is abundance of Freestone in the Island, and great plenty of excellent Limestone in several places, particularly in the Lands adjoining to those, where the above Coal is situated. But though there is every where extensive Heaths capable of being broke up and cultivate to the greatest Advantage with Lime, which the Farmers might procure with Peat Fewel, yet this is a Practice they are entire Strangers to, having never turned their Limestone to any Account as a Manure.

Coral

Besides Sea Shells and Sea Sleech, which abound in many parts of the Shores of Mull, there are large Banks of Coral, situated in several places above the Sea Mark, which is a rich calcarious manure. It is the Corallium album pumilum nostras of Rays Synopsis, page 32, n.l.[15] It grows in great Profusion in several of the Lochs, and is thrown out by the Sea, at high Tides, in such Quantities, that there are a deep Strata above ordinary Floodmark, wholly composed of it. In Cornwall this manure is reckoned so valuable, that it is dredged out of the Sea, from a considerable Depth, and carried both by water and Land Carriage, to a great Distance. But the Inhabitants of Mull are entirely ignorant even of its being a Manure, and make no Use of it, though it lies in Heaps adjacent to the Fields, upon which it would produce the highest Improvement.

Red Granite

In several parts of the South West Extremity of the Isle of Mull, especially in that part of the Parish of Ross which lies opposite to Icolumbkil there are many extensive Rocks of Red Granite.

This stone was known to the Antients by the name of Egyptian Porphyry, by the modern Italians it is called Granite rosso, and by our English Antiquarians, the Red Egyptian Granite.

It is the Stone of which the famous Pyramids of Egypt are built, and abounds in Arabia deserta and upper Egypt; from whence it was transported in a vast Quantities, by the Romans into Italy. Their most superb Edifices were ornamented with it, in whose Ruins there are Masses of it sometimes discovered, which are highly esteemed by the Moderns, and purchased at a great Espence. Many of the antient Monuments at Rome are of this Stone, there are several fine Specimens of it preserved at Versailes, and in the British Museum there is a small antique Pillar of it which belonged to Sir Hans Sloane.[16]

It has been considered by Naturalists and Antiquarians as a Marble, a Porphyry and a Jasper; but in its Properties and Composition it is essentially different from all these Stones. It is found in dispersed Masses, in several parts of England and Scotland, but in the Isle of Mull it is found in fast and extensive Rocks, where the Quarries are still visible from whence the Stones have been extracted of which the Abbey of Icolumbkil is built. Here the Stone is to be had in as great Beauty and Perfection, as any of the Fragments obtained from the Roman Ruins in Italy. Blocks of it also are to be procured perfectly entire, and of any Dimensions, and the Quarries are upon the Sea Shore, which would render the Transportation of the Stone easy to other Places.

If these Quarries were opened, and the Rough Blocks carried to Glasgow, to which Place they can be easily transported, and their [*sic*] wrought into Tables Chimney pieces and other Ornaments, it is not to be doubted, that they might be exported into England and other European Countries to great Advantage. The great Merit of the Stone, its great Scarcity and the high Character it has possessed, both in antient and modern Times, would undoubtedly procure a very extensive Consumption.

Giants Causeway

The Giants Causeway in Ireland, though an extra ordinary Phoenomenon, is not quite singular, as there are Appearances of the same kind to be found in several other Countries. For wherever the same sort of black Whinrock occurs it is found to affect in a greater or less Degree, the same Columnar Disposition.

The Pierre de Stolpen near Dresden described by the German Mineralists is of this kind, and is disposed in perpendicular prismatic Columns. The same Stone and the same sort of Columns are observable in several parts of Scotland, as at the Town of Dunbar in East Lothian, on the South Side of the Mountain of Arthur's Seat near Edinburgh, and in several of the Western Islands. But the most exact Representation of the Giants Causeway in Ireland, is to be seen at the Red Cave of Seba at the South West Extremity of the Isle of Mull.

Here, the Whin rock is disposed in regular prismatick Columns nearly perpendicular, from four to Seven Sides, though they are most usually hexagonal. The Columns are from one to three Feet in Diameter, but are not anywhere so far uncovered, that their whole Length can be seen. They appear hereabouts in several of the Sea Cliffs, but in one place, they form the Beach for above 200 Feet, and being uncovered at Top afford a Causeway to walk upon like that in the County of Antrim, which like that likewise slopes gradually into the Sea beyond the lowest Ebb.

The Pillars of the Giants Causeway in Ireland are jointed at different Distances with a Convex and Concave Surface, but the Pillars of the Causeway in Mull, and in every other place where they have been hitherto discovered are entire from Top to bottom, or at least have no regular Joints.

The Stone of which they are composed, is thought to be the Basaltes of Pliny. Though a compound Stone it is of a very fine Grain, has a good black Colour, admits of a tollarable Polish, and by its extreme Hardness, is admirably fitted for Duration, as appears from the Sepulchral Monuments in Icolumbkil, where it has for Ages stood exposed to the Weather without being the least impaired.

Besides these natural Productions of Mull, there is very fine blue Agate to be found in Plenty about the Giants Causeway above described; and Pearls of considerable Value have been often found in several of the Rivulets.

The Iceland Crystal so remarkable for its Property of reflecting Objects double, is found upon the Shores of Loch Screeden. And Sir Alexander Murray mentions his having discovered several promising Veins of Lead in the Isle of Mull, but takes no notice of the Places where they are situated nor are they known to any of the Inhabitants.[17]

Account of the smaller Islands adjacent to Mull

1st LISMORE which was antiently the Seat of the Bishop of Argyll is situated between the Isle of Mull and the Coast of Appin from which it is only three or four Miles distant. It is 8 Miles long, and from one to two broad, and contains 900 Inhabitants. It abounds in Shell Marle, which is found not only in the Bogs, but under all the Lakes in the Island. It is reckoned the most fertile of all the Hebrides, owing, no doubt to this Circumstance, that the Soil is every where stretched out upon Limestone. It rents at £900 and belongs to several Different Proprietors of the name of Campbell.

The Inhabitants of this Island are remarkable for being of a wan Sallow Complexion, in which they differ from all their immediate Neighbours in the Isle of Mull, or upon the Main Land. This Peculiarity appears to arise from the peculiar Nature of their Fewel. They have neither Coal, nor Peat, nor wood in the Island, but they dig out of some Bogs a Clayey Sort of Soil which they work and form into Lumps, and these when dry, are all the Fewel they have. This sort of Earthy Fewel burns away with a red Heat, but without a Flame, and yeilds a great deal of Smoke, which effectually tarnishes the Complexion of the Inhabitants.

2nd ULVA which lies to the westward of Mull, at the Mouth of Loch-na-Gaul, is an Island about 5 Miles long. It belongs to Macquarry of Ulva, contains 266 People and Rents for about £200.

3rd GOMETRA is situated to the westward of Ulva in the Parish of Kilninian. It is two Miles long and a Mile Broad, contains 50 Inhabitants, rents for £40 and belongs to the Duke of Argyll.

4th INCH KENNETH an Island which lies within Loch-na-Gaul in the Parish of Ross, belonging to the Duke of Argyl, is about half a Mile long, and a Quarter of a Mile broad, contains 8 Inhabitants and rents for £17.

5th ELLAN BACHTA[18] called by the Sailers the Dutchmans Cap, from the exact Resemblance it bears to it, lies near Midway between Mull and the Island of Coll. It belongs to the Duke of Argyll and has no Inhabitants, but there are always Cattle kept upon it. It rents for £10.

6th LUNGA which lies adjacent to Ellan Bachta, also in the Parish of Kilninian and belongs to the Duke of Argyll, rents for £10 but has no Inhabitants.

7th CAIRNBURG[19] lying upon this west side of Mull, though now of no Value and without Inhabitants, was formerly remarkable for the Castle upon it, which belonged to the Chief of the Macleans. It is faced almost round with an inaccessible Rock and surrounded with violent Currents, which in former Times rendered the Fortress upon it impregnable.

8th CALVE ISLAND lies upon the North East Side of Mull in the Parish of Kilninian, at the Entrance of the fine Harbour of Tobirmory. It belongs to the Duke of Argyll, rents for £5 and has only a Family of 6 Persons upon it.

9th KERERA which lies between Mull and the Coast of Appin, is 2 Miles long and one Broad, and rents for about £200. The Earl of Breadalbine, Macdougal of Lorn, and Macdougal of Gallanach are the Proprietors. In this Island according to the Chronicle of the Isle of Man Alexander the 2nd died in 1249.

10th SHEUNA is another Island upon the same Coast, in the Parish of Appin. It consists of one Farm which Rents for £55, and belongs to Stewart of Appin.[20]

COLL

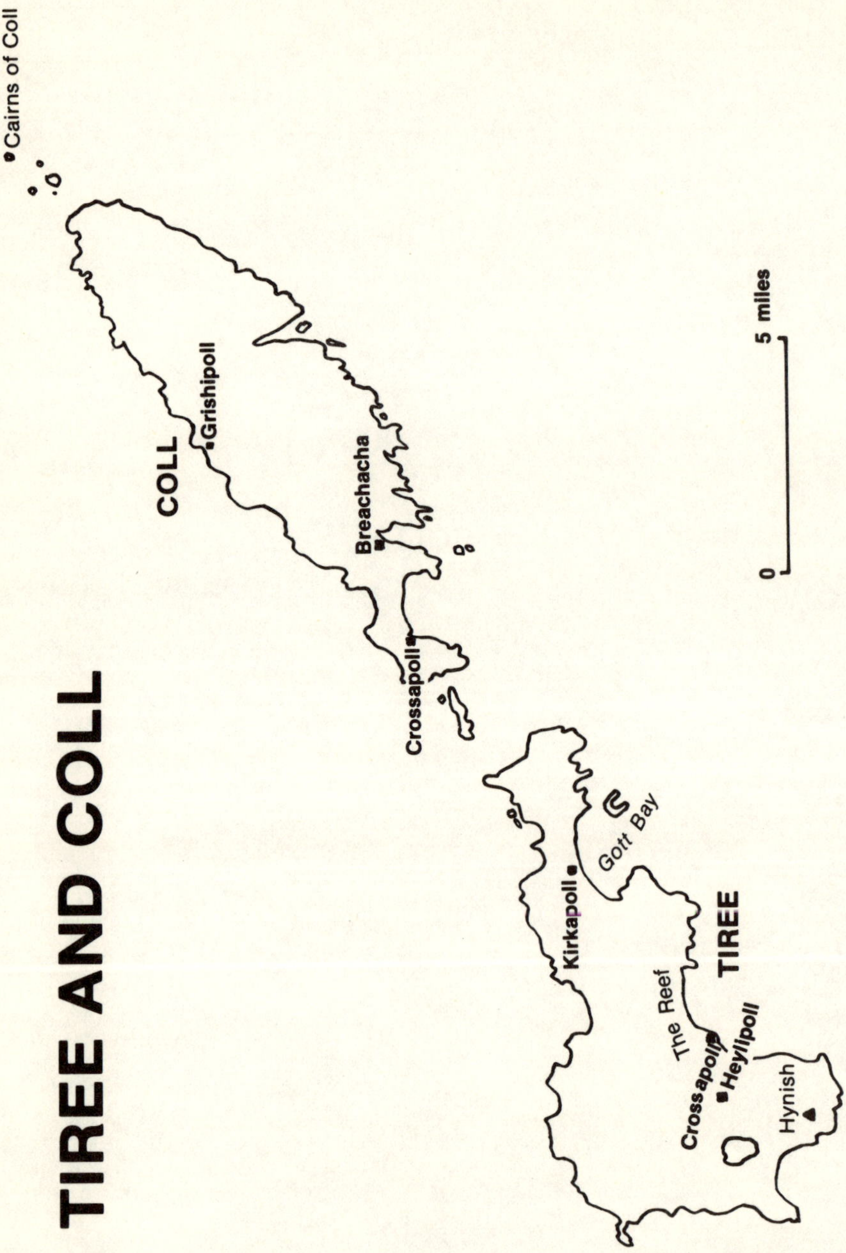
TIREE AND COLL
Cairns of Coll
COLL
Grishipoll
Breachacha
Crossapoll
Kirkapoll
Gott Bay
TIREE
The Reef
Crossapoll
Heylipoll
Hynish
0
5 miles

COLL

Situation and Extent

The Island of Coll, with its neighbouring Island Tirey, is situate at a very considerable Distance from the mainland, and is remote also from any of the other Islands, being about 10 Leagues distant from the South* Extremity of Mull, which is the nearest Land. It is computed at 12 Miles in Length, and three in Breadth; but supposing it 15 measured Miles long, and 3 broad, which will not be far from its Dimensions, at an Average, it then contains 28,800 Acres.

Maclean of Coll is the Principal Proprietor of the Island,[1] and the Rent he draws in it comes to £250 p. Annum. The Remainder belongs to the Duke of Argyll, and amounts to £40 a year. So that the whole Island is at present rented for less than Twopence half penny p. Acre.

Number of People

It contains about 1,200 People, so that there are 24 Acres in it for each Inhabitant, and it sent 40 Men to the late War. The Island composes a Parish, but without any Church, Manse, Glebe or School. By having no Opportunity of being taught to read, the People are in a State of great Ignorance, and the English Language is altogether unknown.

There has been no publick School in the Island for 39 years past, when there was one removed, which had been long supported in it.[2] At that Time, the Inhabitants understood English pretty well, but now it is entirely lost.

Soil

The Island is not mountainous, but much broken by a great number of small Hills, the highest of which is only about 400 Feet above the Level of the Sea.[3] These Hills have little Soil upon them, and yeild nothing but short Heath. Upon every Declivity, the Rock breaks out at the Surface, but is always fast. There are no loose Rocks to be observed upon the Island, as in other Rocky Countries and few Stones are to be obtained for building, but what must be blown with Gun Powder.

These abrupt Hills, however, are interspersed with small Valleys of arable Land, which produce Corn in great Plenty and Perfection. In several parts of

---

**rectius* North (ed.)

the Island also, there are extensive Fields of Excellent Pasturage. The antient Fortress of the Chieftain, and his present House, which is a very good Modern Building, are situate upon the Side of the Bay, by which Vessels have access to the Island, in a much finer Lawn, than many that are modelled by Art.[4] Among several other beautiful Spots of the same kind which occur in this Island, there is one upon the north Side, which in the Month of July appeared very remarkable. It is a circular plain, about half a mile over, like so much bowling Green Ground, surrounded with Hills. It is a rich sandy Soil, which is entirely filled with red and yellow Clover, a variety of yellow Ranunculus's and a vast Profusion of the Bloody Cranesbill and other Flowers, which alltogether, form the most beautiful embroidered Carpet that the Earth perhaps is any where covered with.

The Soil partakes greatly of Sand everywhere, except upon the Hills, and in some parts, the Sand driving from the Shore, has become very detrimental. In one place, there is near 500 Acres of excellent Land, laid entirely desolate. The Sand being now several yards deep, where the People yet alive, have reaped the best Grain in the Island.[5]

Of the number of Acres mentioned above, which this Island is supposed to contain, it is judged there may be about one half or 14,000, that have been cultivate either by the Plough or Spade. About 4,000 Acres incapable of Culture, consisting of Rocks and the Tops of Hills, where there is scarce any Soil, and about 7,000 Acres capable of being reclaimed from their present unprofitable State, which are either thin heathy Land or Sandy Downs. The Grounds in different parts of the Island deluged by Sand, may amount to the remaining 3,800 Acres.

The Prices of Labour and of Commodities are the same here, as in the neighbouring Island of Tirey, in the Description of which, these Articles are Specified.

Natural Productions

This Island is destitute of Coal, Freestone, Limestone and Marle, nor are there any Hopes of discovering any of these Fossils, as the Island is composed entirely of Whin Rock.

The Rock in general runs S.E. and N.W. obliquely across the Island, and all the Veins and Fissures nearly in the same Direction. At a place called Crossapul, on the west side of the Island upon the Sea Shore, I found a considerable Vein of Lead breaking out at the Surface, and bearing Ore at Day, wherever it was uncovered. I traced it above 300 Feet in length, where in several places it is 26 Inches wide and filled with considerable Masses of Lead. It lies in a streight Line, and runs on the one Hand into the Sea, and on the other into the adjacent Hill.

At another place, about a Mile East from the Harbour in a little Bay on the Sea Shore, I found another large Vein, uncovered at Top out of which I picked several Pieces of Lead Ore mixed with Black Talc. This Vein, like the former, rises from the Sea, and runs into the adjacent Hill. It is in different places from 1 to 3 Feet wide, but is mostly choaked up with Earth and loose Stones.

In some parts of the Island, there are Pits of a reddish Clay, which the Inhabitants manufacture into different kinds of Earthern Vessels which they call Crokans.[6] This sort of Ware, the most rude and simple that can be anywhere made, they frame in the following manner. The Clay without any mixture, they form by the Hands, into the Shape of the Vessel required, and then place them in the Sun, till they are thoroughly dry. After this, they are filled with Milk and set upon a strong Fire, where they are kept till the Milk be entirely boiled away, which finishes the Operation. This sort of Ware, though rough and unshapely, is a close firm Substance, and very durable on the Fire. The Milk seems to communicate to the Clay, that Principle which it always loses by Calcination, and by the Loss of which, the Closeness and tenacity of its Substance is impared.

The Island affords about 40 Tun of Kelp annually, which at £4 p. Tun, amounts to £160. Ten years ago, when the first Kelp was made upon the Island, the Minister of the Parish, sold the Liberty of cutting the Sea Weeds upon his Farm, to some English People for two Guineas, and they made upon it 25 Tun of Kelp. So lately were the Inhabitants in entire ignorance concerning the Value of this Commodity, but now they are better instructed how to make their Bargains.

The Island is entirely destitute of Wood, and lies remote from any Place that affords it. It bears neither Tree nor Shrub, except what are in Mr Macleans Garden; and the small grey Willow, which is cut down by the Cattle as fast as it rises. This want of Timber, and the Difficulty of procuring it, distresses the Inhabitants in their Houses, in every Art, and in their whole agrestic Oeconomy. They have little, but what they obtain from Shipwrecks, and with this indeed, they are but too well supplied. The unfortunate Sufferers are sure of being treated with the greatest Honour and Humanity by the Inhabitants, but when the thing happens, the timber of the ship becomes a very convenient Windfall.

In a Country like this, consisting mostly of Pasturage, and that Pasturage, from its wild State, consisting more of Flowers than Grass, the Produce of Bees might be made a very profitable Article. The first Bee Hive, however, was planted in the Island, only two years ago, which has succeeded as well as could be wished, and the Honey it has produced, is of the very finest Quality.

The Sheep which this Island produces, are of a middle Size, but the fine Grass it affords, and the mild Climate it enjoys, renders the Wool upon them of a very fine Quality. Their Pasture is clean and dry all the year round, they have never any Tar or Grease put upon them and they ly abroad all Winter, being never housed, as in other parts of the Highlands. By these means their Wool, is of a Short fine Staple, of a very peculiar kind and widely different from that of any of the Wool in the South of Scotland.

Agriculture

The Agriculture of the Inhabitants, is in a very simple uncultivated State, from the Dissadvantages of their Situation. Their Possessions are very small but equally divided, and capable of furnishing them, with all the necessaries of Life, they seem to have any Demand for. Their Chieftain for whom they have the greatest Affection, governs them with great Equity and Mildness, and lives among them in this Remote Island, like the Master of a Family consisting of above a Thousand People.[7]

They have no knowledge of any Grain except Bear and Oats, and these their Ground yeilds in such Plenty, that after a good Season, they export a considerable Quantity of each, besides a great deal which they consume in their Distillery. Sea weed is their only Manure, and as they do not house their Cattle, they have no other at their Command, except Sea Sleech, which is to be found upon several parts of the Shore, and upon their light sandy Grounds, would have a very considerable Effect.

The Soil being every where light and thin, requires not laborious Tillage, and seems suited to the Feebleness of their Instruments, and the Slightness of their Cultivation. For by want of proper Materials, and bad Mechanicks, their strongest Plough, does not equal the Power of one ordinary Horse. Besides what is laboured by the Plough, a great part of their Land is dug with the Carschrome, or crooked Spade, chiefly in the narrow places among the Rocks, where their Plough with four Horses abreast could not possibly go with ease or Safety. This method of delving, however, in places where it may be necessary, leads them to practice it in places where it is not; and many Fields are to be seen, especially of Bear, manufactured in this way by the Spade, which might be more profitably cultivated by the Plough. It is certain that a Field laboured by the Spade, always produces a larger Crop, than by the Plough, but this advantage must always be greatly overbalanced by the difference between the Value of the Labour of Men and Cattle, at least wherever human Labour can be applied to any useful Purpose.

Two Reasons conspire to render the Use of the Spade so prevalent, in this and many other of the Islands. Most of the Possessions have not employment for a Plough, and even many of them are too small for the fourth part of one; in this case, the small Tenant, keeps no Horse, and finding it difficult to procure the Use of a Plough, manufactures the little arable Land he has with his own Labour. The Tenant again, upon a larger Farm, though he ploughs a considerable quantity of Land during the Winter, yet his Horses, as they never taste a Morsal either of Corn or dry Forage, are so wasted by Labour, that they are incapable of going through the Spring Work, and so the making of the Bear Land, falls to be executed by him and his Servants. The frequency of this Case, has rendered it customary to sow all their Bear upon delved Land. The Custom is pursued, but the Cause of it being forgot, they now look upon it, not as proceeding from Necessity, but as an eligible Practice.

There is exported from Coll a considerable number of black Cattle and Horses, but of a very small Size, and in a much smaller number too, than what the Island might afford if proper Provision was made by the Inhabitants for their Support. They are yet Strangers to the Practice of making Hay, and the Straw of the Grain does little more than serve for Thatch to the Houses. Their

Cattle therefore, though well fed in Summer, are starved in Winter, and in the Spring great Numbers of them die through want, and by the many Diseases, to which all kinds of Cattle are obnoxious when reduced to Leanness.

The Sea Weeds serve as a principle Article of the Sustenance of the Cattle in Winter, which they devour greedily, and though at a great Distance from the Sea, know exactly when to repair to the Shore at the Time of Ebb. They are forced also to have Recourse to the Arundo Arenaria of Linnaeus, a coarse hard Grass, that grows in great Quantity upon the Hills of blowing Sand, and which no Cattle will touch in Winter, except in the greatest Exigency. This however they eat down to the Sand, and feed still more greedily upon it early in the Spring, when its young Shoots are indeed remarkable beyond any Grass we have for their Sweetness. On which Account it goes by the name of Sweet Grass among the Inhabitants of this Island.

The same Grass also is extremely serviceable to them for several other Purposes. Being very tall, and of a tough Substance, with no small Toil, and a great deal of Art they weave it into Sacks, which answer for holding both their Grain and Meal. They frame it into Cordage for Tethers to their Cattle, and Traces to their Ploughs, and even twine it into Ropes and Cables sufficient for their Boats. So powerful is Necessity, in the many cases to produce both Industry and Ingenuity.

Manufacture

The only Species of Manufacture, in this Island, besides Kelp, is the Distillery of Aqua Vitae, which they are oblidged to pursue for the Consumption of their Bear, of which they have a much greater Quantity than they can make use of. There are 9 Distilleries in the Island, one of which will sometimes make use of 70 or 80 Bolls of Bear in the year, and their Boll is to a Triffle double that of Lithgow. But at an Average, each of these Distillers will consume 40 Bolls, which amounts to near 720 Lithgow Bolls of Grain. The Spirits produced from it are dispersed over the other parts of Highlands, and bring Money into the Island, but it would be much more beneficial to raise Hay upon the Land that affords this Superplus Grain.

There is very little Flax raised in this Island, though there was more formerly than at present; for as they never get any Supply of new Flax seed, what they have, being the Product of a great Series of years, is so mightily degenerated, that the Crop it produces is quite insignificant. What they do raise is both cultivated and dressed with as little skill as can well be imagined. They sow it perpetually upon the same dry sandy Soil, and allow it to stand full of Weeds, till it ripens the Seed. After being pulled, they do not water it as usual, but dry it thoroughly, and then beat it with a Stick upon a Stone. It is easy to imagine, what sort of Lint will be produced by this Management, yet it is all they have to provide themselves with a little Coarse Linen, with which they are even very scantily supplied, and any Linen of a fine kind, that they require, they are oblidged to bring from other Places.

Though the general Soil of the Island be dry and sandy, and therefore but ill adapted for Lint, yet there are in some places Fields of a black rich Mold; and in others, a sandy Soil, which is moist and sleechy; both which would answer extremely well for Lint Crops, and there is an extent of both these sorts of Land, capable to raise much more Flax than the People of the Island could Manufacture. But the Disadvantages of the People here, in this branch, are the want of foreign Lintseed, and the want of Knowledge, in raising and dressing Lint. These Defects, are the more to be regretted, as the People, from what they already know, and by the Reports they hear of some other parts of the Highlands, are sollicitous to enter into the Linen Manufacture, and there are at present between 2 and 300 Women in the Island, almost totally idle, who might all be beneficially employed in Spinning.

The Proprietor also is extremely well disposed to assist in carrying on the Manufacture. If it could be introduced, he would not scruple to be at the Expense of £200 for building a Lint Mill upon the Brook that runs near his House, which might serve for both the Islands of Coll and Tirey, for in Tirey, they have no Rivulet that can drive a Mill. But it is likely, that Mr Macphersons Machine,[8] would answer much better than a Lint Mill both for these, and for the other Islands, where the want of Materials, and especially of Wood, would render, both the Building and Machinery of a Lint Mill very troublesome and Expensive. There is a Wright and a Smith in the Island of Coll, both of them very good Mechanicks, who could easily execute Mr Mcphersons Machine, if they had one for a Pattern.

There is another Circumstance, which would be found very convenient in making a trial of the linen Manufacture in this place. There is a house already built which would have very good Accommodation for a Flax Dresser, and also for a spinning School. It is situate near the middle of the Island, upon the Sea Shore, where there is plenty of excellent Fish to be had at all Seasons of the year. The present Coll built it only three or four years ago, upon a Farm of his own, but before it was finished within, he succeeded to the Estate of Coll, by his Brothers Death, upon which he removed to the Family Seat. It is 50 Feet long and 19 Broad, within the Walls, with 3 Floors. It is well built and slated, and well lighted, and excellently adapted for being a Seminary of Industry, to which Purpose, the Proprietor would gladly turn it.[9]

Fishery

Upon both sides of this Island, there is an excellent Opportunity of establishing the Cod Fishing. Upon the eastern Coast, the Sea is 80 Fathoms deep for a great Extent, within two Miles of the Shore, and full of large Cod and Conger Eel. This last Fish which is very large, and of an exceeding good Quality, though little known at present, was cured and exported in great Quantities about 60 or 70 years ago from several parts of the Western Islands. It was in such Esteem abroad, that it always sold in France, at the same Price with Salmon.

Between the Islands of Coll and Canna, there is another extensive Cod Bank, which has been often tried, and always found with Abundance of Fish upon it. Not far from Coll, the Sea is 100 Fathoms deep, but middway upon the Bank, between the two Islands, it is only from 15 to 31 Fathoms, which is the Depth, at which Cod are always found in greatest Plenty. When the weather is so easy, that a Boat can go off to this Bank from Coll by one Days fishing with hand Lines, it returns at Night deeply loaded with large Cod, and sometimes a great Quantity strung upon Ropes at the Stern, which they can not get stowed in the Boat. This makes the Island of Coll, one of the most favourable Situations in the World, for curing dry Cod; but for want of Salt, the Inhabitants have never been able to make the Attempt.

TIREE

TIREY

Situation

The Island of Tirey, or as it is sometimes written Tire-iy or Teree, is the Ethica Insula of Adamnanus. It lies out in the Ocean, at a great Distance from the main Land, and very much detatched from the other Islands. It is situated at about the distance of Ten Leagues to the Northwest of Icolumbkil; and extends in Length nearly from North East, to South West, in the same Direction with its neighbouring Island of Coll.

These two Islands, with the smaller ones that ly in the Sound between them are stretched out in a streight Line, of above 30 measured Miles in Length, which varies but two or three points from the general Direction of the main Land of Scotland, though they are distant from it near 20 Leagues.

Extent

Tirey is above 8 computed Miles long, and in most places about 3 broad, and by a gross Computation, seems to contain about 30,720 Acres. These Acres are presently let, at about the Rate of 6d a Piece, and though the lowness of the Price is indeed surprising, yet Tirey is the highest Rented Land in all the Western Islands. It is the Property of his Grace the Duke of Argyll[1] and is chiefly inhabited by Campbells and Macleans.

Hills

Excepting three or four Hills, the whole Island is one continued Plain, which is everywhere so low, that from a great Distance at Sea, it escapes the View, and only the Hills appear, as so many Islands. The highest Ground in the Island, is at its South west Extremity, where there is a Hill about 400 Feet in Height, which slopes away to the North and East, but is more steep, rocky and abrupt to the South West.[2]

In all the other parts of the Island, the Shore is low and Sandy, running with a very gentle Slope into the Sea; and hence the Shallowness of the Water, in most places round the Island. From the Southwest Extremity, there runs an Extensive Rief of Rocks, with very Shallow water upon them, for 6 Leagues into the Sea, exactly in the Direction of the Island, a thing which never happens in any of the Islands where the Land is high. Both here and in the Island of Coll, the Hills run nearly in a Line, according to the Longitudinal Direction of both Islands.

Harbour

The Flatness of the Country and the Shelving nature of its Shores, is attended with one Inconvenience, the Want of a Harbour. There is not a Creek round all the Island, where a Vessel of any Size can be safe, if the Weather is rough. The only Place of approaching to it, is at the Bay of Gott, which is about the middle of the Island on the East Side. It is called by Adamnanus the Portus Campiluna, being an open Sandy Bay, in the Form of a Crescent. Here our Vessel lay two Days, about half a Mile from the Shore, in four Fathom Water; but the Place is quite Shelterless either from the Winds or the Ocean; and can be visited in Safety only in the Summer Time, and in very easy weather.

Tides

It is remarked by D'Arfeville[3] in his Account of the Voyage of King James the 5th through the Hebrides that along the Coasts of Coll and Tirey, it is high Water, when the Moon is at S. one fourth S.E. But by the Information of the Inhabitants, eastern and western Moons make full Sea at Tirey. The Tide ebbs and flows regularly Six Hours. The Tide of Flood comes upon the Island from the South West, from between Barrahead and Ireland. And thoroughout the whole year, the predominant Wind also is from the South West.

Springs

The Island being so plain, and the Soil in most places deep and Sandy, its Springs are neither numerous nor large, though there is Spring Water sufficient to supply the Inhabitants. There is no standing Water in any Place, except one Lake, towards the Foot of the rocky Hills at the Southwest End of the Island.[4] It is about half a mile long, its Water extremely clear, and its Banks covered with a fine Verdure. It is seldom frozen in Winter, and has usually a great number of Swans upon it. There was one upon it, when we were there, in the Month of July, owing probably to some Missfortune it had met with; for none of the Inhabitants had ever seen any Swan upon the Island before in the Summer Season.

The only running water in the Island, is a small Stripe that issues from this Lake, scarcely sufficient to turn a Mill. And though it were, could not be easily applied to this Purpose, as it glides to the Sea, thorough a deep sandy Plain, in which there is very little Level.

Sea

There are strong Vestiges of the Encroachment of the Sea on both Sides of this Island, and great Alterations it has made upon the Shores, within the Memory of the old People who are yet alive. It has advanced greatly upon the west Side, being the Quarter, from whence comes the heaviest Swell, and the strongest Winds. Here, in an extensive sandy Bay, where the Ocean comes in with a very lofty Surf, it has of late years been continually threatening to break entirely through the Island. The only thing that serves to oppose it, is a Mound of blowing Sand, running along the Shore, in some places, not above Six or eight Feet high. And should this feeble Obstacle give way, there is nothing to interrupt its Progress to the Sea on the other Side. For here, the Island, is a dead Flat, very little elevated above ordinary Flood Mark. The Inhabitants have already been so apprehensive of this alarming Irruption, as to be at pains to heighten and strengthen this sandy Rampart, with Rocks brought from a great Distance, and to repair the Breaches, which the Sea has already made in several parts of it.

Along the Shores of this Island, as in many other places, the Sea itself, forms the most effectual Barrier, against the Violence of its own Billows. Driven by the Tides and Tempests and boiling from the Bottom, it drives along, and deposites upon the Shore, the Sand and Sediment of the deep. This no sooner dries, than it is in motion again by the Winds; and carried forward upon the Coast, forms those Hills of Sand, which are to this Island and to many a Country, its immediate Defence against the Inundations of the Ocean.

Soil

Tirey has always been remarkable, among the western Islands, for its Fertility, and the Goodness of its Crops. The Soil in general, is very deep, sandy, and full of Sea Shells, especially upon the Shores, but in the interior parts, there are many fine Fields, which partake largely of Clay. There is a great deal of Land in it that has been kept perpetually in Tillage, long past the memory of any one alive; bearing every year a Crop either of Oats or Bear, without Intermission, and without any assistance, except a few Sea weeds put upon it, once in Two years. This is an extraordinary Phoenomenon, in the nature of a Soil, not easily accounted for. The great Depth, the Moisture, and pervious nature of the Soil; the Shells with which it is greatly replenished; and the Sea Spray with [which] all the Lands in the Island are liberally watered, may conspire to promote and perhaps to produce, this uncommon Fertility.

Of the 30,720 Acres, which the Island is supposed to contain, there appears, by the nearest Guess, to be fully two thirds, or 20,000 Acres cultivated, which is a much larger Proportion, than is to be found in any other of the Islands. There seems to be about 6,000 Acres, still to be reduced to Culture, consisting chiefly of Sandy Downs on the Sea Shore. The remaining 4,720 may be the amount of the space, occupied by blowing Sand, by the rocky Sides, and Summets of Hills, and other places which may be deemed irreclaimable.

Rieve

The Grass of the Island, as may be judged from the Soil, is extremely fine. It is free from Heath, Ferns, Bushes, and the like Unprofitable Plants, and consists chiefly of such Grasses as usually grow upon Lawns. The numerous small Plains and Hills, covered with this fine Grass and intermixed with Fields of Corn, render the Face of the Island extremely agreeable to the Eye. But there is one Spot, whose Figure, Equality and Verdure, render it one of the finest and most singular Views to be seen in Scotland.

It is a Plain called the Rieve of Tirey, about 8 or 9 measured Miles in Circumference. It is nearly circular, has not the smallest Inequality, but is of the same dead Level throughout; its Soil is dry and its Grass as fine, as that of a Bowling Green. About the first of June when the Cattle are put upon it, it is all over as white as a Cloth, with Daises, and white Clover. In that Season, there may be seen pasturing upon it at once, about 1,000 Black Cattle, 2,000 Sheep and 300 Horses intermixed with immense Flocks of Lapwings and Green Plovers. The Grass upon it is kept always low, but there is not perhaps any where, a Piece of Ground of equal Extent, capable of yeilding more Pasture. After the first of June, it is a common Pasturage, to all the Farmers in the Island, and while it remains so, must remain the finest unimproved spot in Scotland.

Climate

Tirey, by being so champaign, is much less subject to Rains, than the mountainous Islands, and is remarkable for the mildness of its Climate, which feels no Disturbance, but from the South West Wind. It never suffers any considerable Degree either of Heat or Cold. Its Summers are sufficiently hot, for the Vegetation of all the common Crops of Grain and Grass and the Warmth of its Winters, appears to be greater than that of any other part of Britain, or its adjacent Islands. Being far removed from any considerable Tract of Country, having neither high Land, nor wet Soil and surrounded for a great Extent, by the warm streams of the Ocean, the Cold in Winter, very seldom advances to the freezing Degree. Whole Winters do sometimes pass without Snow, and if it happens to fall, by the same Causes and the warm sandy nature of the Soil, it is quickly disolved. It may be justly said of Tirey, with regard to Britain, and for the same Reasons, what Caesar observed of Britain, compared to the Continent: *Coelum Gallico temperatius.*

Crops

Such however, is their summer heat that aided by the forward Nature of the Soil, it is sufficient to produce very quick and early Crops. In the year 1762 the Hordeum vulgare of Linnaeus, the common Bear or square Barley produced a Crop in 35 Days, being sown the 28th of April and reaped the 22nd of July. Linnaeus informs us, that the same plant ripens in Lapland in 58 Days. Being sown the 31st of May the Crop was arrived at Maturity the 28th of July.* This was a Latitude, where the Sun was in the Firmament, during almost the whole Time the Crop was in the Soil. But there are few Places in Britain, capable of ripening this Grain, within the Period above mentioned.

*Linn. flor. lapp. prolegomen. (J.W.)

After the Crop of Bear is reaped at this early Season, the People of Tirey usually plant the same Ground, with red Coleworts, the Brassica rubra of Bauhinus, Pin. p.111 n.2,[5] and they never fail to have a plentifull Crop, which lasts throughout the whole Winter. But some years ago, there was an Instance of a double Crop, much more extraordinary. A Field of Bear having been reaped very early in July, it was immediately ploughed and sown again, with the same Grain. And from this, there was a pretty good Crop reaped about the middle of October. The only Instance perhaps known in Britain, of two white Crops, having been reaped off the same Land, in one Season.

Inhabitants

This Island has about 1,681 Inhabitants, and according to the above Computation of its Dimensions, contains 18 Acres for each Inhabitant. It sent 57 Men to the late War, and of these only 12 returned, most of whom received Chelsea Pensions. It composes a Parish, antiently called the Parish of Soroby, whose Parson was always Vicar of Iona, and Dean of the Isles. The Inhabitants are all Protestants, and there is a School supported in it by the Duke of Argyll: but having little or no Intercourse with Strangers, they have made no Progress in the Acquisition of English, and there are not above 20 Persons in the Parish, who can understand a Sermon in that Language.

As they have no Wood but what they bring by a long voyage in their open Boats from the mainland or the Isle of Mull, their houses and instruments of Agriculture are very mean and simple. They are very ill supplied also with Fewel, as their Island affords but little Peat or Turf. But they are well cloathed and well fed, having plenty of coarse Linen and Woolen Cloth, abundance of Corn and Cattle, and great Profusion and Variety of the finest Fish.

Longaevity

They are in general extremely healthy and long lived. In the year 1764, there was a Gentlewoman living upon the Island, who from unexceptionable authority, was then 103 years old, but who died the year following. At the same Time there were two Men alive of 98, one Man of 90, two of 88, one man and a woman of 83 and three Women and two Men of 80. The whole being a large Quantity of Longaevity among 1,600 People.

Diseases

They are but little subjected to chronical Dissorders and most of them fall, either by Old Age or Epidemic Diseases. The Ague is sometimes prevalent and Mortal. But this is nothing to the Devastation of the small Pox, which rages here with a peculiar Malignity. This Disease visited the Island in the year 1756, and had not again returned in the year 1764. There were then about 105

Children seized with it, but upon enquiring, as is usual, how many of this number had died there could not be found a certain account of one that lived, out of the whole Number. The Chincough[6] also when it appears, is almost equally direfull, and in Winter 1763, cut off 40 children, in the course of two or three Months.

Antiquities

From the Monuments that still remain, this Island appears to have been a favourite Seat of the Danes. The Vestiges of several of their Forts are still to be seen, especially of one or two in the interior part of the Island, which was contrary to the general Practice of fixing them above inaccessible Precipices on the Sea Shore. Pol, which is the antient Scandinavian Word for Town, remains in the names of a great many Places, as Kirkapol, Crossapol, and Heylipol. There are here also several Cairns, and the Remains of some Circles of large single Stones, which seem to be of Danish Origin, both from their Appearance, and the Tradition of the Country.

Agriculture

The Husbandry in Tirey, is conducted much after the same manner as in the other Islands; though by the Equality of its Fields, the finess of its Soil, and the favourable Nature of its Climate, it is better adapted for Improvements in Tillage. The Lands are parcelled out into very small Possessions. The largest Farm is only £30 sterl.p. year and from this they are of various Rents, down to £5. The whole Rents of the Island amount to £773, of which the Proprietor draws £550 exclusive of all Deductions. The Soil everywhere admitts of the Plough, so that there is not that use made of the Spade here, that there is in the other Islands.

Inclosures

A great part of the Fields are inclosed with Walls of Earth, very broad at the Foundation, five or six Feet high, and covered with Grass from Top to Bottom. Without answering in any tollerable Degree the Purposes of Inclosure; being built of a dry sandy Earth, they are perpetually crumbling to Pieces, and create to the Husbandman a constant annual Toil. But were these Mounds of Earth covered with coarse robust Hedges, by being filled with black and white Thorns, Crabs, Brambles, wild Roses and other Hedge Shrubs and Trees; these would not only supersede the present Labour of their Reperation, and fence the Fields from all Inroads; but they would mend the Climate by sheltering the whole Island; and protect the Crops from the Strength of the Winds, which is almost the only Danger they have here to encounter.

Cattle

The Cattle of every kind, range the Fields here all the year round. The Farmers having neither Stables nor Cow Houses, collect no Dung; and Sea Weed is the only manure their Grounds ever received, though immemorially croped. This Treatment of the Soil, never could be productive of a Crop, was it not for its uncommon Natural Fertility, which even assuredly will decay, under this management, but never can be advanced. The first and most important Step therefore, that the Farmers can be put upon here, is, to provide Winter Forage, to house their Cattle, and preserve the Dung. This is but the common Rotine of every Country where Agriculture has made any Progress and every improved Country is a Proof of its being the previous Step, to all other Improvements of the Soil.

Grain

Bear, Oats, Potatoes, and a little Rye, are the only Crops raised in Tirey. The two rowed Barley should undoubtedly be introduced here, notwithstanding the Fears which the Inhabitants express, of its being more easily shaken, than the Square Barley, and therefore less fit for their Climate. There is indeed a little, and but a little Difference, between the two Grains in this Respect, yet any Dissadvantage that might arise from this would be much overbalanced by the superior Qualities of the two rowed Barley. It affords a better Grain, a larger Increase, and ripens in a shorter period. Their Oats likewise, require as great an alteration. For they sow at present, only the small grey Oat, though both the Soil and Climate, would answer for white Oats, as well as in most parts of Scotland.

Change of Seed

The Farmers here, have also great Reason, not only to alter their Grains, but to attend carefully to the Quality, both of those they have; and of those they may acquire. Their Soil in general, is light, dry and sandy, in which all kinds of Grain do sooner degenerate than in any other. Their Grains accordingly are of the smallest Size, not from the Infertility of the Soil, but from the want of Management, and because they never practise any Change of Seed. Grain brought from different Soils, and from distant Places would be the most effectual Change. But even within the Island, there is an Opportunity for this Purpose, which is neglected.

The greater the Difference is, between the Soil that produces the Seed, and that on which it is sown, the greater constantly will be the Advantage. Though the Soil here, is in general Sandy, there are some Tracts in the Island of an adhaesive Clay. Yet the Farmers have never availed themselves of this Advantage; at least never through Design; by transferring reciprocally, the Produce of the one Soil, to the other.

One Experiment of this kind was lately made by Mr Campbell, the Duke of Argyll's Chamberlain in the Island. He brought Bear from Glasgow; and sowed it upon his Farm in Icolumbkil, where the Soil is of the same sandy Nature with that of Tirey. The Grain which it produced he sold one third dearer than any other Bear, that was raised from the Seed upon the Island. This usefull Experiment, it is hoped, will lead others into the same Practice, and though never so often repeated, they may be always assured of the like Success.

Hay

Twelve Years ago, there was no Hay made in Tirey, but upon two Farms. The Practice is since become general, and upon every Farm, there is now some Hay preserved for the young Cattle, which is given them in the Fields, in Winter. The Hay is extremely fine, yet only the Natural Produce of the Soil, though there might be as great advantage reaped here, from sown Grasses, as in any Place whatever. About ten years ago, Mr Lauchlan Maclean Merchant in Glasgow, a native of Tirey, caused Clover and Rye Grass to be sown here for the first Time. But though they throve exceedingly, the Experiment has never been repeated; nor can it be indeed, to any advantage, till there are Inclosures sufficient to protect them against the Cattle, which roam through out the whole Island during Winter, and yet till the Farmers here fall into the Practice of Artificial Grasses, or other Green Crops, they must want a third, if not one half, of the Corn and Cattle, which their Soil might otherwise produce.

Manures

There are few places better provided than Tirey with natural Manures. In the middle of the Island there is a great Body of white Marble, which burns into the finest Lime, but has never been used for any purpose except for Building. As a Remedy, for the general Lightness of the Soil, the Shores in many places are covered with the richest Sleech, and in other Places, there are Banks of Shell Sand, of pure Shells, and of white Coral, which would infuse wonderfull Fertility, into all the strong Soil in the Island. These however have never been used, nor is their use even known, though there is no doubt, but that some Time or other, they will become a Source of great Improvement to this Island.

Were the common Farmers but once prevailed upon to make a fair Trial of these manures, they would not stop, till they had them as far as they would go. For though there are no People more backward to any new Improvement, where they see not the certainty of the Event, yet there are none who can more assiduously pursue any Branch of Industry, when once they are perswaded, and especially when perswaded by finding that it is advantagious.

Turnips

The want of Winter Food for Cattle which is the great Calamity over all the Highlands, might be more easily remedied in Tirey, than any where else. For if Turnips can any where be raised with Success and Advantage for the Purpose, it is in this Island. The Soil is precisely adapted for them, and the Winter is open and free from the Frosts which so generally destroy the Turnip Crops in other places, if allowed to stand in the Ground till late in Winter. For this Reason, they might be preserved in Tirey through out the whole Winter, and the great Losses prevented, to which both the Tenants and Landlord are subjected, by the Death of Great Numbers of Cattle in the Spring, by absolute want of Food.

Price of Commodities

	£	s	d
A Stone of wool containing 22 lbs p. stone and 22 oz p. lb		8	0
A Stone of Butter. Same weight		6	0
A Stone of Cheese. Same weight		3	4
A Stone of Salted Beef. Same weight		7	0
A Stone of rinded Tallow. Same weight		7	0

Price of Labour

Wages of a Man Servant for a year	1	8	0
Wages of a Woman Servant for a year		17	6
Price of a Womans Labour for spinning a spinel of yarn from a lb of Lint weighing 22 oz		1	4
Wages of a Labourer p. Diem with his Victuals	0	0	3

Exports and Imports

Tirey exports annually about 400 Bolls of Bear and Meal, which at an Average may amount to about	240	0	0
Note: The Boll of Tirey and Coll is near double that of Lithgow.			
It affords annually 44 Ton of Kelp, which at £3. 5sh. p. Ton, amounts to	143	0	0
It exports about 150 Barrels of Salted Beef, each Barrel being 32 English Gallons and contains about 200 lb weight of Beef. This may amount to about	230	0	0

The Tallow of these Cattle is also exported.

There are some live Cattle exported, but as the Cattle of this Island when driven, are subject to a fatal Distemper,[7] this oblidges the Inhabitants to Salt the greatest part of their Beef, which they sell at the Ports in the Clyde. A little Linen Cloth and yarn is likewise exported, from 2 Hanks to a Spinel out of the lb of Lint.

A great Quantity of Aqua Vitae is also exported.
They import from the Clyde about 3 Hogsheads of foreign Lintseed annually, which is sold in the Island at 1sh. p. Scots pint.
The Salt with which they cure their Beef is brought from Ireland.

Manufacture

There is not any kind of Manufacture at present in Tirey, except that of a little coarse Linen Cloth and Yarn, which is carried on in the narrow and imperfect manner. And yet there is no Country where the Linen Manufacture could be turned to better Account. The Soil and Climate are excellently adapted for raising Flax, most of the Inhabitants, especially the Women, are not half employed, and the Country affords great Plenty of cheap Provisions.

In the Rental of the Tirey Estate above 150 years ago, the Tenants paid in kind, a certain Quantity of Linen Cloth called Towelling, which shows, that the Linen Manufacture, though it has made no Progress, is of very long standing in this Island. That part of the Rent has since been converted into Money, and is now called Towel money.

They have in this Island above a hundred Generations of the same Lintseed, which is now totally degenerated, that the Crop it affords, is scarce above a Foot long. Of late years, they have got some small Quantities of Foreign Lintseed, from which they always raise exceeding good Crops; but are perfect Strangers to the proper Management of the Lint after it is raised. Even this Lintseed is observed to degenerate quickly, and if due attention was paid to the Lint Crops, there would be no Lintseed sown that is produced in the Island.

The first and most necessary piece of Encouragement therefore, towards promoting the Linen Manufacture in Tirey, is to furnish the Inhabitants with foreign Lintseed at an easy Price. Their access to it at present is difficult and uncertain, but they are already so sensible of its advantage, that they are glad to purchase it in a Retail way, at an extravagant Rate.

As they are already tollerably acquainted with raising a Crop of Flax, they stand not so much in need of a Flax raiser as other Highland Countries. But they stand in great Need of the Assistance and Directions of a Flax Dresser; as they are totally ignorant of the right manner of pulling, watering, grassing and dressing the Flax after it is raised. If an Industrious Artist of this kind, was settled among them, and a Spining School erected under the Care of an experienced Spining Mistress, there is no doubt but in a little Time, the whole Rents of the Island of Tirey might come to paid by the Sale of Linen yarn.

Fishery

The Fishery might be turned to great Account in Tirey. There is not a Net nor long Line in all the Island. There are frequently very favourable Opportunities here, for the Herring Fishing in Summer. But every year, the Herrings constantly abound in great Shoals all about Tirey, from the beginning of October to the end of December which gives the Inhabitants an Opportunity of enriching themselves by the late Fishery. This however they have always neglected, nor ever take any Herrings, though during that Season they are thrown up in vast Quantities upon the Shores, by every violent Gale of Wind.

They are equally negligent with Respect to the Cod and Ling, which are to be found all round the Island in great Plenty and Perfection. Were they furnished with long Lines and Salt a very profitable Trade might here be carried on in drying these Fish, for which the Season and the Shores of the Island are extremely well adapted.

Hemp

As the Inhabitants of the Hebrides are a maritime People, whose chief Occupation should be fishing, this points out the Hempen Manufacture, as one of the most proper for them to pursue. While the Manufacture of Linen may be resigned to the Women, that of Sail Cloth and Cordage should be the Work of the Men; nor can there be a fitter Employment for a hardy and Seafaring People.

It would perhaps be most proper to begin this Manufacture with foreign Hemp, but it would become more Advantageous, if it could be supported with Hemp raised in the Islands, and there is none of them fitter for the Purpose than Tirey. The Climate being more favourable than in most of the other Islands, and the Soil dry, rich and deep in many places, by which Properties, it is excellently calculated for the Production of Hemp.

In all the Islands, I did not see or hear of a Field of Hemp except in the Lewes; where they have begun to raise a little for the Use of their Fishery. The Trial fully answers their Expectation, and I there saw one Herring Buss, fitted out for the Bounty Fishery, whose Nets were wholly made of Hemp which grew in the Lewes. On the 16th of August I measured the Male Plants of the Hemp Crop in the Lewes which are the smallest, and were but just come to the Flower; and found them in general to be about 4 feet three Inches long. This makes a good Crop of Hemp but there is more to be expected from the Soil and Climate of Tirey.

The Iron, Tar, Flax and Potashes of North America, have of late years, greatly diminished our Importation of these Commodities from the Baltick. Hemp has also been tried in several parts of that Continent, especially in New England, but has always failed. A Circumstance which encourages our application to the Culture of this Article in Scotland.

NATURAL PRODUCTIONS

Marble

Towards the middle of the Island, there are extensive Rocks of white Marble, which in one place, have been quarried to furnish large Stones for forming a Barrier against the Sea, where it threatens to cut through the Island. It has also been burnt upon some Occasions for Lime, which it affords of a remarkable Degree of Strength and whiteness.

I brought two Blocks of this Marble to Edinburgh, but found upon Trial, that they would not answer for Cutting. They have many small round Holes which are filled with a Concretion, not so white nor so hard as the Stone. Was it not for these, the substance, Colour and Polish of this Marble would render it extremely valuable. It has never been worked but near the Surface; and it is highly probable, that the Stone at a greater Depth, would be found more solid, and entirely free from these Holes.

Copper

The general Rock of which the Island of Tirey consists, is remarkable in many Countries, for being fruitfull in Metals. It abounds in the mining Countries in Norway, and Sweden, and it is remarked by Linnaeus, as being frequently the Matrix of Copper. Accordingly, upon the Shore, on the South side of the Bay of Gott, I found the Appearance of a great Body of the Pyritical Ore of Copper lodged in this Rock.

It is an Ore of a bright yellow, variegated with green, purple and other Copper Colours. Where I observed it at Day, it did not seem to form any Regular Vein. But a Track of Rocks, between twenty and thirty Feet wide are there impregnated with this Ore, which deserves to be enquired after.

Porphyry

There is great Confusion among many Mineralists concerning Porphyry, nor has it ever been sufficiently distinguished from the Jaspers, Granites and Pudding Stones, which are the Fossils that approach nearest to it. The proper Distinction I imagine, is to be found only in its Composition. The Ground of Porphyry is always a coloured opake Quartz, capable of a fine Polish, and charged with Particles or nodules of a different Colour and Substance, most usually, fusible Spar, Talc, or the Feld Spath of the Germans; but each Sort of Porphyry seldom contains more than one of these Substances.

The most common sort of Porphyry is the Porphyr rubens lapillulis. Waller, mineralog,[8] the Leucosticos of Pliny,[9] and the only Quarries of it now known, or attended to, are the Remains of the Greek and Roman Buildings. There is a fine Pannel of it in Edward the Confessor's Chapel in Westminster Abbey, placed in the Wall, and a large beautifull Table of it at Wilton.

The Porphyry however found in Tirey is very different from this, and much more beautifull. It is the Porphyr rubens, lapillulis nigris. Waller mineralog, or the true Egyptian Porphyry, of which, there are still some Remains in Italy; and from the Account given by M. Esteve in the Memoirs of the Academy,[10] I take the great Antique Urn, in the Temple of Bacchus at Rome, to be this very Stone.

I found several great Rocks of it upon the Sea Shore, near the Ministers House, upon the North West Coast of Tirey, without any Seams or Fissures, and so extremely hard, and solid that for want of proper Instruments, I could only procure some small Specimens of it.

The Ground of the Stone, is a very hard, compact, opake Quartz, of a fine Carnation Colour, interspersed with Spangles of a bright green Talc. It is susceptible of a fine looking Glass Polish, as I have found by Trial, and is a Stone of very great and uncommon Beauty.

In some of the Rocks, the Talc is of a much darker Colour, and in some it is entirely black, which is generally the Case, in the antique Egyptian Porphyry.

At the above Place in Tirey, there might be Blocks of this Stone purchased of any size, and without a Flaw, but on account of its Hardness, the working of it both in the Quarry, and in the Marble Cutters Shop, would be a matter of very high Expence.

RUM

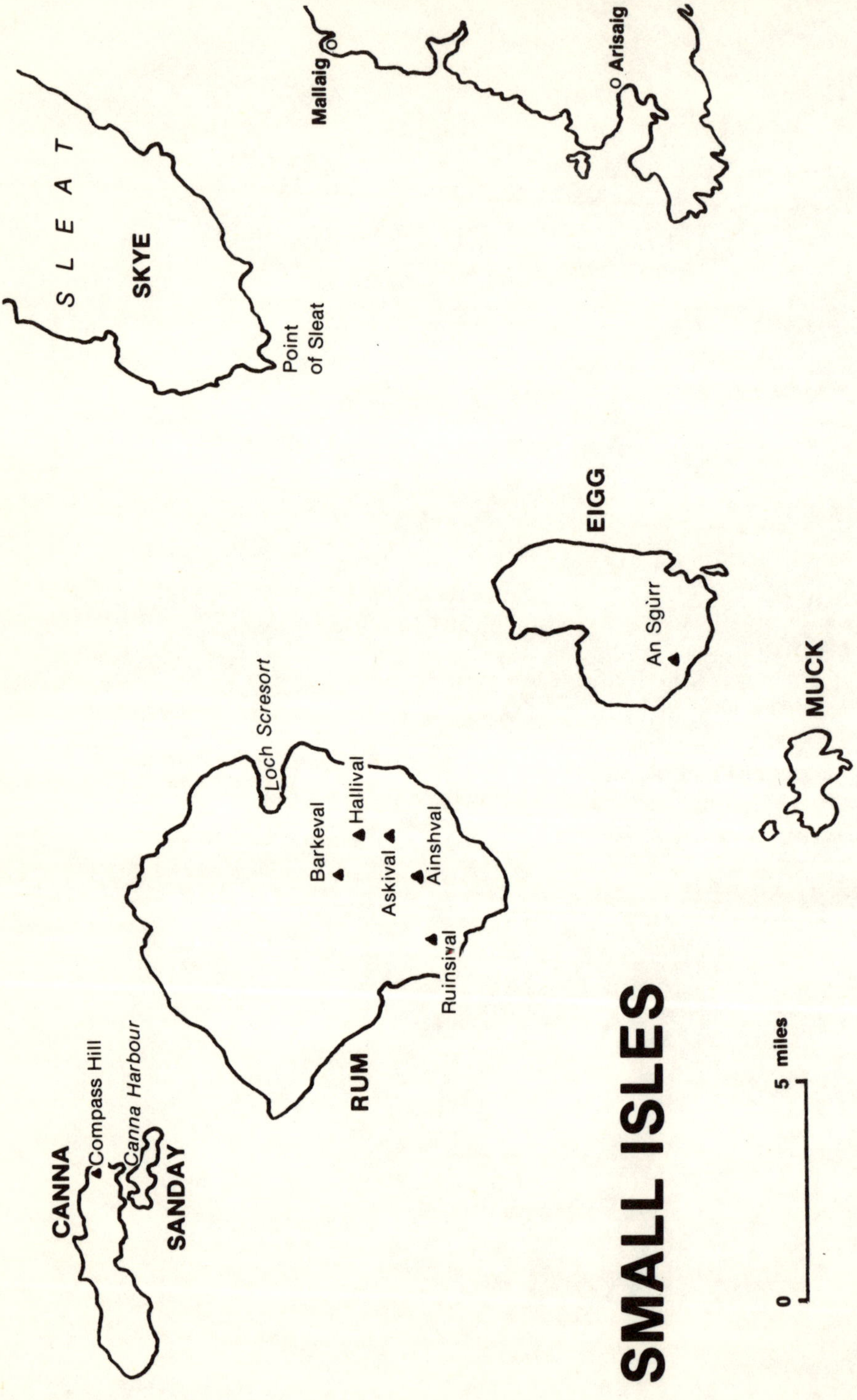
SLEAT
SKYE
Point of Sleat
Mallaig
Arisaig
EIGG
An Sgùrr
MUCK
Loch Scresort
Hallival
Barkeval
Askival
Ainshval
Ruinsival
RUM
CANNA
Compass Hill
Canna Harbour
SANDAY
SMALL ISLES
0
5 miles

RUM

Situation and Extent

This Island is called Rauneya by Torffaeus, and is often mentioned in the Poems of Oscian, by the name of Tongorma, from the Blue Colour of its Mountains. It is situated about 6 Leagues Northward from Coll, and is four Leagues distant from the West Coast of the Isle of Sky; about five computed Miles long from North to South, and three broad from east to west. It is the Property of Maclean of Coll, and inhabited by the People of his Clan.

Soil and Climate

It contains at least, 15,360 English Statute Acres, of which there is a very small Proportion that has ever been cultivated; not above 1,500 Acres; for there is not a Plough in the Island; the Inhabitants cultivating their little Fields on the Sea Shore, entirely with the Spade. It may contain 3,000 Acres of coarse moorish and mossy Grounds capable of being [brought] into Culture, but the Remainder, by far the greatest part, may be judged wholly irreclaimable, consisting of Steep Mountains, deep Mosses and Tracks [*sic*] of Land overspread with Rocks.*

It is an Island of an unfavourable Climate, being much colder, by Reason of the Height of its Mountains, and much more subject to Rains and Winds, than the neighbouring Islands of Egg and Canna, which are lower Land. These Disadvantages of Climate, with its deep wet Soil, must prevent it from being ever profitable in the Production of Corn or Cattle. But as the Bulk of the Island is defended from the Strong South West Wind by a ridge of Mountains, it is likely that Wood would thrive well upon it; nor is it probable that it can ever be turned to so much account, as by being sown entirely with the Seeds of the various Timber, and Converted into a Forest. It has once been well wooded, and in some of the steep Gullies, inaccessable to Cattle, the Oack, the Birch, the Holly, and Rowan Tree, are still to be observed growing vigorously.

Mountains

The whole west Coast of Rum is occupied by five lofty Mountains, which run in a Chain from South to North. At their South Extremity is Loch Scresord, the only Harbour belonging to the Island, where there is a very good Anchorage, on the west Side, close under the High Land. From this Place, I made a Journey to the highest of these Mountains named Ascheval. From the

*The whole Island is rented at present for about £80 so that it is let for little more than a penny per acre. (J.W.)

Shore we ascended through deep Mosses, whose Surface would scarcely carry us, and then passed through several deep pathless Glens, so narrow, and the Bowels of the Earth so mangled with Torrents, as to appear hideous. The rest of the Ascent, was clambering amidst broken Rocks and falls of water; but among these Rocks, and among the straggling Junipers, I found such a Variety of rare Alpine Plants, as amply requited the Fatigue of the Journey. Some of them, the Inhabitants of the highest Alps in Switzerland, and others of Lapland and Spitsberg.

This Mountain by the nearest Computation, is about 2,100 Feet high, above the Level of the Sea. It is divided at Top into a great Number of detatched Rocks, which shoot up perpendicularly like Spires, from 20 to 60 Feet high, which are sadly Tempest beaten, and are entirely divested of any Covering, either of Earth or Herbage. Near the Summit, it is connected with the neighbouring Mountain, by a rocky Ridge, in some places so sharp, that a Man may lean his Breast over it, and look down an inaccessible Precipice, between eight and nine hundred Feet high. The Coldness of this Mountain, may be easily guessed by the following Fact. In one of its perennial Springs, at the Height of 1,600 Feet above the Level of the Sea, Fahrenheits Thermometer on the 19th July, at 3 p.m. stood at 40 Degrees.

Inhabitants

The Island contains 288 Inhabitants, and 53 Acres for each Person. The Number of Families in it are 52, that is above 5 Persons to each Family. The Heads of all these Families are Tenants immediately under the Proprietor, and their Rents are from 10sh. to £4 a piece. Such a Number of People, living in the way of Husbandry, upon so small a Property is not perhaps to be found anywhere else in Europe.

The only Articles exported from the Island, are some Black Cattle and Horses. As for Corn, there is no more of it raised, than what serves the People for Bread a few Months in Winter. During all the Summer, they live entirely upon animal Food, and yet are healthy and long lived. The year before I was there, a man had died in the Island aged 103, who was 50 years of Age before he had ever tasted Bread; and during all the Remainder of his long Life, had never eat of it from March to October, nor any other Food, during that part of the year, but Fish and Milk; which is still the Case with all the Inhabitants of the Island. I was even told, that this old man used frequently to remind the younger People, of the simple and hardy Fare of former Times, used to upbraid them with their Indulgence in the Article of Bread, and judged it unmanly in them to toil like Slaves with their Spades, for the Production of such an unnecessary Piece of Luxury.

So comparative a thing is Luxury.

After his death, the oldest Person, was a Woman aged 92, besides whom there were other three Women above 80. The Island was then accounted populous, as it had not been visited by the Small Pox for 29 years; for by this Disease upon former Occasions, it had been almost depopulate. There were

125 People, 24 of them married Persons who had never had the Small Pox, and who then lived in the greatest Dread, as the Disease had lately appeared in some of the Adjacent Islands.

The Inhabitants of Rum adhaered strictly to the Popish Religion, till about the beginning of this Century, when in one Day, they were all converted from Popery, and in a singular manner. Maclean of Coll, their Chieftain, being himself a Protestant, insisted that they should renounce the Roman Catholick Religion. He came to the Island with a Protestant Minister, and ordered all the People to appear at a certain Place, on Sunday, at publick Worship. They came to the Place, but refused to go into the House, where the Protestant Service was to be administred. The Chieftain reasoned with them, but they became more refractory. At last, he seized the most resolute Man among them, and having drubbed him heartily with his Cane, drove him into the House. Upon this, they all followed, without any further Opposition, and so the Reformation in this Island was accomplished. From that Day, they have ever since continued Staunch Protestants and there are but two Women among them at present of the Popish Perswation. Their neighbours, however, in the Popish Islands of Egg and Canna, still continue to call the Protestantism of Rum, by the name of *Credivk Chall Vuy,* that is, the Faith of the Yellow Stick or Cane.[1]

NATURAL PRODUCTIONS

Animals

There is a large Herd of Red Deer kept upon the Island by the Proprietor, and in all parts, there is great Abundance of Moorfool. Upon the Mountain Ascheval, we found a Nest of the Golden Eagle, the Falco chrysactos of Linnaeus, and brought away the young one. The Puffin of the Isle of Man also builds here, which is reckoned the greatest Delicacy of all Sea Birds. It is rarely to be met with in other places, and keeps the Sea all the year round except in hatching Time. It builds in Holes under Ground, and we found its Nests among the loose Rocks, above a Mile from the Shore.

There is a great Number of Goats kept upon the Island, and here I found an Article of Oeconomy generally unknown in other Places. The People of Rum carefully collect the Hair of their Goats, and after sorting it, send it to Glasgow where it is sold from 1sh. to 2sh. and 6d. p. pound according to its Fineness, and there it is manufactured into Wigs, which are sent to America.

Aira coerulea Linn

The Plants hitherto cultivated in this Country for Hay or Pasturage, are Natives either of the Southern parts of Europe, or of the low fertile Lands in England or Scotland. In Consequence of their native Situation St Foin, Lucerne, Plantain, Rie Grass and the Red, white, and yellow Clovers, do all require a Dale Country, and a rich Soil, and can no where else be cultivated to Advantage.

The mountainous [parts] of Scotland, which must always be a Pasture Country, are but too well known to be extremely destitute of a proper Provision of Hay, both for their Black Cattle and Sheep. In these Countries the above Grasses cannot be raised, but the want may be supplied, by some other Hay Plant better suited to their Soil and Climate, and the most likely place for the Discovery of such a Plant, is among the Natives of these Alpine Countries.

The Plant best adapted for this Purpose I have ever seen, was found in great Abundance in the Island of Rum, which is the Aira coerulea of Linnaeus. It is to be found in some other mountainous parts of Scotland, where it is called by the Shepherds, the Flying bent, but no where in greater Perfection, than in this high cold Island.

It bears long broad grassy Leaves. Its Stem rises between two and three Feet high, and its Foliage is long and thick. It grows in a Soil of pure Moss, and in the most exposed Situation almost to the very Tops of our highest Mountains, where no other Grass of any Value is to be found. It grows generally in a dispersed Manner, but in some places it forms of itself, whole Acres, with scarce any other Plant intermixed, and these, were they inclosed, would make excellent Hay Fields, without any Cultivation.

From the middle of May, to the End of July, it affords the richest Summer feeding that the Sheep have in the high Countries, but when it grows long, they shun it, as they do all Grass of a great Height. It is in its Flower and Strength, and fit to reap, between the 20th of July and first of August. It is a Grass coveted by all kinds of Cattle, when green and affords a heavy Crop of Hay; and its Seeds are very numerous, ripen well, and are easily collected.

This is the only Alpine Grass I have met with which I esteem worthy of Cultivation. It is precisely the Hay Plant that is most wanted in Scotland, which is one, that will grow vigorously, and afford a plentifull Crop, where none of the artificial Grasses at present in Use, can succeed. That is in a Mountainous Situation, and in a wet and mossy Soil.

Coal

I found a Small Seam of Coal, about 6 Inches thick, lodged in a Stratum of Whinrock, upon the west Side of the Island, but saw no appearance of it any where else.

Agate

The Shores of Rum abound with the Chalcedony, and blue and white Onyx, commonly known by the Name of Agates or Pebbles; and I found also some few fine Specimens of the white Cornelian. These Stones are to be found thrown up by the Sea, in the small Bays, on the North East side of the Island, but in larger Masses, and in greater Quantity, upon its North Coast, facing the Sound of Canna. Here, these Stones might be collected and exported with great Advantage to Places, where they are manufactured.

The Business of the Lapidary is an Art lately introduced into Scotland, but is already so far increased, as to merit some Notice, when the Oeconomy of the Country is considered. Two and twenty years ago, there was only one Lapidary in Edinburgh. But at present there are above 30 Workmen closely employed, in cutting Agates, or as they are commonly called Pebbles, for the Birmingham Market. They are chiefly wrought into Sleeve Buttons. Of these, one Man can make 36 Dozen a Week, which sell at Birmingham for 15 Pence the Dozen. The whole therefore, must amount to such a considerable Sum, as renders it questionable, if there are 30 Labourers in any other Manufacture, that bring so much Money into the Country.

The Demand is greater than they are able to Supply, because of the want of Agate. They have hitherto been chiefly furnished, from some places in Angus and Merns, where the Stone is become scarce and high priced, but there is certainly a Stock of it in the Isle of Rum, capable to afford them a large Supply.

Jasper

The Island of Rum affords another Stone, very valuable to the Lapidary. Formerly it was considered as a Jasper, but by Cronsted the late Swedish Mineralist,[2] it is called Petrosilex. It is of a bright Green or blue Colour; has a Degree of transparency, takes a fine Polish, and is a very beautifull Stone for Snuff Boxes, Bracelets or such like Ornaments, and it is found here, in the Sea Cliffs, and upon the Shore of the Sound of Canna in great Quantities, though abroad, it is accounted a rare and Valuable Stone. I got only such Pieces, as were fallen accidentally out of the Cliffs, but by Quarrying there might be Masses got of a considerable size and of an exquisite Colour and Polish.

It is a Stone which the Lapidaries in Scotland should enquire after and Manufacture. It is much esteemed, and more valuable, than the finest Agate, and not only England, but foreign Countries, would afford a very lucrative and extensive Consumption of it.

SKYE

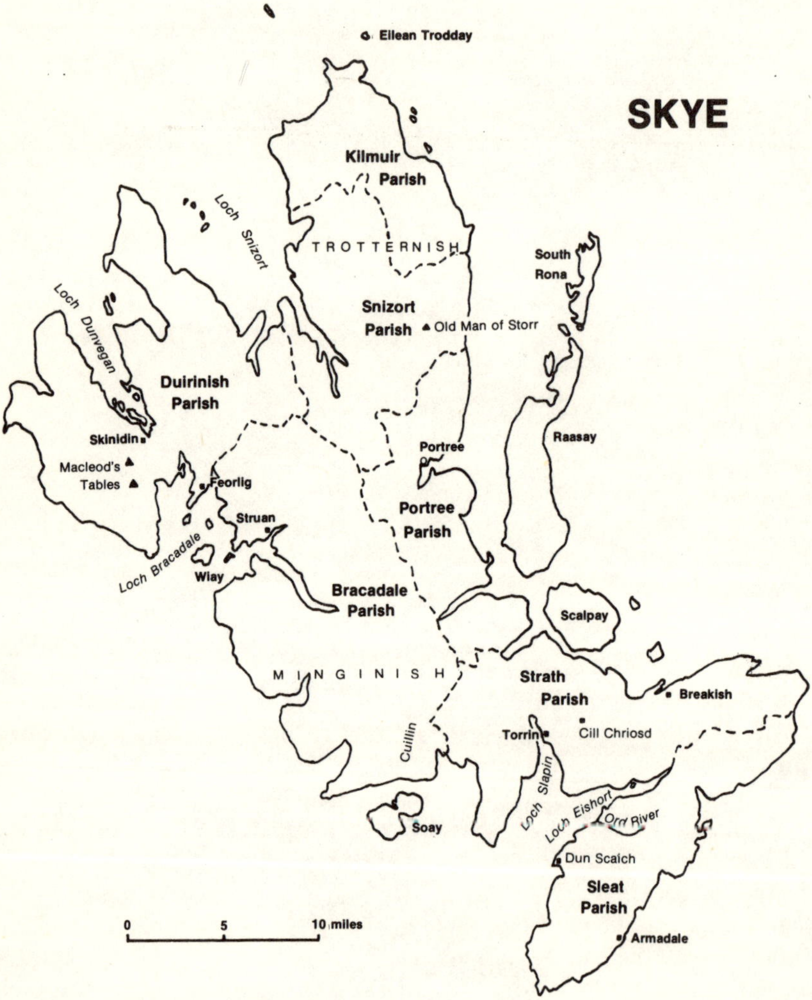
SKYE
Eilean Trodday
Kilmuir Parish
Loch Snizort
TROTTERNISH
South Rona
Snizort Parish
Old Man of Storr
Loch Dunvegan
Duirinish Parish
Skinidin
Raasay
Portree
Macleod's Tables
Feorlig
Struan
Portree Parish
Loch Bracadale
Wiay
Bracadale Parish
Scalpay
MINGINISH
Strath Parish
Breakish
Torrin
Cill Chriosd
Cuillin
Loch Slapin
Loch Eishort
Ord River
Soay
Dun Scaich
Sleat Parish
Armadale
0 5 10 miles

SKY

Situation and Extent

The Isle of Sky stretches along the West Coast of Invernesshire, being separated from the main Land at one Place, by a Sound not a Quarter of a Mile over, but in most places, it is from 4 to 10 Miles distant from the Continent.

It is 40 computed Miles in Length, and in different Places, from 10 to above 20 in Breadth, yet notwithstanding this great Extent of Land, it runs out into so many Promontories, and is so deeply cut by Arms of the Sea, that there is no Part of the Island above three Miles from the Shore.

To take this Extensive Island at a very moderate Computation, and allowing for the great inequality of its Coasts, it may be savely reckoned at an Average, 40 measured Miles long and 10 broad, upon which Supposition, it contains 256,000 English Statute Acres.

The whole Island is in the Hands of three Proprietors. Sir Alexander Macdonalds[1] Rental amounts to £2,500; Macleods[2] to £1,300; and Mackinnons[3] to £140; the Total being £3,940. So that the Island is at present let at about threepence half penny p. Acre.

Inhabitants

This Island contains 7 Parishes, which with the Parish of Eig make up the Presbytery of Sky. These Parishes with their Number of Inhabitants are as follow.

Slait	1,868	Kilmuir	1,900
Strath	1,200	Diurnish	3,600
Bracadale	3,333	Portree	1,466
Snizort	1,700		

The whole Inhabitants of Sky amount then to 15,067 and upon comparing this number with the Number of Acres, the Island contains 16 Acres for each Inhabitant. It sent about 500 Men to the late War, who every where supported the Character of a warlike, faithfull, and high Spirited People.

They belong to the three Clans of Macdonalds, Macleods and Mackinnons, and are all Protestants.

Here Mr Maccaskile Surgeon began the Salutary Practice of Inoculation ann: 1763. Between the first of November in that year and the first of September 1764 he inoculated in the Isle of Skye 287 Persons, of whom only 3 died. At the same Time Mr Maclean the Surgeon inoculated 11 which all lived, and Mr Macleod, Surgeon inoculated 26 of whom 2 died.

In the Parish of Glenelg on the main Land, adjacent to Sky, Mr Maccaskile inoculated during the same Period, 217 Persons, 34 of whom were men and women, and of these, only one died. Some of them who had no sensible Fever, nor any visible Eruption, had a swelling in the axillary Glands of one or both Arms, and in some Cases, this Swelling suppurated and healed in an easy manner. It is to be observed, that the last Time the Small Pox visited the Parish of Glenelg, which was an. 1754, of 200 Persons who were seized, 140 died.

Face of the Country

The Isle of Sky contains no where any Plain Ground of considerable Extent, but in most places towards the Sea, there are large Tracts of arable Land in a shelving Situation, intermixed with small Hills and Glens.

The Quillin Mountains, which are amongst the highest in the British Isles, are situated upon the West Coast, about the middle of the Island. These Mountains, or rather Sceletons of Mountains, appear at a Distance, like a huge Congeries of Buildings and Spires in Ruins; and upon approaching their Summits, all is sharp, ragged and naked, without either Earth or Herbage. Further North, the West Coast rises in a Train of Mountains called by the Sailors, Macleods Tables, from their singular Shape, being each of them pyramidal and flat at the Top, like a truncated Cone.

Upon the East side of the Island, there are also considerable Mountains, but very differently shaped from any of the former, and composed of very different Materials. They consist chiefly of Columnar Whinstone, and are generally flat at Top and abrupt and perpendicular on one Side. This is the Appearance of the Hills at the Giants Causeway in Ireland, of Salisbury Hill at Edinburgh, of the Hill which lies to the North of Stirling, and of many others in the Islands of Mull and Canna. All the Hills of this Figure, are composed of that sort of Whinstone, which generally in some degree or other, affect a Columnar Shape, and is disposed in huge Strata nearly inclined to the Horizon. Of this kind of Stone, there is a most remarkable Column, upon one of these eastern Mountains of Sky, whose stricking Appearance is to be observed at Sea, for many a League. It is called by the People of the Country the Pota Stoir,[4] and is situated upon an Angle or Edge of the Mountain some hundreds of Feet below its Summit. It is an Obelisk, about 100 Feet high, and not above 30 or 40 Feet Diameter at the Base, from which, it tapers gradually to the Top. It stands quite detatched from the Mountain, and what is most remarkable, it is not perpendicular, but juts out from the Side of the Mountain at a considerable Angle.

The Country in general is very destitute of Trees yet formerly it has been filled with Wood, of which there are still some considerable Remains, and the Growth of Trees in several Places, makes it evident, that the want of excellent Timber in this Island is owing to no Defect either in Soil or Climate. At Armadil in Slait, an old Seat of the Mackdonald Family, there is a Garden of very good Fruit Trees, and in the Plantation around the Place, there are many

Ash Trees of as vigorous a Growth and as large a Size, as are to be seen in any Part of Scotland. The Wood of Dunscaich in Slait is also very considerable and thriving, consisting of Birch, Oack, Ash, Alder, Rowan, Holly, Hazel and the Grey Willow. Here I measured an Alder which was 7 Feet in Circumference, at the Height of 4 Feet above the Ground. Adjacent to this Wood, upon an inaccessible Precipice on the Sea Shore, stands the ruined Castle of Dunscaich, an antient Seat of the Macdonald Family, and originally the Fortress of Cuchullin the chief of this Isle of Mist.[5] Upon the Green adjoining to the Castle, there is a Rock, to which, according to Tradition, his Dog Luath celebrated in the Poems of Oscian, used to be chained.

The Moss above the Church of Portree, consisting of some thousands of Acres, is bordered on one Side, by an old wood which occupies above 300 Acres. It consists chiefly of Birch, Hazel, Alder, Hagberry, and water Elder, but contains no good Trees, and in its present State, can never turn to much Account. It stands however upon a good Woodland Soil, and being extremely sparse, with many vacant Spaces, was it inclosed, and these Spaces planted with proper Forest Trees, a Valuable Plantation might be very soon and easily reared; as the old Wood, without incumbering would be sufficient to shelter the young Trees, and without some such shelter it is in vain to attempt the raising of Wood, in this or in any other of the Islands.

The extensive Moss and Heath in the Neighbourhood of this Wood, should also be totally planted with Scots Firs, for which it is exceedingly well adapted. Though at present quite unprofitable, it might in 20 years, be converted by this means, into the most valuable Tract in the Island, considering the high Price of Wood, and the great Scarcity of it in that Country, for every domestick Purpose.

On the North side of the Bay of Oransay there is also a Tract of Land of about 150 Acres, with a good deal of natural Wood upon it, and the remains of some very large Trees of Ash, Birch, Alder, Rowan and Hazel, but all the young Growth miserably stunted by the Grazing of the Cattle. Adjacent to Mackinnons old Castle[6] there are also about 200 Acres of Coppice, chiefly of Ash and Birch, but all open and so eat down by the Cattle, that not a Plant of them has been suffered to arrive to a Tree. By fencing these Tracts they soon would become valuable Woods. They are both surrounded for a considerable way by the Sea, and the compleating their Inclosure, would be a matter of great Advantage to the Proprietors, and of Conveniency to the Country.

Soil and Climate

There are few places in the Island, in which either Clay or Sand predominate greatly in the Soil, but there are extensive Tracts of Fertile loamy Soil, in most of its Districts, which afford excellent Crops both of Corn and Grass. In all the Farms on the Sea Shore there are Fields, which beyond all Memory, have been kept in Tillage affording every Season a Crop either of Oats or Bear, without any other assistance than a Covering of Sea Weeds once in Two years. The

Weighty Crops to be seen on the Fields under this sort of managment are indeed Surprising, and they are remarkable for being more free from Weeds, than any others perhaps in Scotland, which is no doubt one principle Cause of their Luxuriancy, and a natural Consequence of this Train of Culture.

There is nothing so unfavourable here to the Crops raised by Tillage, as the autumnal Rains, which are heavy and sometimes uninterrupted during that Season. The Wind blowing almost the whole year from between the South and West, the Mountains, which stretch along the Coast of the Island in that Quarter, attract and break the Clouds, and produce more Rain perhaps than in most other places. The Country of Strath in particular, about KilChrist, lying immediately under the Quillin Mountains, to the Eastward, would be found upon Trial, if I mistake not, to exceed Lancashire, Argyllshire, and every other part of the British Islands, in Quantity of Rain.

They suffer but little from Frost in this Island, during Winter, and the Degrees of Cold are never so great in that Season, as upon the Continent of Scotland. The first Snow I saw in the Highlands was upon the Evening of the 27th of September which covered all the high Country in Sky, and in the adjacent Continent. Next Day at Noon, it was entirely dissolved in Sky but it continued to ly during that and several succeeding Days, upon the Mountains of the main Land, though much inferior in Height to those of Sky which had been covered with Snow at the same Time. To the same Purpose, having visited a Plantation of american and other exotick Trees, formed by Sir James Macdonald in his Garden at Armadil, I observed, that they had not suffered in their Shoots by Frost in the preceeding Winters, as they always do with us upon the main Land, in consequence of which, they were more thriving and Luxuriant than any Trees of the same kinds to be seen in the Gardens of the South of Scotland.

Price of Commodities

	£	s	d
The Boll of Oat Meal in Sky, for 12 years past, has not sold above	0	11	0
Note. The Sky Boll of Meal weighs rather more than 10 stone, whereas that of Lithgow weighs only 8.			
The Cattle that go annually in Droves to Crieff Fair, sell at an Average, in the Country, at	1	16	0
Note. The Price of driving to Crieff is about 3sh. a Head.			
The Grasing of Cow throught the year	0	6	8

Price of Labour

Wages of a Ploughman for the whole year	1	5	0
Victuals and Wages of a Labourer p. Week	0	3	0
Note. The Labourers wages for a Week is a Merk Scots or 13d, and for his Meat during that time, he receives a Peck and an half of Meal, the Value of which is generally less than two shillings.			

Exports and Imports

	£	s	d
Sky exports annually above 3,000 Black Cattle, which at 1£ 16sh. p. Head amounts to	5400	0	0
About 200 Horses at 4£ each	800	0	0
Two hundred Ton of Kelp at 3£ 15sh. p. Ton	750	0	0
Five hundred and sixteen Barrels of Herrings at 1£ p. Barrel	516	0	0
Four Ton of Dried Cod, in Value about	70	0	0
	7536	0	0
There are only 4 or 5 Stills in the whole Island, so that they import all their Aquavitae from Ferntosh to the yearly Extent of above	1500	0	0

They have Wool to serve themselves, but export none. There is but little Lint sown in the Island, and they buy from other Countries almost all their Linen.

There are great Numbers of open Boats, but not a decked Vessel of any kind in all the Island.

AGRICULTURE

Tenants

The Possessors of Land here, as in most other parts of the Highlands, are of three different kinds, Tacksmen, Tenants and Subtenants. The Tacksmen hold their Land of the Proprietor by Lease; the Tenants hold their Farms without any Lease at the Will of the Landlord; and the Subtenants have small Possessions of Land let out to them from year to year, by the Tacksmen and Tenants.

Most part of the Island is in the Hands of the Tacksmen, who are generally Relations of the Chieftain, and many of them Men of Education. The Farms they possess are from £15 to £55 a year. The Tenants are of a lower Class, and their Possessions run from 10 to £20 p. annum. The Subtenants have small Parcels of Land let to them by the Tenants and Tacksmen, from 15sh. to 40sh, of yearly Value.

A Farm of £30 a year will have 10 such Subtenants upon it, each of whom has a Family: and besides these, 8 Men Servants, 2 Boys, and 6 Women. Such a Number of People, living by Agriculture, upon so small a Property, is not to be found perhaps anywhere else.

The Duration of the Leases hitherto granted has been from 7 to 19 years.

Grain

The only Grains sown in Sky are Grey Oats, Bear and Rye. They have not yet got into the Practice of sowing white Oats, and by this neglect they have not so much Grain by a third part, as the Country might otherwise afford. They urge in Excuse for this, that the Grey Oats are capable of standing bad

Weather much better than the white, and particularly, are not so easily shaken by their Winds which are so high and frequent in Harvest. Mr Macleod however, the Sheriff Substitute in the Country,[7] sowed last year, white and grey Oats in the same Field, for an Experiment. They ripened at the same Time, and he was not sensible, that the white Oats were any more hurt or shaken by the Winds than the other.

The Bear of South and North Wist is remarkable for being much thinner in the Husk, and for yeilding a greater Proportion of Meal, than that of Sky, or any part of the main Land where the Soil is not Sandy.

Here, as in all the other Islands, the Farmers are much to blame, for being too late in sowing their Grain, by which means, they did not begin their Bear Harvest this year till the 1st of September, and frequently it is not even so early as this. The Hazard to which the Crop is exposed by the autumnal Rains, is here the common Complaint, and yet by an atatchment to an idle piece of Superstition, they scruple not to retard both the sowing and reaping of their Grain, as it is a Custom unvariably observed, never to begin either to sow or to reap, except on a Tuesday.

No Pease, Beans, Turnips, Clover or Rye Grass are cultivated without which, their Agriculture must remain in the most imperfect State, and so ignorant are the People of these green Crops, that old Macdonald of Kingsbury, having once raised a Field of Pease, gave out in order to save them from Depredation, that it was a poisonous Plant he had sown, to kill the Foxes.

Hay

The sowing of Rye Grass and Clover would be the best Remedy for that Scarcity of Winter Provender, which is so fatal to the Cattle in this Country; but the Farmers are positive in alledging, that these sown Grasses could not be made into Hay because of the Rains. Wind and Rain, and the Badness of the Climate, is the Universal Objection over all the Islands, against any Innovation in Husbandry. Yet though I was among them four Months, from the first of June to the first of October, the most material Difference I found in the Climate from the Rest of Scotland was this, that in all that Time, there was not the smallest Degree of Frost, except in the Night between the 26th and 27th of September, which is rarely the Case in the Southern parts of Scotland. The Winds and Rains may be somewhat more prevalent and yet the Climate may answer well enough with an industrious People, for the Production of a Crop of Hay from sown Grasses.

The first natural Hay was made in Sky just 30 years ago, and since that Time, the Quantity of cultivated Land has been greatly enlarged by the Planting of Potatoes. By these Means, both the Summer Grass and the Winter Forage has been so far increased, that the Island does at present export one third more black Cattle, and of a larger Size, than before that Period. And yet the Hay made in the Island is sufficient only to fodder their Stirks in Winter. All their aged Black Cattle and Horses run abroad the whole Winter, with out receiving a Mouthfull of dry Forage.

It is scarce to be credited, that in a Country where Cattle is the chief Production, and where there is the greatest Difficulty to support them in Winter, the Inhabitants should burn their Provender. Yet this is really the Case over all the Highlands and Islands in the Manufacture of their Graidin Bread, in which the best part of the Straw is burnt, in order to dry and prepare the Corn for Grinding. The Practice received this year the first Check from Sir James Macdonald, who has given Orders, that after Martinmass next it should be no longer followed on his Estates, but that all the Corn shall be threshed and Kiln dried, as in other places.

Cattle

If a Farmer in Sky keeps 160 Black Cattle upon his Farm, the number of Horses upon it usually amount to 20, the Proportion being as 1 to 8: but the Horses are more numerous in Proportion, upon smaller Farms, being to the black Cattle as 1 to 6. On a Farm of the above Extent, containing 160 black Cattle, there will be 120 Sheep and 20 Goats. These are the general Proportions of the Cattle in Sky, but over all the long Island the Horses are much more numerous.

If the Cows calve before the first of March, it will be sometimes a Month or Six Weeks before they have Milk Sufficient to feed the Calves. The best Cows in the Island afford only a Scots Quart of Milk a Day, of which the Calf gets a Choppin in the morning, and the same Quantity in the Evening, but many of them yeild not daily above a Pint of Milk.

One of the best and one of the worst Milk Cows yeild together, during the Summer Season about 2 Stone of Butter and 4 Stone of Cheese, sometimes in all 7 Stone, but seldom Eight. The Butter they afford is always one third of the Cheese.

The only Reason given for housing their Sheep is to preserve them from the Fox. Some Weather[8] Sheep, being stronger than the others, are allowed to keep abroad in the high, rocky Mountains, where they are so fortified, that the Fox dares not meddle with them; and the Wool of these Sheep is reckoned much more valuable than what is afforded by the Sheep that are housed.

The Gentlemen in Sky did this year enter into a Resolution to extirpate the Fox, and for this Purpose, offered a Premium of three shillings for every Fox that was destroyed. In consequence of this Offer, no less than 112 Foxes were killed this year, in the Country of Trotterness alone.

They mark their Sheep on the Horn, with a red hot Iron having a Letter upon it, and also by cutting the Ear.

Their best Land, which bears a Crop every year, with little or no Manure, is accounted more profitable in Grain than in Grass. But if they are oblidged to manure for a Crop of Oats, the Ground is reckoned more profitable in Grass.

Tillage

The Farmers here put 4 Horses in their Plough, which are yoked abreast, in a very akward Manner. One man drives it, another holds it, and a third follows, to lay down the Turf that is torn off. The want of a proper Mold Board, is the Reason, why the Labour of this additional Man is required to finish the Furrow. So innatentive are the Inhabitants here, to the Mechanism of their Instruments, and to the Value of human Labour.

Before the Introduction of Potatoes, no Care was taken to reclaim any untillaged Earth, but now a great deal of waste Land is yearly broke up, and planted with that Root, in lazy Beds. They always take two and sometimes three Crops of Potatoes off such Land; each Crop being manured either with Dung or Sea Ware. After this they take a Crop of Bear which is also manured with Sea Ware, and then two Crops of Oats without Manure. And when the Soil is thus exhausted, rather than reclaimed, it is left to run to natural Grass.

It is observed, that such wild Land affords a much better Crop of Bear, after the first, than after the second or third Crop of Potatoes, which shows, that this Root is not such a meliorating Crop as is commonly imagined.

Their common Arable Land affords a good Crop of Bear, when manured with Sea Ware, and next, a tolerable Crop of Oats. After which, they are not sensible of the Operation of this Manure in the Soil; yet they sow a second Crop of Oats, which are generally very poor and preserved for Seed Corn. For this is the prevailing and erroneous Practice in Sky, to use the worst of their Grain for the Seed.

The Inhabitants observe, that every fourth Crop in Sky is almost entirely lost, by the lateness of the Harvest and the Inclemency of the Weather. They are rather apt indeed to aggravate this Circumstance as an Apology for their want of Industry in Agriculture, yet it is certainly so far true, as to make it evident, that their Country is better adapted for yeilding Grass, than Grain. Instead of discouraging their Industry, the Observation therefore directs them not to exhaust their Lands, as they do at present with Crops of Corn, but to render their Tillage and their Grain, entirely subservient to the Production of Grass.

Carschrome

A great part of the Land in Sky, instead of being ploughed by Cattle, is cultivated by human Labour; and dug with the Carschrome, or crooked Spade.

A Plough with 4 Horses and three Men labours as much Land in five Days, as will sow a Boll of Bear, or 5 Firlots of Oats. And the same Quantity of Land is dug by 12 Men in the same Time.

The expence of the Plough to the Farmer, is estimate at 6sh. 9d p. Week; and the Labour of 12 Men at 19sh. p. Week.

A Labourer in the Country of Strath will dig as much Ground with the Carschrome in a Day as will sow a Peck of Oats. And if he works assiduously from about Christmas to the end of April, he will cultivate Land sufficient for sowing 5 Bolls.

The Bear upon the delved Land is sown extremely thin, so that a Man takes twice as much Time to dig what will sow a Peck of that Grain, than of Oats. For the Ground that sows a Boll of Oats, will sow only half a Boll of Bear.

If a Boll of Bear raised with the Plough in good Land, yeilds 12 Bolls; raised with the Spade, it would produce 16 Bolls, and in poorer Land, the Proportion is still larger in Favour of the Spade.

In poor lay Land, a Boll of Oats raised with the Plough will bring only 3 Bolls but if raised with the Spade, it will produce 5 Bolls.

But in such Land, the third Crop after the Plough, is always better than the third Crop after the Spade.

It appears in general, that a Field laboured with the Carschrome affords usually, one third more Crop, than if laboured with Plough. Poor Land will afford one half more. But then it must be noticed, that their Land is very imperfectly and scarce half laboured, with the Plough, as their whole Tillage consists only of turning the Clod. The Culture with the Spade, is three Times more Expensive, than with the Plough and the return of one third more Crop, can scarce be an equivalent for this great Difference of Expence.

The Carschrome is a beneficial Instrument, in cultivating those Rocky Tracts in the Highlands, which are innaccessible to the Plough, it is also usefull to the numerous small Subtenants, who having no Horse, cannot otherwise get their little Patch of Ground cultivated. These advantages however are nothing to what the Publick reaps by its Influence on Population. Were it not for this happy Consequence, it is an Instrument which ought to be laid entirely aside, or at least, never to be used, where the Plough can travel.

As an Instance of the extraordinary Produce from Grain sown upon Ground cultivated with the Carschrome, a Farmer in the Parish of Bracadale, in the year 1763, being in Scarcity of Seed Bear, sowed five Lippies extremely thin upon rich delved Land. From this he had 5 Bolls in Return, which amounts to 64 Fold.

MANUFACTURE

Kelp

Besides the making of Kelp, there is Scarce any thing in Sky, that can be called Manufacture. The Island produces about 200 Ton annually yet this is but a small Quantity compared to what it might produce with proper Improvement.

The Planting of Sea Weeds is the Improvement here meant. The most simple of all kinds of Cultivation, but if I mistake not, would turn out the most profitable.

All submarine Plants when burnt produce the lixivial Salt called Kelp, so necessary in many extensive Manufactures, and which already brings a great Sum of Money annually to the Western Coasts of Scotland. But nine Tenths of all the Kelp manufactured in the Hebrides, are produced from the three following Plants.

FUCUS serratus. Linn.
vescculosus Linn.
nodosus. Linn.

These three Plants cannot grow either upon Sand or Sleech, but must always be rooted upon Stone. They generally cover all the fast Rocks within ordinary Flood mark, but the greatest Crop of them is to be observed where a Sandy or Sleechy Shore, is thick covered with loose Rocks and Stones of such a Size, as to be seldom or never moved by the Violence of the Waters. It is also to be noticed, that they are of a quicker and more vigorous Growth, according as they are situated near the Mark of the lowest Ebb; and gradually from a less luxuriant Crop, as they Approach Flood mark. Their Growth also is greatly promoted by Shelter; for they arrive at a larger Size, in a Landlocked Bay where the Water is calm, than upon an exposed Shore.

To cover the Shores, especially near the Mark of Ebb, with loose Stones from 50lb to 200 Weight, is all that is required, to raise these profitable Plants in great Abundance. The Sea is everywhere full of their Seeds, and they adhaere to and grow upon every Stone, capable of lying in the Sea Water, without Mouldering.

There are none of the Hebrides, in which, the Quantity of Kelp might not be greatly augmented by this Improvement and in Sky in particular, it might be prosecuted to a great Extent. In the Lochs of Fallart, Arnisort, Snizort, Bracadale, Slapan and Eyshort, there are some thousands of Acres, on which no Sea Weeds grow at present, but which might all be planted in this manner for the Production of Kelp. The Sides of these vast Lochs, like almost all the other Shores in the Highlands, are thick covered with loose Rocks and Stones fit for the Purpose, and all the Trouble and Expence attending this Improvement, is to Carry them off the Ground, a few hundred yards within Floodmark.

The Profit attending this simple Piece of Improvement, must be very extraordinary; yet it could not be exactly ascertained as in all the Islands, I could not find an Accurate Answer to this Question how much Kelp is produced from an Acre of Sea Weeds. The Islanders employed in the Manufacture have no Idea of an Acre, and they were as much at a Loss, as to the Weight of Kelp, producible from any certain Weight or Quantity of Sea Weeds.

I had the Pleasure of finding this proposed Cultivation of Sea Weeds, admitted by some of the most intelligent Gentlemen in the Western Islands, both as practicable and highly profitable and upon Enquiring into the most proper Method of carrying it into Execution, they agreed in this. That if the great Proprietors of the Islands, who live all at a Distance, did not think proper to engage in the Trouble and expence of this Improvement; their Tenants might plant the Shores, with Stones, in the manner described above; upon the Assurance of receiving from them three Crops of Sea Weeds, Rent free which would require about 12 years. In this way the Landlords at the Expiration of 12 years, might have the Rental of their Estates greatly increased, without any Trouble or Expence whatever.

Some People in the Country of Arisaig, opposite to Sky, manufactured in the year 1764, 157 Barrels of Fern Ashes, for which a Gentleman in Sky paid 7 shillings p. Barrel and exported them to Liverpool. A great Quantity of such Ashes might be produced in Sky especially in the Parish of Portree. The Farmers Profit upon this Article is not confined to the Sale of the Ashes. By the Destruction of the Fern, his Pasturage also is greatly increased and improved.

The Linen Manufacture is not yet introduced into Sky. There is but little Linen of any kind made by the Inhabitants and they bring from other Countries the greatest part of what is required for their own Consumption, yet of late, they have several Times sown some small Quantities of foreign Lintseed, from which they had a great Crop of Lint, measuring three feet long, exclusive of the Root and Panicle.

FISHERY

Cod

The valuable Cod Fishery about this Island, is inexcusably neglected, both by the Inhabitants, and the Publick. There are Cod Banks off most parts of the Island, particularly between Sleat, and the Countries of Knoidart and Arisaig upon the main Land. Large Cod are likewise Caught midway between Sleat and the Isle of Rum, in 24 Fathom water, when any Boats happen to Fish there. But the best known Bank about the Island is that which reaches from Dunvegan Head, towards Roudil in the Harris. It reaches within a League of Dunvegan Head, and extends near to the Middle of the Channel. It stretches N.E. and S.W. It is 16 Fathom deep, and has 60 Fathom Water on each Side of it. The Inhabitants sometimes cure a little Cod from this Bank, but it is only when they meet accidentally with a Quantity of Salt for the Purpose.

Herring

The Herrings vary their Residence, during the Spawning Season in different years; yet usually they are for a few years constant to the same Place. The Highland Lochs, or embayed Arms of the Sea, are the Places in which they spawn, and wherever they take up their Residence for this Purpose, there is the Seat of the Winter Fishery.

During five years, from 1759 to 1763, the Herrings spawned in the Lochs of Sky, and especially in Loch Slapan and Bracadale, where the Busses upon the Bounty resorted for the Winter Fishery. Into these Lochs the Fish entered about the Beginning of November and continued Stationary for several Weeks, during which Time, one Buss has been known to take and cure 14 Lasts of Herring in 48 Hours.

The following Observation, though little attended to, by the Herring Fishers, may be of great Use, in directing them to the Seat of the Winter Fishery. The Herrings do seldom or never visit in the Spawning Season, or in Winter, those places they frequented, in the Summer and autumnal Months. They always appear among the Hebrides about the beginning of July, yet during the 5 years above mentioned, though they entered many others of the Highland Lochs, they never were seen in Loch Slapan or Bracadale, till the Spawning Season, about the first of November.

Though the Herring Fishery continued so many years in Sky, it was entirely [neglected] by the Inhabitants, and only pursued by the Bounty Vessels. During this Period, the whole Island might have been enriched by the Fishery, but the Opportunity was lost for the Want of Salt and Casks and year past after year without any Attempt by the Inhabitants to procure them.

Some Individuals at last, with great Difficulty, procured a Quantity of these Materials, and Set about the Fishery. Mr Donald Macleod in Fiorlag, upon Loch Bracadale, made in the year 1763, during the Winter 20 Lasts of Herring, and exported them to Dublin, which was more than was taken in Sky, that Season, by any Buss in the Fleet.

During the years that the Herrings were in Loch Slapan and Bracadale in Winter, they always visited the Loch of Dunvegan in Summer. Here they appeared in July and August, when in the greatest Perfection, but the People of Sky, though furnished with Boats and Nets, and with sufficient Skill both in catching and curing them, having neither Salt nor Cask, took no more of them, than what were consumed fresh.

At length in the year 1764 Mr Alexander Morison Taksman of Skiniden near Dunvegan, having procured Salt and Cask, began in the Spring, to fish for Cod and Ling, of which he cured and exported 4 Ton. Against the 6th of July, the Herrings appeared in the Loch, when he, and Mr James Macdonald Postmaster at Dunvegan, set the Country People to Work, from whom they purchased the Herrings at 6d p. Hundred. Of these, they cured before the 1st of September, 276 Barrels, which they exported to Newry.

These two Gentlemen have, at their own Expence established a Cooper at Dunvegan, so that the Command of Salt, is now the only thing wanted to render that little Port considerable in the Fishery. It is the most centrical and proper Place in all the Hebrides, for establishing a Magazine of Materials for the Fishery.

Salmon

It is remarkable here, as in all the other Western Islands, that the Salmon enter Rivulets and Brooks of a much smaller Size, than they ever appear in upon the Coast of Scotland or England. This Fish is to be found in above 20 Brooks in Sky, some of which are so inconsiderable that it is surprising how a Salmon should enter them. The Two small Rivers of Stot and Kilmartin in Trotternish, are the only ones however that afford them in any Quantity, and from those, Two Lasts of Salmon are sometimes taken, which are cured and exported by the Inhabitants.

The River of Kilmartin and the River of Ord in Slate, do also contain the Pearl Muscle in great Abundance, and the Pearls it affords, are many of them of an excellant Quality. It was thought that some Englishmen who came here on Purpose, in the year 1763, collected Pearls out of these Rivers to a great amount. But they taught the Inhabitants the manner of fishing for them which they now practise with pretty good Success.

NATURAL PRODUCTIONS

Coal

I found an Appearance of Coal; at two Different Places in Sky. The first at Rhigouan in the Farm of Struhan, on the North Side of Loch Bracadale in Macleods Country. Here there is a small seam of Coal of Six Inches, by the Side of a Brook, having a Staple of Earth above it 4 Feet thick. Below it, there is a blackish blue Vitriolick Earth, and under that, a hard Bastard Sandstone. Another Seam of the same kind appears in the Rocks on the South Side of the Loch of Portree.

Limestone

There is Limestone in several parts of the Country of Trotternish, and at Braccis in Strath, along the Sea Shore, there are extensive Tracts of coarse Limestone filled with petrified Shells, and with Cornua Ammonis, a Figured Fossil, which has not yet been discovered anywhere else in Scotland. These Rocks ly all horizontal and strech East and West, but are intersected by Whinrock Dykes, from one to four Feet broad, which run South and North, inclined to the Horizon at an Angle of above 80 Degrees.

There are also Strata of very good Freestone in several parts of the Island.

Statuary Marble

There is a pure white Marble of a fine Grain, found in two different places in the Country of Strath in this Island. The one near the Church of Kil-christ, and the other about 2 Miles distant at the Village of Torrin upon Loch Slapan, a land locked Arm of the Sea, which is an excellent Harbour.

There are extensive Strata of it at both places, and the Minister's House of the Parish of Strath, which stands near the Church of Kil-christ, is wholly built of it. The Strata in which it is disposed as they appear at the Surface, are from one to three feet thick, very solid and entire, without Cracks or Fissures, so that it might be raised in very large Blocks, sufficient for any Purpose of Architecture. How deep these Strata extend is not known, as little more than their Surface has hitherto been uncovered or Quarried. Where they are fully exposed to the Weather, the Surface becomes blackish, as the antient Statuary

Marble does in the same Situation. But where the Surface is screened from the Violence of the Weather, it assumes that mild Cream coloured Tint, observable in the fine antique Statues, which I take to be of the very same sort of Marble with this.

The modern Artists distinguish between the Parian and Statuary Marble, though with Naturalists, they are the same Species. The Parian admits of the most bright glossey Surface, in a thin Plate; it is half transparent, and one can see a great way into it, when highly polished. The Statuary again, is more opake, of a milder white Colour, softer and more easily wrought, yet susceptible of as fine a Polish, and judged more advantageous and valuable for Statues.

Both these sorts of Marble, are to be seen in great Abundance, among the antique Statues; but I have observed that the Bustos are generally of the former, and the full length Statues of the latter kind.

Upon a Comparison with the antique Statues, it has been found, that this Sky Marble is the same with the antique Statuary, or at least approaches nearer to it, than any other Marble at present known to, or wrought by the Moderns. For the whole Grecian Marble from Paros and Antiparos and that of Saligno, Carara, and Padua, which are at present wrought by the European Statuaries, are all of the Parian kind, the Quarries of the antique Statuary being unknown.

From the View I had of the Strata of this Marble, I have strong Hopes, of its being found in the largest Masses to a great Depth, and of a pure white, without Blemishes or Stains, such, as are not at present to be obtained, even from Italy. The finest Statues of Roubilliac and Rysbrack of Carara Marble, being greatly blemished with Spots and Veins of other Colours.

The Marble Cutters, who have dressed some Pieces of it, are greatly pleased with it. They never saw a Marble, that wrought more kindly, as they express it, with the Tool or that took a finer Arras. And that in a large Mass it would still admit of a finer Polish, than what they could put upon such small Specimens of it, as I brought from the Island.

Other Marbles

In the neighbourhood of the above Statuary Marble, there is another sort to be found in very great Quantities, for there is a Hill about 500 Feet high, that is almost wholly composed of it. The Ground of it is white, with Spots of a green coloured Spar, which does not however prevent its taking a very fine Polish. I brought away with me only one Specimen of it, as I did not apprehend it to be so fine a Stone, as I now find it to be, upon seeing it polished.

Another black and white Marble I found in the Country of Strath, where I observed several deep Strata of it. It is of a very unpromising Appearance when rough, but when dressed, is a Stone of great Beauty. It works easily yet takes a finer Polish, than that of most Marbles; its Colours become vivid upon polishing, and are disposed in large Spaces.

Upon the Mountain S.E. from Kil-christ in Strath, I found also another Marble of great Merit, disposed in thick and extensive Strata. It very much resembles, and is undoubtedly equal both in Colours and Polish to the Dove Coloured Italian Marbles, which are veined with white.

There is not by all Accounts, any Spot in Europe, north of Italy, in which, there is found Marbles of so much Beauty, of so great Variety, and in such Quantity, as in this Country of Strath. Like the Italian Marbles, they are all calcarious, and afford the purest Lime.

Huana

This is a very Singular Sort of Earth found in the Country of Strath. It is purely calcarious and has been used Successfully in some small Trials as a Manure. It is therefore considered by the Inhabitants as Marle. No Marle can indeed be superior to it, for the Purposes of Manure, yet it is a very different Earth from all the kinds of Marle hitherto discovered in Britain.

It is found in several places not far from the Statuary Marble, above described. It is disposed in thick Strata, reaching near to the [surface] of the Earth, and in the same Position as the Marble. It is of a pure white Colour, and of a rough, friable, powdery Substance, when dry; exactly resembling the Substance of the Marble when reduced to Powder. It is from the Strata of this Earth, that the Strata of the white Marble are evidently found. Though it is of the greatest Value as a Manure it has hitherto been shamefully neglected. It is to be had in inexhaustible Quantity, and at the easiest Rate, and is capable to enrich to a high Degree, all the adjacent Country.

Smectis[9]

I was very glad to find this Fossile, which is commonly called Spanish Chalk, in great Abundance in the Isle of Sky, as it is a very rare one, and so usefull for several mechanical Purposes as to be an Article of Commerce.

It is commonly used, everywhere, as a Detergent for cleaning and scouring Cloths, and there is a considerable Quantity of it imported annually from abroad. The consumption of it for this Purpose might render the raising of it in Sky, advantageous to the Proprietor. But its great Excellency in Manufacture of China, is an Article of much greater Consideration.

This is precisely the Earth adapted to form the most elegant and most perfect China Ware, and from all that I have been able to learn of the eastern Manufacture, I judge it to be the very Substance, which is the Basis of the oldest and finest Porcellane.

The best China hitherto manufactured in England has been formed from the Soap Rock of Cornwal, a Talky Earth of the same kind, though not near so fine. But so far as I have been able to learn, there has been little or none manufactured from it of late, because of its Scarcity. Instead of this, all the

English Manufactures of China at present, are carried on with a fine apyrous Clay, found at Stourbridge and other places. And indeed, if some Accounts from China are to be depended on, it is a Clay of the same Nature of which at least all the coarser China is formed, that is at present brought from the East.

There is no Doubt however, but that a Talc, such as the Soap Rock, is capable of affording a finer Porcellane, than any Clay whatever, and I have as little Doubt, that this Talc of Sky, is superior to the Soap Rock. It is of a most pure and impalpable Substance, of itself, the most unalterable in the Fire perhaps, of any Fossile, Gold only excepted. It is white, with a Degree of Transparency and untinged by any extrinsick Mineral Substance. Whereas, the Soap rock is always of a coarser Substance, and generally tinged more or less, with red, brown, or yellow Colours, which are very detrimental.

The fine Talc here described, appears in several Places of the Isle of Sky, where it might be had in considerable Quantitys. I brought a Barrel of it from thence, with a view to have it tried in the China Manufacture, but have not yet had an Opportunity.

Black Lead

The great Scarcity of this Fossile is the reason why it is so little known and so imperfectly described by the Mineral Writers. The most remarkable Place for it abroad, is the Country of Hesse, and the only considerable Mine of it in the World, is at Keswick in Cumberland, from whence all the other Nations of Europe are supplied with their Pencils.

Upon the Shore of Glenelg opposite to Sky, I found two different Veins of this Metal about two Miles distant from each other, and another very promising Appearance of it in the Country of Glengary. In each of these Places, the Metal appears at day, and gives great Encouragement for pursuing a black Lead Mine, which might turn out both profitable to Adventurers, and Advantageous to the Publick.

The three principal Uses of black Lead, are the Manufacture of Pencils and Crucibles, and its removing the Friction of Wood Machines, preferably to any other Substance.

The finest black Lead for Pencils sells in Retail, at upwards of 20sh. p. lb and the Powder produced by sawing the Pencils sells at the Rate of 250£ p. Ton, for making Crucibles.

The Black Lead I found in these Veins, would not answer for fine Pencils, not being of so fine a Quality, as what lies probably at a greater Depth. But it is perfectly well adapted for Machines and for making Crucibles, for which Purposes, it would bring a high Price.

The Quantity of Black Lead afforded by the Mine in Cumberland, for making Crucibles is so inconsiderable, that there are 50,000 black Lead Crucibles imported annually into Britain from Passau, the only Place in Germany where they are made. But the Opening of Mines at the above Places in the Highlands would no doubt put an immediate Stop to this Importation.

Amiantus

In Loch Huron, opposite to Sky, there is a Species of Amiantus in vast Quantities. Sir Andrew Balfour[10] and Sir Robert Sibbald[11] in the last Century had Specimens of this Fossile from the same Place, but both of them acquiesced in the Traditional Opinion of the Natives of the Country, who all suppose it to be petrified Holly, a Wood which grows naturally in abundance upon the Banks of the River where it is found; though a genuine Amiantus, it has indeed a most exact Resemblance of petrified Wood, in its Colour and Structure, yet upon a narrow View of its Fibres, it is easy to discern, that they never have belonged to any Plant.

It is of a very pure impalpable Substance, so soft as to be easily reduced to Powder, and bids fair for being a valuable Material in the Manufacture of China.

EIGG

EIG

THE Island of Eig, called by the Latin Writers Egea, is situated about 6 Leagues South from the Isle of Sky, and lies, in Invernesshire, though its three neighbouring Islands of Rum, Muck and Canna belong to Argyllshire. It rises towards the West, into several Rocky Hills, of which the highest may be about 7 or 800 Feet above the Level of the Sea; but from these, it shelves towards the East, where there are many fine Fields both of Grass and Corn.

It is 4 computed Miles long and 2 broad, but supposing the length to be only 5 English miles and its breadth 3, it then contains 9,600 english Acres. The present Rent is £152 so that it is let for about 3d. p. Acre. Excepting a small part, in the Possession of Macdonald of Morer,[1] the whole Island belongs to Clanronald,[2] and is all inhabited by his Macdonalds or by People belonging to the inferior Tribes of his Clan, which have other Names, as Maccaskil, Mackinish, Mackeachen, Macleolan, Mackisaac, and Maccormic.

The Island contains 461 Inhabitants, and about 20 Acres for each Person. The Number of Protestants amounts only to 74; the People here having always been kept firm in the popish Perswation, by the Residence of a Priest among them. There is no School in the Island, and of all the Inhabitants there are only 24, who can read English, who are mostly Protestants.

The only Harbour in the Island, is a Creek upon the South east Side, landlocked by a small Islet, with a narrow Entry on each Side, not to be attempted without a Pilot. The South west and Northwest Coast, is composed of a singular Species of white Cliffery Rock, which is hollowed out into Caves in many Places, by the Force of the Waves and Weather. One of these Caves is so large as to be capable of containing many hundreds of People, and indeed the whole Inhabitants of the Island perished in it in one Day, by a mortal Feud which subsisted between them and the Macleods, about the Time of the Reformation.

In the Sea Cliffs there are several Veins of Coal, some Inches thick, to be observed. There is Freestone in the Island, and great Abundance of hard blue Limestone. But the Inhabitants have never yet thought of burning it, either for Manure or Building, though they have also plenty of Peat for the Purpose.

The four Islands of Eig, Rum, Muck and Canna, compose what is called the Parish of the Small Isles. I was anxious to obtain an accurate List of the People, in one of the Parishes of the Hebrides, and pitched upon this for the Purpose. I engaged with this View a sensible and careful Man, who is Catechist in the Parish, to make an Accurate Roll of the Inhabitants in the Course of his annual Visitation. To mark the Number of Families, and how many persons were contained in each; the Number of Marriages and of Children; and the Age of each individual in the Parish. The following Table and Observations, comprehend the Substance of his Report, which was very accurate and particular; and the Facts founded upon them, will be found applicable, I believe, with very little Variation, to all the other Parishes of the Western Islands.

Table of the Inhabitants in the Parish of the Small Isles

UNDER Years of Age	Numbers in Rum	Numbers in Eig	Numbers in Muck	Numbers in Canna	Total in the Parish	Years of Age	Numbers in Rum	Numbers in Eig	Numbers in Muck	Numbers in Canna	Total in the Parish	Years of Age	Numbers in Rum	Numbers in Eig	Numbers in Muck	Numbers in Canna	Total in the Parish
1	6	8	—	—	14												
1	8	7	1	—	16	34	4	1	1	2	8	67	3	2	—	—	5
2	14	15	4	2	35	35	1	6	2	1	10	68	1	—	1	—	2
3	9	12	—	9	30	36	4	12	6	2	24	69	—	—	—	—	—
4	9	17	7	6	39	37	9	5	4	4	22	70	2	4	—	—	6
5	10	12	7	10	39	38	1	2	1	2	6	71	—	1	—	—	1
6	10	9	7	6	32	39	2	5	2	3	12	72	—	3	—	—	3
7	16	18	8	13	55	40	8	14	8	7	37	73	—	1	—	—	1
8	5	9	—	7	21	41	—	5	4	5	14	74	1	1	—	—	2
9	8	15	7	12	42	42	5	1	3	2	11	75	—	—	—	—	—
10	7	6	3	14	30	43	1	—	1	—	2	76	1	3	2	—	6
11	3	7	—	5	15	44	2	1	—	—	3	77	—	—	—	—	—
12	8	13	6	13	40	45	—	3	1	—	4	78	—	—	—	—	—
13	2	4	2	7	15	46	—	—	1	2	3	79	—	1	—	1	2
14	1	5	5	3	14	47	2	3	—	4	9	80	1	1	1	1	4
15	7	1	2	3	13	48	1	1	—	1	3	81	1	—	—	—	1
16	7	7	4	2	20	49	1	6	1	1	9	82	—	—	—	—	—
17	7	5	3	7	22	50	8	11	2	10	31	83	—	—	—	—	—
18	3	10	1	1	15	51	1	6	1	4	12	84	—	—	—	—	—
19	9	7	2	5	23	52	4	6	1	5	16	85	—	1	—	—	1
20	5	7	3	5	20	53	2	—	—	—	2	86	—	—	—	—	—
21	5	10	1	10	26	54	2	1	1	—	4	87	—	—	—	—	—
22	3	9	1	6	19	55	—	2	—	—	2	88	—	—	—	—	—
23	4	6	—	2	12	56	3	3	—	3	9	89	1	1	—	—	2
24	3	14	5	—	22	57	1	4	1	1	7	90	—	—	—	—	—
25	2	4	—	2	8	58	—	1	—	—	1	91	—	—	—	—	—
26	7	8	1	2	18	59	—	5	—	2	7	92	1	—	—	—	1
27	11	16	3	7	37	60	7	12	1	5	25	93	—	—	—	—	—
28	3	7	—	5	15	61	1	8	1	3	13	94	—	—	—	—	—
29	5	9	1	2	17	62	2	2	—	4	8	95	—	—	—	—	—
30	8	15	5	5	33	63	2	2	—	—	4	96	—	—	—	—	—
31	1	6	2	2	11	64	3	2	3	—	8	97	1	—	—	—	1
32	6	12	2	5	25	65	—	—	—	—	—	Col. 3	13	19	4	2	38
33	2	—	—	—	2	66	—	—	—	—	—	Col. 2	77	130	46	73	326
	214	310	93	178	795		77	130	46	73	326	Col. 1	214	310	93	178	795
												GRAND TOTAL	304	459	143	253	1159

Observations

1. RUM contains among 304 Inhabitants, one Man of 81, one Woman of 89, another of 92, one of 97 and a Man of 80.
2. The Males are 147; the Females 157.
3. It contains 68 Fencible Men, above 16 and under 60 years of age, that is one fourth and $\frac{32}{68}$ of the whole Inhabitants.
4. The Number of Families are 57, so that each Family contains at an Average $5\frac{19}{57}$ Persons. Of these Families, the least numerous consists of. two Persons, of which; there are only two upon the Island, and the most numerous of 9, of which there are also but two.
5. There is a Marriage in each of the 57 Families, of which, either one or both Parties are alive.
6. So many Families and none without Marriage, is very remarkable.
7. In the 57 Families, the Number of Children are 153, that is $2\frac{39}{57}$ Persons in each Marriage.

   Note. Many of the Children of these Marriages have left the Country; and many are servants in other Families: so that scarcely a half of the Children of these Marriages, can be supposed to remain in the Families. These things considered, the Average Produce of each Marriage cannot be supposed less than 5.

1. EIG among 459 Inhabitants contains a Man of 80, a Woman of 85, and another of 89.
2. The Males are 183, and the Females 276.
3. It contains 110 Fencible Men, from 16 to 60 that is one fourth and $\frac{19}{110}$ of the whole Inhabitants.
4. The Number of Families are 88. So that the Families contain at an Average $5\frac{19}{21}$ Persons. Of these Families, the least Numerous consists of two Persons, of which there are 8 upon the Island and there are only 3 Families, which contain 9, 10 and 11 Persons.
5. In 10 Families, in Eig there is no Marriage. In the remaining 78 Families, there is a Marriage in each; and the Number of Children in these Families is 186, that is $2\frac{30}{78}$ Children to each Marriage.

1. MUCK among 143 Inhabitants, contains only one Woman of 80.
2. The Males are 72, the Females 71.
3. It contains 32 fencible Men from 16 to 60 that is one fourth and $\frac{15}{32}$ of the whole Inhabitants.
4. The Number of Families is 28. So that the Families contain at an Average 5 $\frac{3}{28}$ Persons. It has but one Family of 9 Persons and one under three.
5. There is a Marriage in each of the 28 Families. And the Number of Children in the marriages is 82: that is $2\frac{26}{28}$ Persons for each Marriage.

1. CANNA among 253 Inhabitants, contains only one Man of 80.
2. The Males are 124. The Females 129.
3. It contains 61 fencible Men, between 16 and 60 which is $\frac{1}{4}$ and $\frac{9}{61}$ of the Inhabitants.
4. The Number of Families is 44; so that they contain at an Average 5 and $\frac{33}{44}$ Persons. Of these Families, there is but one that contains two Persons, and none above 8 excepting two, of which one has 9 and the other 11 Persons.
5. All the Families in Canna have a Marriage, except 3, and of the 41 Marriages, there live in the Families 134 Children, that is 3 and $\frac{11}{41}$ Persons for each Marriage.

CANNA

CANNA

Canna is a very pleasant and fertile small Island with a fine Harbour: much frequented by the Ships which pass through the Hebrides.

It is about four measured Miles long and one broad; containing 2560 Acres, and Rents for 1,600 Merks Scots yearly. It is let at about 4d.½ p. Acre, contains 253 Inhabitants, and 10 Acres for each Person. It is the Property of Clanronald, and is inhabited by the People of his Clan who are all Papist excepting 16 Persons. There went 14 Men from this Island to the late War, of which 3 were slain in America, 3 returned with Chelsea Pensions, and the remaining 8 are still in the Army.

The Island contains 10 Ploughs and there is a great deal of Ground also dug with the Spade. It exports a good many Cattle, but no other Article.

There are several Cod Banks within reach of the Island, but the Inhabitants never fish but to supply themselves.

There is no Species of Industry carried on, either in this, or the three adjacent Islands of Rum, Eig and Muck, so that the People are idle to the Last Degree. It would be happy for them, was there a Spinning School erected in Canna for the Use of the four Islands.[1]

In one of the Hills in this Island, there are several Strata of Whinstone Columns, mostly hexagonal, and exactly resembling those of the Giants Causeway in Ireland. They stand nearly perpendicular and each Range or Stratum of the Columns is about 20 Feet high. Between the Strata there is interjected an horizontal Stratum of irregular Rock.

I was told that when Ships came near a certain Mountain in this Island, which they often do, as it lies upon the Sound of Canna, a much frequented Passage, their Compasses deserted the North; and veered to other Points. Being anxious to be further informed concerning this extraordinary Fact, I travelled to the Top of the Mountain, and carried along with me, two Accurate Mariners Compasses.

Being arrived at the Summit, I set down one of the Compasses upon the Grass, and the Needle stood immediately at W. b. N. The other, I placed at two yards Distance, in which the Needle stood directly at E.N.E.

I had then the two Compasses removed and set precisely in each others Place, upon which the former veered about to E.N.E. and the latter to W. b. N.

One of the Compasses, being placed in the middle between the above two Stations, the Needle there, stood at N. b. W.

In short every Time, either of the Compasses was removed, a yard, a Foot, or even a few Inches, the Direction of the Needle was altered. And in different Places traversed the whole Circle from North to South.

FINIS

NOTES

Introduction

1. James Sutherland was Intendant of the Edinburgh botanical garden founded by Sir Robert Sibbald and Sir Andrew Balfour, and first Professor of Botany in the University of Edinburgh. His catalogue of the garden was published in 1683, and a copy was in Walker's library.

2. Tytler, Alexander Fraser, Lord Woodhouselee, 'Memoirs of the Life and Writings of Lord Kaimes', (1806), Vol. 2, App. ii, p. 24.

3. Thomson, John, 'Life, Lectures and Writings of William Cullen M.D.', (1859), Vol. 2, p. 507.

4. *Ibid.,* p. 731.

5. Harold W. Scott, in his introduction to '"Lectures on Geology" by John Walker' (1966), suggests that Walker was the subject of a poem published in the 'Scots Magazine' in 1772, praising a Mr Walker's preaching in most bombastic terms. It is far more likely that John Walker's contemporary, Mr Robert Walker, minister of the High Kirk, St Giles, was the source of the poet's inspiration.

6. Scottish Record Office (S.R.O.) GD/24/1/502/8-11.

7. S.R.O. GD/24/1/517/12-19.

8. S.R.O. GD/24/1/581/3-4.

9. S.R.O. GD/24/1/502/12-13.

10. S.R.O. CH1/1/55.

11. *Ibid.*

12. See Scott, H. W., '"Lectures on Geology" by John Walker', (1966), and Gillespie, Charles Coulston, ed., 'Dictionary of Scientific Biography' (1976).

13. Quoted in Taylor, George, 'John Walker, D.D., F.R.S.E., a Notable Scottish Naturalist', Transactions of the Botanical Society of Edinburgh, 38, (1959), p. 178.

14. A very nearly complete bibliography of his works is to be found in Scott, H.W. (1966).

15. S.R.O. E 721/7, 5th March, 1764.

16. Edinburgh University Library (E.U.L.) La. III. 352/1.

17. S.R.O. E 727/16/2, 30th July, 1764.

18. Walker, John, 'Essays on Natural History and Rural Economy', (1812), 'History of the Island of Jura'.

19. Jardine, Sir William, 'Memoir of John Walker D.D.', in 'The Birds of Great Britain and Ireland', (1842) Vol. 3, pp. 24, 26.

20. *Ibid.*

21. Walker wrote a letter to Lord Bute, 29th January, 1765, in many details similar to this one to Kames, but he gives the statistics of the tour as, 'sailed, 1894; rowed in a boat, 420; rode, 1630 and walked, 792', making it a far longer expedition. S.R.O. GD/18/5118 and E.U.L. La. III. 352/1. (Undated).

22. S.R.O. GD24/1/571/5 and E.U.L. La. III. 352/1.

23. *Ibid.*

24. S.R.O. GD/18/5118 and E.U.L. La. III. 352/1.

25. National Library of Scotland (N.L.S.) MS 98 ff. 39-40.

26. S.R.O. CH1/1/55.

27. Jardine, (1842), pp. 32-39.

28. S.R.O. GD24/1/571/5 and E.U.L. La. III. 352/1.

29. S.R.O. CH1/1/55, pp. 589-628.

30. See Jardine, (1842), pp. 32-39.

31. S.R.O. E727/63/4, 11th March, 1771.

32. S.R.O. CH1/1/63, pp. 126-135.

33. S.R.O. GD/18/5118 and E.U.L. La. III. 352/1.

34. E.U.L. La. III. 352/1.

35. E.U.L. La. D.C. 2-37-38.

36. S.R.O. CH1/5/43.

37. E.U.L. La. D.C. 2-37-38.

38. Fraser Darling, Sir Frank, 'West Highland Survey', (1955), pp. 36-56.

39. Walker, John, 'Economical History of the Hebrides and Highlands of Scotland', (1808), Vol. 1, p. 7.

40. *Ibid.*

41. Maitland Club, Miscellany, vol. iii.

42. N.L.S. MS 976 f. 143.

43. N.L.S. MS 68 ff. 31-2.

44. S.R.O. CH1/5/119.

45. *Ibid.*

46. Anson, Peter F., 'Underground Catholicism in Scotland', (1970), p. 150.

47. Forbes, F. and Anderson, W. J., 'Annual Lists of the Clergy in the Highland District 1732-1828', Innes Review, Vol. 17, (1966).

48. S.R.O. CH1/1/55.

49. S.R.O. CH1/5/79.

50. Jardine, (1842), pp. 32-39.

51. See 'Scottish Population History from the 17th century to the 1930's', ed. Flynn et al. (1977).

52. Walker, John, 'Essays on Natural History and Rural Economy', (1812), p. 103.

53. See N.L.S. MS 976, f. 143, N.L.S. MS 976, f. 154, S.R.O. CH2/557/5/252.

54. S.R.O. CH1/5/119.

55. S.R.O. CH1/5/43.

56. S.R.O. CH1/5/79.

57. See Kyd, J. G., 'Scottish Population Statistics' (Scottish History Society) 1975.

58. Walker, John, 'Essays in Natural History and Rural Economy' (1812), p. 103.

59. Walker, John, 'Economical History of the Hebrides and Highlands', (1808), Vol. 1, pp. 24-27.

60. S.R.O. RH2/4/386.

61. MacDonald, Rev. Roderick, 'The Highland District in 1764', Innes Review, vol. 15, 1964.

62. Boswell, James, 'Tour to the Hebrides', ed. Pottle, F.A. (1936), p. 257.

63. Cregeen, E.R., 'Argyll Estate Instructions', Scottish History Society, (1964), p. xxviii.

64. Walker, John, 'Essays on Natural History and Rural Economy', (1812), p. 103.

65. *Ibid.*

66. *Ibid.*

67. Monro, Alexander, (Primus), (1697-1767), 'Account of Inoculation of the Small Pox in Scotland', (1765).

Lewis

1. Rubh Eorrapidh or the Butt of Lewis.

2. Kenneth Mackenzie of Seaforth, known as the 'little lord', inherited the estate in 1761 on the death of his father, Lord Fortrose. He died in 1781 on his way to India with the 78th Regiment, of which he was Lieutenant-Colonel. His grandfather, William, fifth Earl of Seaforth, had been attainted for his part in Jacobite risings and the family had retained the estates only by various devious ploys. The 'little lord' reaped the benefit of Lord Fortrose's support for the Government during the '45 rebellion and was granted a Crown charter of the Seaforth properties in 1763, and the titles of Baron Ardelve and Viscount Fortrose in 1766. He was created Earl of Seaforth in 1774.

3. Eye.

4. Uig.

5. Barvas.

6. Martin Martin (1716) mentions spirits four times distilled as well as trestarig, made before the years of scarcity in the 1690's when corn was plentiful on Lewis. It was called 'Usquebaugh baul'. Martin commented, 'two spoonfuls of this last Liquor is a sufficient Dose; and if any Man exceed this, it would presently stop his breath, and endanger his life.'

7. Trade by sea to Glasgow from Lewis is said to have started about 1710. Before this, exports had gone across the Minch and then by packhorse through Glenelg to Inverness.

8. Sulasgeir.

9. This is a form of 'graddaning' less destructive of the straw than others followed in some parts of the Highlands where the whole length of the straw was burnt with the heads. Walker deprecated the loss of the straw but realised that this method of drying the grain and grinding with the quern was 'a natural and necessary contrivance for turning the grain immediately into bread, before kilns and water mills were introduced'. 'Economical History of the Hebrides and Highlands', II, 368.

10. Barkin Isles, Loch Leurbost.

11. Loch Ouirn.

12. The Government provided further support for the herring fishery by granting a bounty of 30s per ton by an Act of 1749, under certain conditions. The bounty was raised in 1757 to 50s per ton.

13. Walker provides valuable evidence on the spread of the habitat of the eider. Harvie-Brown and Buckley ('Vertebrate Fauna of the Outer Hebrides' (1888) and 'Vertebrate Fauna of Argyll and the Inner Hebrides' (1892)) considered there were two centres of expansion of the species, from Heiskeir, off North Uist, and Colonsay. Walker states that local people on Colonsay maintained that the eider was a recent arrival, having appeared within eight or nine years of his visit.

14. Marten.

15. Saithe or half-grown coal fish.

Harris

1. Towards the end of 1771, when Macleod of Macleod wanted to sell Harris and St. Kilda to settle debts, there was difficulty in describing the estate. A copy of the report was used but it was criticised for inaccuracy in the figures for the extent of Harris. It was maintained that it was 16 miles by five or six miles. (E.U.L. La. III 352/1, William Fraser W.S., 21st December, 1771).

2. Norman Macleod (c. 1706-1772). An early agricultural improver, with a strongly paternalistic attitude towards his people. He died heavily in debt.

3. Unlike many proprietors, the Macleods had erected a parish school early in the eighteenth century. It was at Rodil, not well sited to serve the whole parish, and appears to have had long periods without a schoolmaster.

4. At the time of the sale of Harris, Macleod of Macleod maintained that Harris exported three hundred tons of kelp per annum. (E.U.L. La. III 352/1, 21st Dec., 1771.)

5. This plough is very different from the old Scots plough which was thirteen feet in length and very heavy. The plough described by Walker has become known as the 'thrapple' plough. It is thought to have developed from the primitive Norwegian 'ard'. There were differences in construction in the various islands but all were light and depended on the use of the ristle. See Fenton, Alexander, 'Early and Traditional Cultivation Instruments', P.S.A.S., xcvi (1965).

6. Alexander Macleod of Pabbay, Steward and Tacksman of St Kilda and Tacksman of Pabbay where he occupied the farm of Kirktown. He emigrated to North Carolina in 1773 with Donald Campbell of Scalpay, with whom he had been engaged in a business venture, probably based on fishing. He appears to have attempted to develop a fishing industry on Harris in the 1730's.

7. Donald Campbell of Scalpay (1690-1783). He held the office of Forester and was responsible for the prevention of poaching in the deer forest of Harris. He was not a Jacobite but sheltered Charles Edward Stuart in 1746 for four days. He emigrated to North Carolina and died there in 1783.

St Kilda

1. Walker did not visit St Kilda in 1764 and he had not managed to reach it in 1762, despite efforts to arrange for a boat to take him. He overestimates its size – Hirta is only just over 1,500 acres and the entire group, including all the stacs, is only 2,000 acres.

2. Another account of the smallpox epidemic on St. Kilda is given by Kenneth Macaulay, Minister of Ardnamurchan, who visited the island in 1758 on behalf of the S.P.C.K. Macaulay records ('Voyage to St. Kilda', 1764) that out of twenty-one families, four adults and twenty-six orphans survived, together with three men and four boys who had been on Boreray, making thirty-seven survivors in all compared to Walker's eighteen. By 1758 the population had reached 88.

3. This appears to contradict evidence from an S.P.C.K. minute of 1731 which refers to Hirta soon becoming populous again, 'by the yearly transporting of people to it'. Macaulay, however, found that the St. Kildans spoke a distinctive kind of Gaelic and did not have the same knowledge of dyeing as the people of the Long Island, which suggests that the old population was not swamped by incomers from the Harris estate or Uist.

4. Walker is referring to 'tetanus infantum' which in the nineteenth century was to have a devastating effect on the island's population. As Martin Martin, who was a physician and was fascinated by illnesses and their cures, did not mention it, the disease was probably an eighteenth-century development. Macaulay describes it in detail.

5. From the details Martin Martin gives in his 'Late Voyage to St. Kilda', it seems quite likely that the disease was true leprosy.

6. Sir William Monson, Bart. (1569-1643). Admiral Monson's 'Naval Tracts' were published in Vol. iii of 'A Collection of Voyages and Travels' by William Churchill in 1732.

7. The Commissioners and Trustees for Improving Fisheries and Manufactures in Scotland were instituted in 1726.

North Uist

1. Walker is quite rightly cautious in making this statement. Dispute over the exact boundary between Harris and North Uist was longstanding but had been intensified as the value of kelp rose. In 1765 Donald Macleod of Berneray brought a case before the Court of Session which was not settled until 1781.

2. It is difficult to identify Heray as Walker describes it. It seems most probable that he is referring to Grimsay, which has the small island of Eilean na h-Airidh lying off its west coast. On his way north Walker probably passed across the north ford to Eilean na h-Airidh and then on to Grimsay. Since he later refers to 'Grimsay', he may have simply transposed the names.

3. James Macdonald (1741-1766), 8th baronet. He was renowned as a brilliant scholar and linguist, and had plans for agricultural improvement and the establishment of industries on his estates. His early death has been considered a tragedy for Skye and North Uist.

4. Eachkamish.

5. Charles I's Company of the General Fishery of Great Britain, founded in 1633, is more usually associated with Lewis. The company appears to have traded up to at least 1640; there are no records of activity after the civil wars, although the charter was not annulled until 1690. Martin Martin stated that the ruins were on 'Vacksay,' identified as Faihore in Lochmaddy harbour. He is the source of Walker's statement about the fishing industry in the seventeenth century.

Benbecula

1. Ranald Macdonald, younger, son of Old Clanranald, Ranald Macdonald, who succeeded in 1730. Old Clanranald played a mainly passive role in the '45, although he was suspected of the illegal possession of arms by Captain John Barlow in 1753. (N.L.S. MS 10691 f.14.) He died in 1766.

2. Alexander Macdonald of Boisdale was old Clanranald's half-brother (1698-1768). During the Jacobite rebellion he remained loyal, but he was arrested for harbouring the Prince. Two of his sons were among the men from Benbecula who fought and died in America in the Seven Years' War.

3. The family's seat at Ormaclett in South Uist was burned in 1715. The Clanranalds lived at Nunton, Benbecula.

4. This is erroneous. The hill is named Rueval and it is generally accepted that Benbecula's name is derived from Beinn a' bh-fhaodhla, the mountain of the fords.

5. Uskavagh.

South Uist

1. Ranald Macdonald, younger, had played a very active part in the '45 in support of Charles Edward Stuart. In 1753 he had taken over the running of the estates from his father. By Walker's visit he had become a Protestant. He died in 1777.

2. Daliburgh.

3. The native Hebridean sheep were a blend of two wild types, the moufflon and the urial, and their ancestors go back at least to the Bronze Age. Multi-horned sheep were still to be found until the 1930's. Their type is best seen today in the black park sheep known as the St. Kilda.

4. It was the custom in the Lowlands to smear the sheep with a mixture of tar and butter at the end of October. It was held that the process increased the quantity and improved the quality of the wool and that it kept the sheep from becoming too wet. Its main object was to prevent scab, a disease brought to the Highlands by the big southern sheep.

5. Gaspard Bauhin (1560-1624) was important in botany for his work in classification; he was one of the first to distinguish genus and species. His 'Pinax' was published in 1621.

6. The Disarming Act of 1746 probably only exacerbated an already difficult situation. Martin Martin had found the geese making similar depredations at the end of the seventeenth century, although then they were both shot and trapped.

7. It is true that the primitive sheep have shorter tails; this is one of their distinguishing features, as wild sheep have about twelve vertebrae and some domestic sheep over twenty.

Barra

1. It has been suggested that Walker meant Hellisay instead of Fuday, but the dimensions of the island leave no room for doubt that Fuday was meant. (See Thompson, F. 'The Uists and Barra' 1974.) The next island mentioned by Walker, Feala, is probably Fiaray.

2. Roderick Macneill (1693-1763), 39th Chief, was succeeded by his grandson, Roderick (d. 1822), his son having been killed at Quebec.

3. Donald Macneill of Vatersay had been brought up a Catholic, but was a Protestant by the 1720's. It was largely owing to his representations that the S.P.C.K. opened the school on Barra in which Walker found the teacher, 'at the greatest pains to make the Popish children mandate those passages of Scripture that are most subversive of Popery, and to ground them in our catechisms and Confession of Faith'. (Walker, 'Report to the S.P.C.K.', 1765.) Vatersay was ruling elder.

4. James Grant (1706-1778). Educated at the Catholic school at Scalan and the Scots College in Rome; ordained in 1734 and worked as priest in Lochaber, South Uist and Barra; in 1746 he was arrested and imprisoned; made bishop in 1755 with the title of Bishop of Sinita in Numidia *in partibus;* he lived at Presholme in Banff until 1761, when he went to Aberdeen. The education of Macneill was undertaken by the Rev. Angus Macneill, heir to Donald Macneill of Vatersay. He became a Protestant.

5. The Traigh Mhor or Cockle Strand.

6. I.e. Portrush fishers.

Islay

1. I.e. Outram, Eilean Craobach, Eilean a'chuirn, Eilean Bhride, Eilean mhicMhaolmhoire, Orsay, Eilean nan Caorach, Nave and Texa.

2. Daniel Campbell of Shawfield (d. 1777).

3. Walker appears confused over the parishes of Islay. In 1765 they were the united parish of Killarow which already included Kilmeny, and Kilchoman which included Kilchiaran; and the united parish of Kildalton and Kilnachton.

4. I.e. polecat.

5. *Hordeum distichon.*

6. Sediment found in river estuaries and on clay shores. 'It is a mass of all the animal and vegetable substances of the sea, in a putrid state, accompanied with a considerable portion of calcarious matter and sea salt . . . . On the surface it is of a grey colour; but at the depth of a foot or two, it is of a blueish or blackish cast . . . . When dug, it is soft and smooth like the most tenacious clay, but falls to powder in the air or in the earth.' Walker, 'Economical History of the Hebrides and Highlands', Vol i, 152 & 3.

7. Support for the idea of building an Argyllshire canal continued to the end of the century. In 1793, the necessary Act for the Crinan Canal was passed and the canal was opened, though still incomplete in 1801.

Jura

1. Parts of this section of the report are nearly identical to a MS 'History of the Island of Jura', which was one of the few sections Walker appears to have completed of his 'Natural History of the Highlands'. The MS of the 'History' includes far longer sections on 'Eddies and Whirlpools' and the Paps of Jura experiments, and concludes with sections on plants and fossils which are not in the 'Report on the Hebrides'. It does not include the sections on the parish and agriculture which appear here. The MS 'History of the Island of Jura' is in the Laing collection in the Library of the University of Edinburgh and a published version is in 'Essays on Natural History and Rural Economy' (1808).

2. This description is not quite accurate. One of the western summits is lower than one of the others: Beinn an Oir, 2571′ and Beinn a' Chaolais, 2407′ are on the west; Beinn Shiantaidh, 2477′ is very close to the east side of Beinn an Oir and from many viewpoints is hidden by it; Corra Bheinn, 1867′, lies to the north east.

3. Abhainn a' Chnuic Bhric.

4. Perhaps Lussa.

5. Loch na Mile.

6. In 1764, it had not yet been determined exactly what was the relationship between atmospheric pressure and heat. Fahrenheit had discovered that the boiling point of water varied according to atmospheric pressure. Mairan had found that the point at which water boiled was greater at the foot than at the top of a mountain. Walker wanted to settle the relationship exactly.

7. Halley, Edmond (1656-1743), mathematician, geophysicist, astronomer and archaeologist.

8. Mairan, Jean-Jacques d'Ortous de (1678-1771), physicist and member of the Royal Societies of London, Edinburgh and Uppsala. Published 'Dissertations sur les variations du Baromètre', Bordeaux (1715).

9. Fahrenheit, Dante Gabriel (1686-1736).

10. This contrasts with Martin Martin's assertion that, 'This Isle is perhaps the wholesomest plot of Ground either in the Isles or Continent of Scotland, as appears by the long life of the Natives, and their state of health.' 'Description of the Western Isles of Scotland', (2nd edition, 1716, repr. 1976), p. 232.

11. Pennant (1772) recorded that he came across 'some obscure account' of 'the Fillan, a lettle worm of Jura, small as a thread and not an inch in length which insinuates itself under the skin, causes a redness and great pain, flies swiftly from part to part'. The remedy was a poultice of cheese and honey. ('Voyage to the Hebrides', 1774 edition, p. 213.) Cases of 'fillean', however, were confined neither to Jura nor to the late eighteenth century. Martin Martin, at the end of the seventeenth century, recorded a case on Skye and another in the Outer Hebrides and added that the 'fillan' had been in 'several persons in the Isles'. ('Western Islands of Scotland', 1716 edition, pp. 41 and 191.) James Robertson, a botanist touring the Highlands in 1767, while in Lochaber heard of 'an animalcule that nestling in (people's) legs or other places causes exquisite pain'. (N.L.S. MS 2507.) As late as the beginning of this century, Alexander Carmichael came across a man in Gairloch who had suffered from the 'fiollan fionn' and told him a charm against 'the worm'. ('Carmina Gadelica', Vol. II, p. 302.) It is not clear whether the details of Walker's description of the worm were given him on Jura or whether they come from a very similar account in Martin Martin (p. 191). Although the 'fillean' is difficult to identify positively, it appears to be some kind of fillaria. The symptoms are most similar to those produced by a fillaria now found only in the tropics.

12. An extract of this plant was also used against animal lice. It contains glycoside aucubin, which is poisonous to insects.

13. Maol Buidhe.

14. John, 4th Duke of Argyll (1693-1770).

15. Belnahua.

16. Garbh Eileach. The name of the group of islands is more commonly given as Garvellachs.

17. Eileach an Naoimh.

18. Gigha.

19. Roger Macneill of Taynish.

Colonsay and Oronsay

1. Adamnan, Abbot of Iona (628-705), author of 'Vita S. Columbae' (ed. A.O. and M.O. Anderson, 1961).

2. In 1700, Argyll sold Colonsay to Donald Macneill of Crear. In 1765 the Laird was Donald Macneill of Colonsay.

3. *Arctostaphylos* or *Arbutus uva-ursi,* the bearberry, a small shrub with evergreen leaves, used for dyeing in the Hebrides.

4. A small shrub of the St. John's Wort family, slightly aromatic, with yellow flowers and red berries. On Colonsay, tutsan was said to induce madness.

5. Buchanan, George (1506-1582), author of 'Rerum Scoticarum Historia', 1582.

6. The Gaelic 'colc' means eiderduck.

7. This suggests that Harvie-Brown, J. A. and Buckley, T.E., 'A Vertebrate Fauna of Argyll and the Inner Hebrides' (1892), came to the wrong conclusions about the spread of the eiderduck.

8. John of Islay, Lord of the Isles, is said to have founded the priory whose ruins Walker saw, in about 1350.

9. There is no evidence to show at what period the Macduffies came to Colonsay. They were in occupation from at least the second half of the fourteenth century and held it until 1623, when Malcolm Macduffie or Macphee was killed by Coll Ciotach at Eilean-nan-Ròn, south of Oronsay.

10. There is a tradition that Murdoch (Murdardus) oppressed his people, who rose against him and killed him in 1539.

Iona

1. Another version of this section, a MS 'History of the Island of Icolumbkil', is among Walker's papers in the Laing collection in the Library of the University of Edinburgh and was published posthumously in 'Essays on Natural History and Rural Economy'. The version here has less full accounts of the early history of the monastery and ecclesiastical history, and omits entirely sections on the 'fossil, vegetable and animal kingdoms' and details of shells, insects and birds.

2. In the Laing MS 'seperated sound' appears as 'aspirated sound', which makes sense of the sentence.

3. Bede, 'Ecclesiastical History of the English People', ed. Colgrave, B. and Myers, R.A.B. (1969).

4. Adamnan translated the name of the island as 'Ioua Insula', which, misread, became Iona.

5. The highest hill is not Druim an Aoineidh on the south west to which Walker is probably referring, but Dùn on the north east.

6. Port na Curaich.

7. William Sacheverell (? d. 1715), Governor of the Isle of Man, visited Iona when he was engaged in an expedition to Mull to raise the wreck of the 'Florida' in Tobermory Bay. He gives an account of his visit in 'Account of the Isle of Man', (1702).

8. Probably the Duke of Argyll's Chamberlain of Tiree.

9. Neil Macleod, Minister of Kilfinichen and Kilvickeon, 1756-1780. Johnson described him as the cleverest man he had met with in the Western Islands (Boswell, 'Journal' (O.U.P., 1924) p. 388), and a man whose elegance of conversation and strength of judgement would make him conspicuous in places of greater celebrity. (Johnson, 'Tour', *ibid.,* p. 139)

10. Columba died in 597. The abbey was plundered for the first time in 795, again in 801 and 806 when 68 monks are said to have been killed at Martyrs Bay, in 925 and in 986 when the abbot and fifteen monks were slain at the 'White Strand of the Monks'. Magnus Barelegs seems to stand alone in his reluctance to devastate Iona, when he visited it in 1097 and prayed in the church.

11. The main buildings of both the abbey and nunnery date from the twelfth century, when Reginald, Lord of the Isles and son of Somerled, rebuilt the former and founded the latter.

12. Ray, John (1627-1705), botanist. Published 'Synopsis Stirpium Britannicorum'.

13. Martin Martin described the altar as 'large, and of as fine marble as any I ever saw'. ('Western Islands of Scotland', 1716 edition, p. 257.) By the time Bishop Pococke saw it in 1760, it had already been damaged by the 'common people', who broke pieces off to use 'as a Medicine for man or beast in most disorders, and especially the Flux'. ('Pococke's Tours in Scotland', Scottish History Society, First Series, I, p. 82.) When Pennant visited the island in 1772, only a very little of the slab remained, and he added to the desecration by taking a piece as a souvenir. By the time Dr Johnson reached Iona in 1773, the altar had disappeared entirely.

14. John Mackinnon, abbot of Iona from at least 1489 until his death in 1509.

15. Pliny, 'Historia Naturalis'.

16. Among Walker's papers in the Laing collection are his notes on the Scottish kings based on Boece.

17. Identification of this cross is uncertain and intriguing. Reliable accounts establish that by mid-nineteenth century there were three crosses still standing in the precincts of the Cathedral – St Martin's, entire, as it is today (from the detailed description, Walker's second cross) and the two stumps of St John's and St Matthew's. This cross is unlikely to be St Matthew's which has a stepped base similar to the one which Walker describes as an apparently distinguishing feature of the St Martin's cross. Is this then the magnificent St John's cross seen still almost entire before its first destruction? This is possible, yet drawings made of an Iona cross by Edward Lhuyd in 1699 have been identified as being of 'fragments' of the St John's cross. ('Edward Lhuyd in the Scottish Highlands', J. L. Campbell and D. Thomson, 1963, p. 306).

Other visitors' accounts only add to the difficulties of identification. Martin Martin refers to one cross, St Martin's; Bishop Pococke mentions two, St Martin's and a higher one to the west; Boswell recorded one and, perhaps wisely, left the name blank in his MS; Dr Johnson refers to two, St John's and St Matthew's. (Martin Martin, *ibid.*, p. 259; 'Bishop Pococke's Tours', p. 85; 'A Tour to the Hebrides', ed. F. A. Pottle, 1936, p. 334; 'Journey to the Western Islands', O.U.P., 1924, p. 137.)

Whether this is St John's or St Matthew's cross, Walker is erroneous in dating it. Both are tenth century.

18. St Martin's Cross; also tenth century.

19. Maclean's Cross; fifteenth century.

20. John Fraser (1647-1702), Minister of Tiree and Coll, son of Farquhar Fraser.

Mull

1. Torfasson, Thormadur, c. 1640-1720.

2. For Mr J. Cowley, see 'The True Interest of Great Britain' by Sir Alexander Murray.

3. John Maclaine of Lochbuie, Laird 1759-1775; Hector Maclean of Torloisk, Laird 1748-1765; Hugh Maclean of Coll, Laird 1754-1786; Alan Maclean of Drimnin, (1724-1792); Charles Mackinnon of Mackinnon (b. 1753). His estate on Mull was sold in 1774.

4. If Walker is correct, his opinion refutes that of the present day which considers that, by the mid-eighteenth century, population pressure on land resources had made the economy precarious. (MacNab, P. A., 'The Isle of Mull', 1970, p. 81).

5. Loch na Lathaich.

6. William Sacheverell's expedition.

7. Probably Portencross.

8. Foxes had been so successfully extirpated from Mull by the end of the nineteenth century that Harvie-Brown and Buckley (*op. cit.*) did not believe evidence that they had been native to the island.

9. Archibald, 3rd Duke of Argyll (1682-1761).

10. Achnahaird.

11. Not identified.

12. Shiaba.

13. Beinn an Aoinidh. The seam was first worked in the sixteenth century and for a time coal formed part of the farm's rent.

14. Sir Alexander Murray of Stanhope, Bt. (d. 1743). Pioneer in the development of mining in the west of Scotland, and an agricultural improver with a strong interest in drainage.

15. Ray, John (1627-1705), author of 'Synopsis Stirpium Britannicorum'.

16. Sloane, Sir Hans (1660-1753). Physician and botanist, member of the Temple Coffee House Botanic Club, the earliest natural history society in Britain; President of the Royal Society; his library, manuscripts and collection of curiosities formed part of the original collections of the British Museum.

17. Sir Alexander Murray of Stanhope, author of 'An Abstract of an Essay on the Improvement of Husbandry and Working of Mines' (1733). Walker's notes on Murray's works are in the Laing MSS in the Library of the University of Edinburgh.

18. Bac Mòr.

19. Cairn na Burgh. It was used as a fortress up to the end of the seventeenth century, as Martin Martin records a 'small garrison of the standing forces . . . at present'.

20. Dugald Stewart of Appin (d. 1769).

Coll

1. Hugh Maclean of Coll, Laird 1754-1786.

2. This had been an S.P.C.K. school. Not only had the school been removed but the Minister, Aulay Macaulay, had taken the S.P.C.K. library with him when he was translated to the Long Island.

3. Ben Hogh.

4. Breachacha castles. The New Castle where Boswell and Johnson stayed in 1773, and described in detail, was built in 1750. In a sour mood, Johnson said it was a 'tradesman's box'.

5. By 1726 two farms had been so overblown that the houses had to be moved a mile away. (S.R.O. TE/ 9/13)

6. Craggans.

7. Shortly after Walker's visit, Hugh Maclean took up residence in Aberdeen.

8. Robert Macpherson was a clerk in the office of the Board of Manufactures. He developed his machine – which broke, scutched and beat the flax – in the early 1760's. It was said to allow one man to do the work of three and was adopted by the Commissioners of the Annexed Estates in their campaign to improve flax production in the Highlands and Islands. (S.R.O. E727/28/1 and E728/23.)

9. The White House of Grishipoll.

Tiree

1. John, fourth Duke of Argyll (1693-1770).

2. Ben Hynish.

3. Arfeville, Nicolay de Nicolay, sieur d' (1517-83), author of 'Voyage en Ecosse'.

4. There were more lochs then in Tiree. See the map, 'Isle of Tiree, 1768-9', in Cregeen, E.R., 'Argyll Estate Instructions' (1964).

5. Bauhin, Gaspard, author of 'Pinax' (1621).

6. Whooping cough.

7. The cattle of Tiree, Canna, Muck and Coll to some extent suffered from a deficiency disease. 'They (sc. the cattle) become extremely hard in the belly, then pass bloody urine, after which they die in one, two or a few days.' Walker, 'Economical History of the Hebrides and Highlands of Scotland', II, 64.

8. Wallerius, Johan Gottschalk (1709-1785), Swedish natural scientist. His 'Mineralogie' was published in Stockholm in 1747.

9. Pliny, 'Historia Naturalis'.

10. Estève, Louis (fl. 1750-65).

Rum

1. More commonly known as 'creideamh a'bhata bhuidhe'. The reputed date of this conversion is 1726/7. It was not nearly as traumatic as the story suggests. Rum had been becoming Protestant over a number of years: early in the century both Catholic and Protestant sources claim the island was totally Catholic; in 1718, it was said to have a mixture of Protestant and Catholic; in 1720, about one third were Catholic; in 1726, about a half were said to be Catholic; from the late 1730's all except a handful were Protestant. The same story is told of Alexander Macdonald of Boisdale and his tenants on South Uist.

2. Cronstedt, Axel Frederik (1722-1765). A pupil of Wallerius, noted for his work in classification and arrangement. His 'Foisch' was translated into German in 1760, and William Cullen translated this into English for Walker and outlined the new classes shortly before the 1764 journey. Walker was a great admirer of Cronstedt, describing him to his students in Edinburgh as 'a man of deep research and great genius' and his essay as a 'work of prodigious merit'.

Skye

1. Walker is being inconsistent here. In the section on Harris, Sir James Macdonald of Sleat is said to be proprietor. Sir James died in July, 1766 and was succeeded by his brother, Sir Alexander Macdonald, who became the first Lord Macdonald in 1776. He died in 1795.

2. Norman Macleod succeeded as an infant in about 1706. He was an early agricultural improver – he was sowing clover as early as 1728 and in 1736 became a member of Cockburn of Ormiston's Agricultural Club. He tried to promote fishing and linen industries and to persuade his tenants to attempt agricultural improvements. He died in 1772 heavily in debt.

3. Charles Mackinnon, b. 1753, succeeded in 1756; he held the lands of Strathaird.

4. The 'Old Man of Storr'.

5. Macpherson, in 'Ossian', related that Cuchullin, son of Semo, grandson of Cathbaird, some time in the third century was chief of Skye and had his headquarters at Dunscaith.

6. The Mackinnons had two castles, Caisteal Maol on the west shore of Kyle Akin and Dunringill on the shores of Loch Slapin.

7. Macleod, Alexander (b. 1692), 2nd son of Roderick Macleod of Uilinish.

8. I.e. 'wedder', castrated male sheep.

9. A kind of fuller's earth.

10. Balfour, Sir Andrew (1630-1694), a botanist, assisted Sibbald in the Botanic Garden in Edinburgh. He left his curiosities and MSS to Sibbald.

11. Sibbald, Sir Robert (1641-1722). Qualified in medicine and an ardent naturalist. A founder of the Edinburgh Botanic Garden and the Royal College of Surgeons in Edinburgh. Walker did a considerable amount of research on his papers.

Eigg

1. John Macdonald of Morar (d. 1809).

2. Ranald Macdonald, chief 1730-1766.

Canna

1. In mid-1766 the Commissioners of Annexed Estates gave Donald Macleod, Tacksman of Canna, a flax machine, reels and lintseed 'in order to encourage the raising and manufactury of flax'. (S.R.O. E721/9. f. 170).

INDEX

Achnahaird, Loch Scridain, Mull, 150 (map), 162
Adamnan, St. (d. 705) *abbot of Iona,* 123, 137, 139, 146, 151, 179, 180, 238
agate, 165, 198-9
Agricultural Society of Edinburgh, 2
Agriculture, Board of, 2, 12
ague, 183, *see also diseases*
aira caerulea, see purple moor grass
Airidh, eilean na h-, North Uist, 26, 63, 235
alder, 205, *see also trees*
amiantus, 219
Annexed Estates, Commissioners of the, 2, 6, 8, 9, 10, 33-4, 46, 244
Aoneidh, Druim an, Iona, 138, 239
Aonidh, Beinn an, Carsaig, Mull, 150 (map), 162, 241
arable land, 12-13, 15
  in use, 40, 54, 63, 64, 69, 74, 86, 99, 117, 129, 137, 153, 170, 181, 195, 210
  potential, 41, 54, 64, 69, 74, 86, 99, 123, 137, 153, 156, 170, 181, 195
Ardtun, Mull, 162
Arfeville, Nicolay de Nicolay, sieur d' (1517-83), 180, 242
Argyll, Archibald, third duke of (1682-1761), 160
Argyll, John, fourth duke of (1693-1770), 105, 111, 120, 137, 151, 162, 165, 166, 179, 183
Armadale, Skye, 124, 202 (map), 204, 206
arms, 79, 159
army –
  Fencible men, 225, 226
  men sent from –
    Arisaig, 73
    Barra, 30, 86
    Benbecula, 30, 69
    Canna, 229
    Coll, 169
    Harris, 30, 54
    Islay, 30, 97, 99
    Lewis, 40
    Moidart, 73
    Mull, 30, 152
    North Uist, 30, 64
    Skye, 30, 203
    South Uist, 30, 73
    Tiree, 30, 183
  pensioners, 40, 54, 183, 229
Arnisort, Loch, *see Greshornish, Loch*
Aros, Mull, 150 (map), 152
arundo arenaria, see marram grass
Ascrib Isles, Loch Snizort, Skye, 27
ash, 102, 124, 205, *see also trees*
Askival, Rum, 194 (map), 195-6, 197

Bac mor, eilean, Treshnish Isles, 150 (map), 162, 166
badgers, 100
Baleshare, North Uist, 13, 62 (map), 64
Balfour, Sir Andrew, Bt. (1630-94), *physician and botanist,* 219, 224
Ballygrant, Islay, 96 (map), 106
Barkin Isles, Loch Leurbost, Lewis, 38 (map), 44
barley (*hordeum distichon* L.), 14, 117, 185
  need for two-rowed, 15, 100, 185
  ripening of, 15, 185
  see also bear
barometric experiments, 7, 114-5, 237
Barra, 8, 12, 13, 14, 17, 18, 19, 20, 26, 27, 29, 34 (map), 72 (map), **85-90**
Barvas, Lewis, 25, 38 (map), 39, 40
basalt, 14, 147, 164
Bauhin, Gaspard (1560-1624), *botanist,* 11, 183, 236, 242
beans, 15, 100, 208
bear (*hordeum tetrastichum (Koern.), h. vulgare*), 14
  cultivation on –
    Barra, 14, 86, 87, 88
    Benbecula, 69
    Coll, 172
    Harris, 14, 55
    Iona, 139, 186
    Lewis, 14, 42, 43
    Mull, 153, 155, 157
    North Uist, 65, 208
    Skye, 14, 205, 207, 210, 211
    South Uist, 14, 75, 77, 78, 208
    Tiree, 14, 181, 182, 185, 186
  harvesting of, 43

price of, 41, 155, 187, 206
ripening, 78, 87, 139, 153, 182, 183, 208
weights and measures, 14-5
whisky from, 14, 155, 173
yield of, 14, 55, 78, 88, 211
bearberry (*arctostaphylos uva-ursi* (L.) Spreng.), 123, 239
Beatons of Pennycross, Mull, 151, 154
Bede, St. (673-735), *historian,* 137
Bee, Loch, South Uist, 72 (map), 74
bees, 75, 100, 171, *see also honey*
beeswax, 100
Beinn an Aonidh, Carsaig, Mull, 150 (map), 162, 241
Belnahua, isle of, Jura, 26, 110 (map), 119 (map), 120
Benbecula, 8, 12, 13, 14, 17, 18, 19, 26, 27, 34 (map), 62 (map), **69**
Ben Hogh, Coll, 169
Ben Hynish, Tiree, 168 (map), 179
Ben More, Mull, 150 (map), 152-3
bent, *see marram grass, purple moor grass*
Berneray, isle of, Barra, 72 (map), 85
Berneray, isle of, Harris, 8, 13, 38 (map), 53, 54, 62 (map)
Bhride, eilean, Islay, 96 (map), 97
Bhruist, Loch, Berneray, Harris, 38 (map), 54
birch, 102, 124, 195, *see also trees*
birdsnest, (*daucus carota* L.), 76
Boece, Hector (1465-1536), *historian,* 11, 240
bolls, *see weights and measures*
Boreray, isle of, North Uist, 26, 62 (map), 63
Bracadale, Skye, 27, 202 (map), 203, 211
Bracadale, Loch, Skye, 202 (map), 212, 213, 214, 215
Breachacha Castles, Coll, 168 (map), 170
Breadalbane, John, third earl of (1696-1782), 166
Breakish, Skye, 202 (map), 215
Buchanan, George (1506-82), *historian and classicist,* 11, 48, 125, 145, 239
Bunessan, Mull, 150 (map), 152
burdock, great (*arctium lappa* L.), 75
Burgh, Mull, 150 (map), 162
Bute, John, third earl of, (1713-92), 8, 10, 231
butter, 14
dairy yields of, 65, 209
exports of, 54, 65, 77, 100
prices on –
Barra, 88
Coll, 170
Islay, 99, 100
Lewis, 41
Mull, 155
North Uist, 65
South Uist, 77
Tiree, 187
weights used in measuring, 16, 41, 65, 77, 155, 187
buttercup, 170

Cairn na Burgh, isles of, Treshnish isles, 145, 150 (map), 166, 242
Calve island, Mull, 26, 150 (map), 154, 166
Campbell, Archibald of Jura (d. 1764), 111
Campbell, Daniel of Shawfield (d. 1777), 97, 100, 103, 111
Campbell, Donald of Scalpay, Harris (1690-1783), 56, 234
Campbell, Donald of Shawfield (1670-1753), 101
Campbell, Major Donald, chamberlain of Tiree (c. 1744- after 1810), 140, 186
Campbeltown, 7, 34 (map), 56, 59, 105
fishing rendezvous at, 44-5, 103
Canna, 8, 17, 18, 19, 20, 22-4, 27, 28, 34 (map), 175, 194 (map), 195, 198, 204, 223, **229**
Canna, Sound of, 199
Caorach, eilean nan, Islay, 96 (map), 97
Cara, isle of, Gigha, 26, 27, 96 (map), 120, 133
cas-chròm, 14, 15, 43, 172, 210, 211, *see also plough*
Catholics, 4, 17-21, 22, 27, 28, 53, 63, 69, 73, 85, 152, 183, 197, 223, 229, 236, 243
cattle, 13, 81, 86, 88, 98, 139, 182, 185-6
diseases of, 173, 187, 243
exported from –
Barra, 87
Benbecula, 77
Canna, 229
Coll, 172
Harris, 54
Islay, 100
Jura, 117
Lewis, 42
Mull, 155
North Uist, 63, 65
Rum, 196
Skye, 206-7, 208
South Uist, 77
hay for, 43, 78, 172, 186, 198, 208-9
prices of grazing for, on –
Barra, 88
Islay, 99
Lewis, 41
Skye, 206
South Uist, 77
salted beef, 42, 54, 65, 87, 170, 187
selling prices on –
Coll, 170
Islay, 100
Lewis, 41, 42
Mull, 155, 157
Skye, 206
South Uist, 77
Tiree, 187
yields of dairy produce, 65, 209

chalcedony, 198
cheese, 14
  exported from islands, 54, 65, 77, 100
  prices of, on –
    Barra, 88
    Coll, 170
    Islay, 99
    Lewis, 41
    Mull, 155
    North Uist, 65
    South Uist, 77
    Tiree, 187
  weights used in measuring, 16, 41, 155, 187
  yields of, 65, 209
'chincough', *see whooping cough*
Chnuic bhric, abhainn a', Jura, 110 (map), 112
'Chohinruagh', Mull, 162, 164
Chuirn, eilean a', Islay, 96 (map), 97
churches, 20, 117, 152, 169
Cill Chriosd, Skye, 202 (map), 206, 215, 217
Cille Bharra, Barra, 88
climate, 87, 99, 114, 139, 153, 171, 182, 195, 206, 208
Clisham, Harris, 38 (map), 54
clover, 100, 157, 186, 208
  red (*trifolium pratense* L.), 75, 170, 197
  white (*t. repens* L.), 75, 105, 182, 197
  yellow (*t. campestre* Schreb.), 170, 197
Clyde, goods exported to the, 42, 46, 77, 82, 87, 101, 107, 118, 187, *see also Glasgow*
coal, 98, 105, 106, 133, 162, 170, 198, 215, 223
cod, 81
  banks, 43, 55-6, 59, 69, 89-90, 104, 161, 174-5, 189, 213, 214, 229
  exported, 42, 43, 89, 207
  see also fisheries
'colewort' (prob. a brassica or rape), 183
Coll, 8, 12, 13, 14, 16, 17, 19, 27, 28, 34 (map), 166, 168 (map), **169-75**, 179, 195
Colonsay, 8, 12, 17, 19, 20, 25, 26, 27, 34 (map), 116, 117, **123-6**, 233
Columba, St. (521-97), 137, 138, 139-40, 141, 146-7, 240
'conger', 124
conger eel, 81, 174
copper deposits, 106, 118, 190
coral, 15, 143, 163, 186
cornelian, 198
cornua Ammonis, 215
Corryvreckan, whirlpool of, 110 (map), 113, 119 (map), 120
Cowley, Mr J., 151, 241
'Crackbreac', *see Chnuic bhric, abhainn a'*
craggans, 171
cranesbill (*geranium sanguineum* L.), 170
Craobhach, eilean, Islay, 96 (map), 97
creideamh a' bhata bhuidhe, 197, 203
Cronstedt, Axel Fredrik (1722-65), *metallurgist,* 199, 243
Crossapol, Coll, 168 (map), 170
Crossapol, Tiree, 168 (map), 184
crosses on Iona, 146-7, 240-1
crystal, 165
Cuillins, Skye, 202 (map), 204, 206
Cullen, Professor William (1710-90), *physician,* 1, 5, 6, 29, 243

Daliburgh, Loch, South Uist, 72 (map), 74
Darling, Sir Frank Fraser (1903-79), *ecologist,* 12
Darwin, Charles (1809-92), *naturalist,* 5
deer, red, 54, 75, 118, 197
  venison, 14
diarrhoea, 115
  see also disease
Dick, Rev. Robert (1722-82), *minister of the Tron, Edinburgh,* 6, 20, 21, 22
diet, 14, 49, 65, 89, 90, 115, 196, 197
  see also potatoes, shellfish
Disarming Act, 17, 46, 79, 159, 236
disease, 29, 73
  see also ague, diarrhoea, dysentery, fever, fillean, inoculation, jaundice, leprosy, measles, rheumatism, scurvy, smallpox, tetanus infantum, whooping cough
distilleries, 14, 42, 77, 87, 172, 173, 207
  see also whisky
dogfish oil, 41, 42, 46, *see also fisheries*
drainage, 15, 54, 64, 66, 69, 74, 88
Druim an Aoneidh, Iona, 138, 239
Duart Castle, Mull, 150 (map), 154
duck, eider, 48, 25, 233, 239
Duirinish, Skye, 27, 202 (map), 203
Dunscaich, Skye, 202 (map), 205
Duntuilm, Skye, 21
Dunvegan, Skye, 214
Dunvegan Head, Skye, 213
Dunvegan, Loch, Skye, 202 (map), 214
Dutchman's Cap (*eilean Bac mor*), Treshnish Isles, 150 (map), 162, 166
dysentery (bloody flux), 73, 97
  see also disease

Eachkemish, North Uist, 62 (map), 64
eagles, 54, 75, 157, 158
  golden, 197
eggs, prices of, 99, 155
eider duck, *see duck*
Eigg, 8, 17, 18, 19, 20, 22-4, 27, 28, 34 (map), 194 (map), 195, 223-6, 229
eileach an Naoimh, Garvellachs, 26, 119 (map), 120
eilean na h-Airidh, North Uist, 26, 63, 235
eilean Bac mor (Dutchman's Cap), Treshnish Isles, 150 (map), 162, 166

eilean Bhride, Islay, 96 (map), 97
eilean na Caorach, Islay, 96 (map), 97
eilean a'Chuirn, Islay, 96 (map), 97
eilean Craobhach, Islay, 96 (map), 97
eilean Mhaolmhoire, Islay, 96 (map), 97
Eishort, Loch, Skye, 202 (map), 212
elder, 205, *see also trees*
emigration, 24, 30
  from –
    Iona, 140
    Islay, 30, 97-8
    Mull, 30, 153
    Rum, 225
enclosure, 15, 78, 102, 184
English speakers, 40, 53, 63-4, 69, 73, 85, 140, 152, 169, 183, 223
Ensay, isle of, Harris, 8, 38 (map), 53
Eorrapidh, Rubh', Lewis, 38 (map), 39
Episcopalians, 17-21
Eriskay, isle of, South Uist, 26, 72 (map)
Estève, Louis (fl. 1750-65), *physician and chemist,* 190
Eye, Lewis, 19, 20, 38 (map)

Fahrenheit, Dante Gabriel (1686-1736), *natural scientist,* 87, 114, 139, 153, 196, 237
Faihore, Lochmaddy, North Uist, 235
Fallart, Loch (Loch Dunvegan), Skye, 212
'Feala', *see Fiaray, isle of*
feathers, export of, 42, 48, 100
fencible men, *see army*
Feorlig, Skye, 202 (map), 214
fern ash, 17, 125, 155, 213
fever, 73, 115, *see also disease*
Fiaray, isle of, Barra, 72 (map), 85, 236
fillean, 115-6, 238, *see also disease*
fir, Scots, 102, 124, 205, *see also trees*
fisheries, 43, 81, 235
  bounty on, 44-5, 59, 189, 213, 214, 233
  Commissioners for improving f. and manufactures, 59, 234
  economics of, 81-2
  nets, 81, 104, 161, 188, 189
  potential development of, on –
    Barra, 89-90
    Benbecula, 69
    Coll, 174-5
    Harris, 56, 234
    Islay, 103-4
    Lewis, 43-46, 89
    Mull, 161-2
    North Uist, 66
    St. Kilda, 60
    Skye, 213-5
    South Uist, 81
    Tiree, 188
  prices of, 41, 42, 56, 77, 82, 89, 207, 214
  see also Campbeltown, cod, dogfish oil, flounders, herring, ling, mackerel, mudfish, mullet, saithe, salmon, salt
Fladda, isle of, Lunga, 26, 110 (map), 119 (map), 120
Flannan Isles, Lewis, 25, 34 (map), 42, 48
flax, *see linen and lintseed*
Flodigarry, Skye, 27
Florida, wreck of the, Tobermory, 154, 239
flounders, 81, *see also fisheries*
flux, bloody, *see dysentery*
Forrester, Rev. Alexander (1701-80), *priest on South Uist,* 19
foxes, 100, 158-9, 208, 209, 241
Franklin, Benjamin (1706-90), *natural scientist,* 1
Fraser, Rev. John (1647-1702), *minister of Tiree and Coll,* 148, 241
Fuday, isle of, Barra, 72 (map), 85, 236

galium verum, see Lady's bedstraw
Garvellach Islands, 26, 34 (map), 110 (map), 119 (map), 120
geese, 78-9, 100, 118, 236
geranium sanquineum, see cranesbill
Giant's Causeway, 98, 144, 164-5, 204, 229
Gigha, 26, 27, 34 (map), 96 (map), 120, **133**
Gillanders, factor on Lewis, 11
Glasgow, exports to, 65, 89, 125, 197, 232, *see also Clyde*
glass, potential development of, 105
goats, 99, 157, 197, 209
  goat hair, 197
  goat tallow, 116
Gometra, isle of, 26, 150 (map), 165
Gott Bay, Tiree, 168 (map), 180, 190
gradan, 43, 155, 209, 233
granite, 142-3, 163-4
Grant, Rev. James (1706-78), *Catholic bishop of Aberdeen,* 86, 236
graphite, 218, *see also lead deposits*
Greenock, 7, 56, 59, 87
Greshornish, Loch, Skye, 218
Gress, Lewis, 19, 20
Grimsay, isle of, North Uist, 26, 62 (map), 63, 235
Grishapoll, Coll, 168 (map), 174
Gruinart, Loch, Islay, 96 (map), 98, 104
Gruinart, river, Islay, 104

hagberry (*prunus padus* L.), bird cherry, 205
Hall, Sir James (1761-1832), *geologist and chemist,* 4
Halley, Edmond (1656-1743), *natural scientist,* 22, 114
Harris, 8, 12, 14, 19, 25, 27, 34 (map), 38 (map), **53-6**, 233
hay, 43, 75, 78, 99, 172, 186, 198, 218-9
hazel, 102, 205
Heisker, isle of, North Uist, 26, 34 (map), 62 (map), 63, 233
Hellisay, isle of, Barra, 72 (map), 236

hemlock dropwort (*oenanthe crocata* L.), 76
hemp, manufacture and cultivation of, 48, 189
'Heray', *see eilean na h-Airidh*
herring –
  development of fishing for, 44-5, 56, 66, 69, 161, 188-9, 213-4
  exported, 42, 44, 207, 214
  prices of, 41, 42, 56, 207, 214
  see also fisheries
Heylipoll, Tiree, 44, 168 (map), 184
Highland and Agricultural Society of Scotland, 2
Hirta, *see St. Kilda*
Hogh, Ben, Coll, 169
holly, 153, 195, 205, *see also trees*
honey, 75, 100, 171
Hooker, Sir William (1785-1865), *botanist,* 5
horses, 172, 182, 209
  exported, 155, 172, 196
  grazing for, 99, 208
  price of, 155, 207
Hourn, Loch, Inverness-shire, 219
'huana', 217
hyacinths, 153
Hyndman, Rev. John (1723-62), *minister of Lady Yester's, Edinburgh,* 6, 20, 21, 22, 27, 28
Hynish, Ben, Tiree, 168 (map), 179

improvement, agricultural, 5, 15
  see also, barley, bear, clover, hay, leases, marle, oats, rye, sheep, turnips, vetch, wheat
Inchkenneth, isle of, Mull, 26, 150 (map), 165
'Inchomish', *see Eachkemish*
inoculation, 29-30, 73, 86, 97, 203-4, *see also smallpox*
Iona, 8, 26, 30, **137-48**, 150 (map), 152, 163, 165, 179, 186
Iona, Sound of, 137
iron ore, deposits of, 118
Islay, isle of, Loch Dunvegan, Skye, 27
Islay, 7, 12, 14, 17, 19, 21, 26, 27, 29, 96 (map), **97-107**
Islay, Sound of, 34 (map), 96 (map), 105, 112, 113, 114

Jameson, Robert (1774-1824), *mineralogist,* 4
Jardine, Sir William, Bt. (1800-74), *naturalist,* 5
jasper, 163, 190, 199
jaundice, 29, *see also disease*
juniper, 196, *see also trees*
Jura, isle of, 7, 12, 14, 17, 19, 20, 25, 26, 27, 34 (map), 96 (map), 110 (map), **111-20**
Jura, Paps of, 7, 111, 114, 237

Kames, Agatha Drummond, Lady, 3, 4
Kames, Henry Home, Hon. Lord (1696-1782), *jurist and agricultural improver,* 1, 2, 3, 5, 6, 7, 8, 9
Keal, Loch na, Mull, 150 (map), 154, 165
kelp –
  on –
    Barra 87, 88
    Benbecula 69, 77
    Coll 171
    Colonsay, 125-6
    Harris, 54, 233
    Islay, 100, 104
    Jura, 118
    Lewis, 41, 42
    Mull, 155, 161
    North Uist, 65
    Skye, 207, 211-2
    South Uist, 76, 77
    Tiree, 187
  prices, 41, 42, 54, 65, 76, 77, 125, 155, 171, 187, 207
  and rents, 63, 65, 69, 212
Kerrera, isle of, Lorne, 34 (map), 166
Kilbarra, *see Cille Bharra*
Kilbranan, river, Islay, 106
Kilchiaran, Islay, 96 (map), 97, 237
Kilchoman, Islay, 7, 26, 96 (map), 97, 237
Kilchrist, Skye, *see Cill Chriosd*
Kildalton, Islay, 26, 96 (map), 97, 237
Kilfinichen, Mull, 150 (map), 152
Killarow, Islay, 96 (map), 100, 101, 237
Killarow, river, Islay, 104
Killegray, isle of, Harris, 38 (map), 53
'Killiren', Islay, *see Kilchiaran*
Kilmartin, river, Trotternish, Skye, 215
Kilmeny, Islay, 96 (map), 97, 237
Kilmore, Mull, 152
Kilmory, Scarba, 110 (map), 119 (map), 120
Kilmuir, Skye, 27, 202 (map), 203
Kilnachton, Islay, 237
Kilninian, Mull, 26, 152, 166
Kiloran, Colonsay, 125
Kilvickeon, Mull, 26, 152
Kinlochspelvie, Mull, 150 (map), 152
Kintour, river, Islay, 96 (map), 104
Kintyre, 97, 98, 99, 104, 105, 107, 111, 120, 133
Kirkapoll, Tiree, 168 (map), 184
Kirkibost, isle of, North Uist, 26, 62 (map), 63
Knox, Rev. Andrew (1559-1633), *bishop of the Isles,* 19

Lady's bedstraw (*galium verum* L.), 13, 90
Laggan, river, Islay, 96 (map), 104
lakeweed (*polygonum amphibium* L.), 76
Lang, Andrew (1844-1912), *journalist and historian,* 10
lapwings, 182

Lathaich, Loch na, Mull, 150 (map), 154
lead deposits, 106, 108, 118, 170, *see also graphite*
leases on –
Islay, 101, 103
Mull, 156, 159-60
North Uist, 65
Skye, 207
see also steelbow, sub-leasing, tacksmen, tenants
leather, tanning potential, 123
leprosy, 59, *see also disease*
Leurbost, Loch, Lewis, 44
Lewis, 12, 14, 16, 17, 19, 20, 21, 25, 27, 34 (map), 38 (map), **38-49**
Lightfoot, Rev. John (1735-88), *naturalist,* 5
limestone, 15, 98, 104, 105, 106, 118, 133, 163, 165, 170, 215, 223
linen and lintseed –
flax seed, quality and origin, 47, 55, 66, 79-80, 100, 103, 118, 133, 161, 173, 188, 213
linen production on –
Benbecula, 69
Canna, 244
Coll, 173-4
Harris, 55
Islay, 101, 103
Jura, 118
Lewis, 46-7
Mull, 155, 161
North Uist, 66
Skye, 207, 213
South Uist, 79, 80
Tiree, 187
spinning schools, 42, 46-7, 174, 188, 229
yarn production, 42, 55, 100, 118, 133, 187
ling –
on –
Barra, 89
Lewis, 41, 42, 43
Mull, 161
Skye, 214
South Uist, 77, 81, 82
Tiree, 189
prices, 41, 42, 77, 82, 89
Linnaeus, Carl (1707-78), *botanist,* 1, 8, 11, 48, 76, 124, 182, 190, 197
lint, *see linen and lintseed*
Lismore, isle of, 10, 34 (map), 150 (map), 165
Loch Arnisort, *see Grashornish*
Loch Bee, South Uist, 72 (map), 74
Loch Bhruist, Berneray, Harris, 38 (map), 54
Loch Bracadale, Skye, 202 (map), 212, 213, 214, 215
Lochbuie, Mull, 150 (map), 154
Loch Daliburgh, South Uist, 74
Loch Dunvegan, Skye, 202 (map), 214
Loch Eishort, Skye, 202 (map), 212
Loch Fallart, Skye, 212
Loch Greshornish, Skye, 212
Loch Gruinart, Islay, 96 (map), 98, 104
Loch Hourn, Inverness-shire, 219
Lochindaal, Islay, 96 (map), 98, 104, 105
Loch na Keal, Mull, 150 (map), 154, 165
Loch na Lathaich, Mull, 150 (map), 154
Loch Leurbost, Lewis, 44
Lochmaddy, North Uist, 62 (map), 66, 235
Loch na Mile, Jura, 110 (map), 112
Loch Ouirn, Lewis, 38 (map), 44
Loch Roag, Lewis, 38 (map), 43, 44
Lochs, Lewis, 19, 20, 25, 38 (map), 39, 40
Loch Scresort, Rum, 194 (map), 195
Loch Scridain, Mull, 150 (map), 151, 152, 154, 162, 165
Loch Seaforth, Lewis, 38 (map), 44
Loch Sealg, Lewis, 38 (map), 44
Loch Shell, Lewis, 38 (map), 44
Loch Slapin, Skye, 202 (map), 212, 213, 214, 215
Loch Snizort, Skye, 202 (map), 212
Loch Stornoway, Lewis, 44
Loch Tarbert, Harris, 38 (map), 44, 56
Loch Tarbert, Jura, 110 (map), 112
Loch Uskavagh, Benbecula, 62 (map), 69
longevity, 28-9, 40, 86, 115, 183, 196, 225, 226, *see also population*
lucerne (*medicago sativa* L.), 197
Luing, isle of, 10, 34 (map), 110 (map), 119 (map)
Lunga, isle of, Jura, 26, 110 (map), 119 (map), 120
Lunga, isle of, Treshnish Isles, 150 (map), 166
Lussa, river, Jura 110 (map), 112

Macaskill, Mr, *surgeon,* Skye, 203-4
Macaulay, Rev. Aulay (c. 1673-1758), *minister of Harris,* 242
Macaulay, Rev. Kenneth (1723-79), *minister of Ardnamurchan,* 234
Macdonald, Sir Alexander of Sleat, Bt., first Lord Macdonald (d. 1795), 203, 243
Macdonald, Alexander of Boisdale (1698-1768), 69, 74, 76, 81, 82, 235, 243
Macdonald, Alexander of Kingsburgh (1698-1772), 208
Macdonald, Colin, younger of Boisdale (d. 1800), 11
Macdonald, Rev. Hugh (1699-1773), *Catholic bishop in the Highlands,* 18, 27
Macdonald, Sir James of Sleat, Bt. (1741-66), 63, 206, 209, 235, 243
Macdonald, James, *agriculturalist,* 12
Macdonald, James, *postmaster, Dunvegan,* 214

Macdonald, John of Morar (d. 1809), 223
Macdonald, Rev. John (1727-79), *Catholic bishop in the Outer Isles,* 19
Macdonald, Ranald of Clanranald (1692-1766), 69, 73, 75, 80, 223, 229, 235
Macdonald, Ranald, younger of Clanranald (d. 1777), 11, 30, 73, 235
Macdougall of Gallanach, 166
Macdougall of Lorne, 166
Macduffies of Colonsay, 130, 139
Macgillivray of Pennyghael, 151
Mackenzie, Sir Kenneth of Gairloch, Bt. (1832-1900), 10
mackerel, 45, 90, *see also fisheries*
Mackinnon, Charles of Mackinnon (b. 1753), 151, 203, 241, 244
Mackinnon, Rev. John (d. 1509), *abbot of Iona,* 144, 240
Maclaine, John of Lochbuie (d. 1785), 151, 241
Maclaughlan of Kilbride, 120
Maclean, Alan of Drimnin (1724-92), 151, 241
Maclean, Rev. Hector (1696-1775), *minister of Tiree and Coll,* 28
Maclean, Hector of Torloisk (d. 1765), 151, 241
Maclean, Hugh of Coll (d. 1786), 151, 171, 172, 174, 195, 241, 242
Maclean, Lachlan in Glasgow, 186
Maclean, Mr, *surgeon,* Skye, 203
Maclean, Murdoch of Kilmory, Scarba, 120
Macleod, Alexander of Pabbay, 56, 234
Macleod, Alexander (b. 1692), *sheriff of Inverness,* 208, 244
Macleod, Donald of Berneray, 235
Macleod, Donald of Canna, 244
Macleod, Donald in Feorlig, Skye, 214
Macleod, Mr, *surgeon,* Skye, 203
Macleod, Rev. Neil (1729-80), *minister of Kilfinichen and Kilvickeon, Mull,* 141, 240
Macleod, Norman of Harris (c. 1706-72), 12, 53, 59, 203, 233, 243
Macleod's Tables, Skye, 202 (map), 204
Macneill, Alexander of Oronsay, (d. 1780), 129
Macneill, Rev. Angus (1723-73), *minister of Barra,* 236
Macneill, Donald of Colonsay, 11, 111, 123, 125, 239
Macneill, Donald of Vatersay, 86, 236
Macneill, Roderick of Barra (1693-1763), 85, 86, 236
Macneill, Roderick of Barra (d. 1822), 86, 236
Macneill, Roger of Taynish, 120, 133
Macnicol, Rev. Donald (1735-1802), *minister of Lismore,* 10
Macpherson, Mr, *linen factor, Lewis,* 47
Macpherson, Robert, *clerk in the office of the Board of Manufactures,* 174, 242
Macquarrie, Hector of Ormaig, 151
Macquarrie, Lachlan of Ulva (1715 × 1722-1818), 151, 165
magnetism, experiments with, 229
Magnus III 'Barelegs', *king of Norway* (c. 1073-1103), 142, 240
Mairan, Jean-Jacques d'Ortous de (1678-1771), *physicist,* 114, 237, 238
Manufactures, Commissioners for improving fisheries and, 59, 234
manure, 15, *see also coral, limestone, marle, sea-shells, sea-sleech*
Maol Buidhe, Scarba, 119 (map), 120
marble, 144, 163, 186, 189-90, 215-7
marle, 118, 170
  rock, 15, 105
  shell, 15, 105, 165
marram grass (*ammophila arenaria* (L.) Link.), 13, 173
marten, 48
Martin, Martin (d. 1719), *topographer and physician,* 7, 11, 18, 29, 232, 234, 235, 236, 238, 242
measles, 29, *see also disease*
mercury deposits, 106-7
metrology, *see weights and measures*
mhic Mhaolmhoire, eilean, Islay, 96 (map), 97
Milbuie, *see Maol buidhe*
Mile, Loch na, Jura, 110 (map), 112
milk yields, 14, 65, 209
Mingulay, isle of, Barra, 72 (map), 85
Mitchill, Hon. Samuel Latham (1764-1831), *physician and U.S. Senator,* 5
Monro, Alexander, *primus* (1697-1767), *physician and anatomist,* 30
Monro, Rev. Donald (d. 1576), Dean of the Isles, 11
Monson, Sir William (1569-1643), *mariner,* 59, 60, 234
moorfowl, 124, 197
More, Ben, Mull, 152-3
Morrison, Alexander of Skiniden, Skye, 214
Muck, 18, 19, 20, 22-4, 27, 28, 34 (map), 194 (map), 223, 229
mudfish, 42, 43, 49, *see also fisheries*
mugwort (*artemisia vulgaris* L.), 75
Mull, 12, 14, 16, 17, 19, 20, 21, 26, 28, 34 (map), 45, 142-3, 144, 150 (map), **151-66,** 183, 204
Mull, Ross of, 140, 150 (map), 151-2, 162, 163
Mull, Sound of, 8, 90, 150 (map)
mullet, 69, 104, *see also fisheries*
Murray, Sir Alexander of Stanhope, Bt. (d. 1743), 5, 11, 118, 162, 241, 242
mussels, 89, 215

Naoimh, eileach an, Garvellachs, 26, 119 (map), 120
Natural History Society of Edinburgh, 2
Nave, isle of, Islay, 96 (map), 97
Necker de Saussure, Louis Albert (1786-1861), *geologist and mineralogist,* 5
Ness, Lewis, 39
Newcastle, Thomas, third duke of (1693-1768), 9
'Nissa', *see Lussa*
North Rona, isle of, Lewis, 25, 34 (map), 48
North Uist, 8, 12, 13, 14, 16, 17, 19, 21, 26, 27, 29, 30, 34 (map), 62 (map), **63-66**
Nunton, Benbecula, 62 (map), 69, 235

oak, 102, 124, 195, *see also trees*
oatmeal –
  import of, 65, 69, 155
  Mull boll, 17, 155
  price of, 155
  Skye boll, 17, 206
oats, 14
  cultivation on –
    Barra, 86
    Benbecula, 69
    Coll, 172
    Harris, 55
    Iona, 139
    Islay, 100
    Jura, 117
    Lewis, 42
    Mull, 153, 155
    North Uist, 65
    Skye, 205, 206, 207-8, 209, 210, 211
    South Uist, 74, 77
    Tiree, 14, 181, 185
  grey oats (*avena strigosa* Schreb.), 14, 42, 55, 65, 69, 77, 100, 157, 185, 207-8
  spirits made from, 42
  white oats (*a. sativa* L.), 15, 100, 155, 208
  yield of, 14, 78, 211
oenanthe crocata, see hemlock dropwort
onyx, 198, *see also agate*
Orbost, Skye, 21
Ord, river, Skye, 75, 202 (map), 215
Ormaclett, South Uist, 72 (map), 235
'Oransay', bay of, Skye, 205
Oronsay, isle of, Colonsay, 20, 25, 26, 27, 104, 116, 117, **129-30**
Oronsay, isle of, North Uist, 26, 62 (map), 63
Oronsay, isle of, Skye, 27
Orsay, isle of, Islay, 96 (map), 97
osier, 102
Ossian, 4, 10, 35, 195, 205, 244
otters, export of skins, 54, 75
Ouirn, Loch, Lewis, 38 (map), 44
Outram, isle of, Islay, 96 (map), 97
oysters, 90, 154

Pabbay, isle of, Barra, 72 (map), 85
Pabbay, isle of, Harris, 8, 13, 14, 38 (map), 53, 54, 62 (map)
Paps of Jura, 7, 111, 114
parishes, 19-20, 39, 63, 73, 85, 97, 116-7, 123, 140, 151-2, 169, 183, 203
pearls, 165, 215
pease, 100, 208
pedicularis palustris, see red rattle
Pennant, Thomas (1726-98), *traveller and naturalist,* 6, 11, 24, 238, 240
Pennygown, Mull, 150 (map), 152
plane, 124, *see also trees*
plantain, 197
Pliny (G. Plinius Secundus), (A.D. 23-79), *natural historian,* 144, 164, 190
plough –
  use on –
    Canna, 229
    Coll, 172
    Harris, 55
    Lewis, 43
    Rum, 195
    Skye, 210, 211
    Tiree, 184
  see also cas-chròm, ristle
plovers, 182
polecat, 100
polygonum amphibium, see lakeweed
population, 21-30
  on –
    Airidh, eilean na h-, 26, 63
    Barra, 13, 26, 27, 29, 85, 86
    Belnahua, 26, 120
    Benbecula, 26, 27, 69
    Berneray, Barra, 85
    Boreray, 26, 63
    Calve, 26, 166
    Canna, 23, 24, 27, 28, 223-4, 225, 229
    Coll, 27, 169
    Colonsay, 25, 26, 27, 123
    Eigg, 23, 24, 27, 28, 223-4, 225
    Fiaray, 85
    Fladda, 26, 120
    Fuday, 85
    Garvellachs, 26, 120
    Gigha, 26, 27, 120, 133
    Gometra, 26, 165
    Harris, 25, 27, 55
    Heisker, 26, 63
    Inchkenneth, 26, 165
    Iona, 26, 139
    Islay, 26, 27, 29, 97
    Jura, 25, 26, 27, 115
    Lewis, 25, 27, 39-40
    Lismore, 165
    Mingulay, 85
    Muck, 23, 24, 27, 28, 223-4, 225
    Mull, 26, 28, 152, 153
    Naoimh, aileach an, 26, 120

North Uist, 26, 30, 63
Oronsay, 26, 27, 129
Pabbay, 85
Rum, 23, 24, 27, 28, 29, 196-7, 223-4, 225
St. Kilda, 25, 29, 59, 234
Sandray, 85
Scarba, 26, 120
Skye, 27, 28, 30, 203
South Uist, 26, 27, 28, 73
Tiree, 27, 30, 183
Ulva, 26, 165
Vallay, 26, 63
Vatersay, 85
by decades, 23-4, 40, 224
disease and, 29, 115, *see also disease*
examinable persons, 22-3, 28
fertility, 24, 225, 226
and potatoes, 78, 101
Walker's and Webster's figures, 23-5, 28-9
see also emigration, longevity
porphyry, 163, 190
Port Askaig, Islay, 96 (map), 113, 118
Port na curraich, Iona, 138, 150 (map)
Portencross, 154
Portree, Skye, 19, 27, 202 (map), 203, 205, 213, 215
potatoes, 15, 29
grown on –
Barra, 13, 88
Colonsay, 123
Islay, 101-2
Jura, 115
Lewis, 43
Mull, 156
Skye, 102, 208, 210
South Uist, 78, 102
Tiree, 185
and population, 78, 101
prices –
bear, 41, 155, 187, 206
butter, 41, 65, 77, 88, 99, 100, 155, 170, 187
cattle, 41, 42, 54, 65, 77, 100, 155, 157, 170, 187, 206, 207
cheese, 41, 65, 77, 88, 99, 155, 170, 187,
cod, 207
dogfish oil, 41, 42, 46
eggs, 99, 155
fern ash, 125, 155, 213
goats, 99
goat hair, 197
herring, 41, 42, 56, 207, 214
horses, 155, 207
kelp, 41, 42, 54, 65, 69, 76, 77, 125, 155, 171, 187, 207
ling, 41, 42, 77, 82, 89
lintseed, 47, 188
oatmeal, 155, 206
rabbit skins, 100, 125
salmon, 41, 42
salted beef, 170, 187
sheep, 77, 88, 99, 155, 157
whisky, 41, 42
wool, 41, 170, 187
see also rent, wages
Proaig, river, Islay, 96 (map), 104
Ptolamy (Claudius Ptolemaeus), *astronomer and geographer,* 11
puffin, 197
Pulteney, Sir William, Bt., M.P. (1729-1805), 2
purple moorgrass (*molinia caerulea,* (L.), Moench) flying bent, 197-8

quartz, 190-1

Raasay, isle of, Skye, 19, 27, 34 (map), 202 (map)
rabbits, export of skins, 100, 125
ragwort (*senecio jacobaea* L.), 75
Ramsay, Professor Robert (d. 1775), *natural historian,* 2
rape, *see 'colewort'*
Ray, John (1627-1705), *botanist,* 11, 143, 163, 240, 241
red rattle (*pedicularis palustris,* L.), 116
Reef, Tiree, 168 (map), 179, 181-2
rent, 158
on –
Barra, 85, 88
Benbecula, 69
Berneray, 85
Calve, 166
Canna, 229
Coll, 169
Dutchman's Cap, 166
Eigg, 223
Fiaray, 85
Fuday, 85
Garvellachs, 120
Gigha, 133
Gometra, 165
Harris, 53
Inchkenneth, 165
Islay, 99, 101
Kerrera, 166
Lewis, 39, 41
Lismore, 165
Lunga, Jura, 120
Lunga, Treshnish, 166
Mingulay, 85
Mull, 151, 156
Naoimh, eileach an, 120
North Uist, 63
Pabbay, 85
Rum, 195, 196
St. Kilda, 59
Sandray, 85

Scarba, 120
Shuna, 166
Skye, 203, 207
South Uist, 73
Tiree, 179, 184, 188
Ulva, 165
Vatersay, 85
see also kelp
rheumatism, 29, *see also disease*
ribwort (*plantago lanceolata* L.), 75
ristle, 55, *see also plough*
Roag, Loch, Lewis, 38 (map), 43, 44
Robertson, James (fl. 1760-70), *botanist,* 238
Rockall, 34 (map), 59, 93
Rodil, Harris, 213, 233
Rona, isle of, Skye, 27, 34 (map), 202 (map)
Rona, North, isle of, Lewis, 25, 34 (map), 48 (map)
Ronay, isle of, North Uist, 26, 62 (map), 63
Ross of Mull, 140, 150 (map), 151-2, 162, 163
Roubiliac, Louis-Francois (1695-1762), *sculptor,* 216
Rousseau, Jean-Jacques, (1722-78), 1
rowan, 195, 205, *see also trees*
Royal Bounty Fund, 20-1, 40, 64, 116, 152
Royal Highland and Agricultural Society, 2
Royal Society of Edinburgh, 2
Rueval, Benbecula, 62 (map), 235
Rum, 8, 11, 14, 17, 18, 19, 20, 22-4, 27, 28, 29, 34 (map), 194 (map), **195-9**, 213, 223, 229
rye (*secale cereale* L.) –
cultivated on –
Benbecula, 69
Harris, 55
Islay, 100
North Uist, 65
Oronsay, 129
Skye, 207
South Uist, 74, 77, 78
Tiree, 185
yield of, 78
rye-grass (*lolium peranne* L.), 75, 99, 100, 157, 186, 197, 208
Rysbrack, Jean Michel (1693-1770), *sculptor,* 216

St. Kilda, 25, 29, 34 (map), **59-60,** 93, 233, 234
Sacheverell, William (perh. d. 1715), *governor of the Isle of Man,* 11, 140, 144, 239
sainfoin (*onobrychis viciifolia* Scop.), 197
saithe, 49, 233, *see also fisheries*
salmon –
on –
Islay, 104
Jura, 112
Lewis, 41, 42, 45
Skye, 214-5
see also fisheries
salt, 43, 44, 45, 59, 81, 82, 175, 188, 189, 213, 214
sand for glass-blowing, 105
sandblow, 13
on –
Barra, 13, 86, 87, 88
Benbecula, 13, 69
Berneray, 13, 54
Coll, 13, 170, 173
Harris, 13, 54
Iona, 137
Lewis, 41
North Uist, 13, 63, 64
Pabbay, 13, 85
South Uist, 13, 74-5, 78
Tiree, 13, 81
Sandray, isle of, Barra, 72 (map), 85
Scalpay, isle of, Harris, 38 (map), 53, 56
Scalpay, isle of, Skye, 27, 202 (map)
Scarba, isle of, Jura, 10, 20, 26, 34 (map), 110 (map), 113, 116, 119 (map), 120
Scarp, isle of, Harris, 38 (map), 53
schools, 21, 40, 53, 64, 69, 85, 116, 125-6, 140, 152, 169, 183, 223, 233, 236, 242
Scottish Society for the Propagation of Christian Knowledge, 2, 6, 7, 9, 11, 18, 20-1
Scresort, Loch, Rum, 194 (map), 195
Scridain, Loch, Mull, 150 (map), 151, 152, 154, 162, 165
scurvy, 29, *see also disease*
Seaforth, Kenneth, fourth earl of (d. 1701), 21
Seaforth, Kenneth, earl of (d. 1781), 39, 40, 47, 232
Seaforth, Loch, Lewis, 38 (map), 44
Seaforth, William, fifth earl of (d. 1740), 232
Sealg, Loch, Lewis, 38 (map), 44
seals, exports of skins, 54
sea-shells, 88, 104, 143, 163, 186
sea-sleech, 15, 104, 163, 172, 186
seaweed –
used as cattlefood, 173
as manure, 14, 15, 42, 55, 63, 65, 77, 88, 104, 172, 181, 185, 205, 210
see also kelp
Seil, isle of, Lorne, 10
'Selma', 4, 10
sheep –
on –
Coll, 171
Iona, 139

Islay, 98
Jura, 117
Mull, 155, 157, 158
Oronsay, 129
Rum, 198
Skye, 209
South Uist, 77, 80
Tiree, 182
foxes prey on, 157-8, 159, 209
marking, 209
native breeds, 7, 74, 80, 171, 236
new breeds, 74, 80, 129-30, 157
prices of, 77, 88, 99, 155, 157, 158
prices of grazing, 77, 158
'rooing', 43
skins exported, 42, 54
smearing, 74, 80, 99, 171, 236
see also wool
Shell, Loch, Lewis, 38 (map), 44
shellfish, 89, 90, 154
Shiaba, Mull, 150 (map), 162, 164
Shiant Isles, Lewis, 25, 34 (map), 38 (map), 39
Shuna, isle of, Loch Linnhe, 119 (map), 150 (map), 166
Sibbald, Sir Robert (1641-1722), *physician and antiquary,* 7, 11, 219, 244
silver deposits, 106
Skiniden, Skye, 202 (map), 214
Skye, 8, 14, 17, 18, 19, 20, 21, 27, 28, 30, 34 (map), 75, 194 (map), 195, 202 (map), **203-20,** 223
Slapin, Loch, Skye, 202 (map), 212, 213, 214, 215
slate, 120, 143
Sleat, Skye, 19, 20, 27, 194 (map), 202 (map), 203, 204, 205, 213
Sloane, Sir Hans (1660-1753), *physician and collector,* 163, 241
smallpox, 29, 115
inoculation against, 29-30, 73, 86, 97, 203-4
visitations of, 29-30, 59, 73, 86, 97, 183, 196-7, 204, 234
see also disease
smectis, *see Spanish chalk*
snakes, 124
Snizort, Skye, 19, 20, 27, 202 (map), 203
Snizort, Loch, Skye, 202 (map), 212
Soay, isle of, Skye, 27, 202 (map)
South Uist, 8, 12, 13, 14, 16, 17, 18, 19, 20, 26, 27, 28, 34 (map), 72 (map), **73-82**
Spanish chalk, 217-8
spermaceti, 49
spinning schools, *see linen and lintseed*
steelbow tenancy, 160-1, *see also leases*
Stevenson of Belnahua, 120
Stewart, Charles, *printer,* 5
Stewart, Dugald of Appin (d. 1769), 166
Stornoway, Lewis, 7, 8, 19, 20, 21, 25, 38 (map), 39, 40, 42, 43, 44-5, 46-7, 49, 56
Stornoway, Loch, Lewis, 44
Storr, Old Man of, Skye, 202 (map), 204
'Stot', river, Skye, 214
Strath, Skye, 19, 20, 27, 202 (map), 203, 206, 215, 216
strontianite, 2
Struan, Skye, 202 (map), 215
sub-leasing, 101, 160, 207, *see also leases*
Sulasgeir, 34 (map), 42, 48
Sutherland, Professor James (d. 1705), *botanist and numismatist,* 1, 230
swans, 180
Swinton, John of Swinton, Hon. Lord Swinton (d. 1799), *jurist,* 16, 17

tacksmen, 101, 160, 161, 207, *see also leases*
tallow, 187
Taransay, isle of, Harris, 38 (map), 53
Tarbert, Loch, Harris, 38 (map), 44, 56
Tarbert, Loch, Jura, 110 (map), 112
tenants, 41, 103, 160, 207, *see also leases*
tetanus infantum, 59, 234, *see also disease*
Texa, isle of, Islay, 26, 96 (map), 97, 105
thermometer, experiments with, 87, 114-5, 139, 153, 196
thistle –
spear, (*cirsium vulgare* [*savi*] *Ten.*), 75
way, (*cirsium arvense (L.) scop.*), 75
thorn –
black, 102, 184
white, 102, 184
Tiree, 8, 12, 13, 14, 16, 17, 19, 27, 28, 29, 30, 34 (map), 168 (map), **179-91**
Tobermory, Mull, 150 (map), 154, 166, 239
Torfasson, Thormadur (Torffaeus) (c. 1640-1720), *historian and antiquary,* 151, 195
Torosay, Mull, 150 (map), 152
Torrans, Loch Scridain, Mull, 150 (map), 152
Torrin, Skye, 202 (map), 215
Traigh mhor, Barra, 88, 90
trees, 102, 124, 153, 184, 195, 196, 205
see also wood, woodland
'trestarig', 42, 232, *see also whisky*
trifolium, see clover
Trodday, isle of, Skye, 27, 202 (map)
Trotternish, Skye, 202 (map), 209, 214, 215
Turnbull, James, *land surveyor,* 28
turnips, 15, 187, 208
tutsan (*hypericum androsaemum* L.), 124, 239

Uig, Lewis, 19, 20, 25, 38 (map), 39, 40, 43
Uig, Skye, 19, 20
Ulva, isle of, 26, 150 (map), 152, 165
Uskavagh, Loch, Benbecula, 62 (map), 69

Vallay, isle of, North Uist, 8, 26, 62 (map), 63
Vatersay, isle of, Barra, 72 (map), 85

vetch –
kidney (*anthyllis vulneraria* L.), 75
tufted (*vicia cracca* L.), 75

wages –
on –
Barra, 88
Coll, 170
Islay, 99
Lewis, 41
Skye, 206, 210
South Uist, 76, 79
Tiree, 187
for fishermen, 81
Walker, Rev. John (1731-1804)
agricultural improvement, 5, 15
barometric experiments, 7, 114-5, 237
botanical work, 1, 2, 3, 5, 8, 11
and Catholicism, 4
demographic interests, 10, 21-31
education of, 1
on education in the Hebrides, 7, 9, 19
family of, 1
and Gaelic, 8, 9
geology, 1
and Lord Kames, 1, 2, 3, 5, 7
library of, 11
and Linnaeus, 1
magnetism, experiments with, 229
manuscripts, 5, 11
metrology, 15-17
mineralogy, 1, 2, 4
ministry, 1, 2-4, 8
Moderatism, 2-3
Ossian, 4, 10
Report of 1764, 2, 6, 9, 33-4
thermometric experiments, 7, 87, 114-5, 139, 153, 196, 237
University of Edinburgh, 2
Walker, Rev. Robert (1716-83), *minister of the High Kirk, Edinburgh,* 230
Wallerius, Johan Gottschalk (1709-84), *chemist and geologist,* 11, 190, 243
weasels, 100
Webster, Rev. Alexander, (1707-84), *minister of the Tolbooth, Edinburgh,* 11, 22, 23, 24, 27, 28, 29
weights and measures, 15-7, 156
beef, 187
dairy measures, 16, 41, 65, 77, 155, 187
fern ash, 17, 125
grains, 16-7, 41-2, 78, 155, 173, 187
liquid, 41, 42
meal, 16, 17, 155, 206
tallow, 187
wool, 158, 187
wheat (*triticum aestivum* L.), 101
whetstone, 98, 118
whinrock, 106, 144, 146, 147, 162, 164, 170, 198, 204, 215, 229
whisky, 41, 42, 77, 155, 161, 172, 173, 188, 207, 232
see also 'trestarig'
whooping cough, 29, 184, *see also disease*
willow –
grey, 102, 205
laurel-leaved, 102
see also trees
wood, shortage of, 88, 102, 124, 153, 171, 183
woodland –
destroyed, 102, 123-4, 195, 204-5
need to encourage, 88, 102, 124, 153, 195, 205
see also trees
wool –
exported from –
Harris, 54
Jura, 18
Lewis, 46
Oronsay, 129
Skye, 207
prices on –
Coll, 170
Lewis, 41
Mull, 158
Tiree, 187
see also sheep

yarn, linen, *see linen and lintseed*